Alethea Kontis

BEAUTY AND DYNAMITE

ISBN (Hardcover): 9781942541318
ISBN (Paperback): 9781942541325

2008 Apex Publications: 9780977668175
2014 Alliteration Ink (Revised Edition): 9781939840158

Cover design by Chris Kridler and Cait Greer
Interior design by Caitlin Greer
https://www.authorcaitlingreer.com/

Alethea Kontis
PO Box 512
Mims, FL 32754
USA
www.aletheakontis.com

To Hank Reinhardt
A gentleman and a scholar
who wore a fine hat and had no
compunction about handing a girl a sword
when she needed one

~and~

To Max
Some things are meant to be,
and some things are just meant to be great stories.
He was the greatest story of my life.

Table of Contents

THE STORY MAGNET

THE LIFE OF HYMIE

POINTS FOR BRAVERY

Ask yourself if you are living
One against the world
One eye to watch the sunsets
One heart to feel the seasons reborn
One ear to hear the birds singing
And one mind to think in return
That this life you didn't choose
Wouldn't have chosen, and yet
Its beauty is beyond comprehension.

~from *One*, 1993

Elements of Dynamite

I never thought my young life would be a story worth telling…until I told it. Just the other day—some ten years after the original publication of this book—Casey mentioned how much she enjoys that my real life is still just as much of an adventure as my stories.

Well, I can't say I didn't ask for that.

Beauty & Dynamite was created so I would have something to sell at all the conventions I enjoyed frequenting. I figured I'd collage in some old poetry and a few fun essays written by my other—far more famous—friends, and stick a pretty cover on it. If Mom was proud enough of the finished product to show it off to her friends, then I'd done my duty.

I did not expect *Beauty & Dynamite* to become a quiet cult phenomenon. I did not expect readers to compare it to *Eat, Pray, Love.* I did not expect my older sister—who never reads anything longer than a magazine article—to not only devour it from cover to cover, but also buy a copy for Danny Jarvis to remind him that I'd been in love with him my whole childhood. (Ah…sisters.)

I did not expect that when my itty-bitty memoir went out of print, used booksellers at Amazon would jack up the price to thousands of dollars. (Now, that's just silly.)

Nor did I expect *Beauty & Dynamite* to be the time capsule it has become: an encyclopedia for my fading memory to use as reference. A chunk of amber in which some of these voices will live forever. (Pic, I miss you every day.)

So…here we are. Ready to tell my story, once again, from the top.

Third time's the charm, right?

1.) Soteria / Sami & Lee

I have three siblings: An older sister (Cherie), an older brother (West), and a younger sister (Soteria). Soteria is named after our paternal grandfather Soterios/Sotos, who was called "Sam" in America. For this reason, our family called Soteria "Sami" when she was a kid. She eventually grew into her name, but I often refer to "Sami" in these essays so don't be confused. (Absolutely no one else is allowed to call her "Sami," so don't ask. You have to be legacied in. You know if you are.)

Similarly, when I was ten, during the summer before middle school started, I decided that my forever-nickname should be "Lee." Now, you don't have to be legacied in to call me Alethea, Lee, or Princess. Just pick whichever one you're sure you can pronounce correctly.

2.) Bookville

While writing the blogs and essays for this manuscript, I worked as a Buyer for a major book wholesaler. I loved my job, and it facilitated the meeting of many friends whom I still hold dear to this very day.

That company and I have since parted ways. Because I would rather be cautious than not, I have changed the name of that corporation to "Bookville" within the context of this book.

3.) Max

In previous editions of *Beauty & Dynamite*, I revealed a lot more about Max. Too much more. This time around, no spoilers. Just sit back and enjoy the story.

Much love and many hugs!
ox

—Princess Alethea Kontis
Space Coast, Florida
2018

Sex and Flying Meat

AN INTRODUCTION
by Brian Keene

I have been asked... nay, *commanded*, to tell you about how I met Alethea Kontis.

I met Alethea Kontis at an orgy.

With meatloaf.

Several years ago, I was a guest of honor Hypericon, a small convention in Nashville, Tennessee. It was the convention's first year. As a result, Hypericon seemed to be searching for an identity. The people in attendance included elves, fairies, Jedi Knights, zombies, S&M enthusiasts, furries, role playing gamers, and several dozen overweight adults dressed as Harry Potter. There were also many authors in attendance—Tom Piccirilli, Sherrilyn Kenyon, Bryan Smith, Deborah LeBlanc, Glen Cook, James Newman, and several others. The weekend's programming featured the obligatory convention staples. There were panels and readings, a dealer's room, gaming, people in colorful costumes, and the aforementioned orgy.

I'm not sure how the orgy came about or who organized it or who the participants were, because it happened on Saturday night after a long day of drinking. Everyone was inebriated, including myself, and chaos reigned. Bryan Smith wandered the hotel hallways clad only in a purple feather boa and humming unreleased Guns and Roses songs. Sherrilyn Kenyon and Glen Cook had started an impromptu country line dance in the elevator. Deborah LeBlanc downed fifty-seven shots of tequila and suddenly decided it would be a good idea for her to run for President of the HWA (Horror Writer's Association). James Newman sat in a potted plant, sobbing uncontrollably, distraught over the fact that he couldn't grow a pubic hair mullet. It was a bad scene, man.

Filled with fear and loathing, I tried to escape it all by fleeing back to my room. With my trusty bodyguard, Big Joe Maynard, at my side, I battled my way through drunken writers, sweaty gamers, and angry Vulcans. We were nearly mugged by a group of Jedi Knights who'd been smoking crystal meth in a misguided attempt to feel the Force. Then we ended up caught in the middle of a rumble between some Harry Potter fans and Lord of the Rings enthusiasts. They were arguing over who would win in a fight—Gandalf or Harry Potter. We were cut off from our room, and the hordes swarmed.

Big Joe picked the lock on a hotel room door and we escaped just in time.

But we went from the frying pan to the fire.

"Those people," Big Joe gasped, "are having sex!"

"Quick," I ordered him, "get me some bleach for my eyes."

Seems we'd walked into an orgy, already in progress. Naked, sweaty bodies glistened and gyrated. Moans and gasps filled the air. The nightstand was covered with various lubricants and flavored lotions and a wide array of impossibly-sized rubber penises. Big Joe asked me what they were and I explained to him that they were toys.

He frowned. "Don't look like *G.I. Joe with Kung-Fu* grip to me."

"You've led a very sheltered life."

I glanced around the room with a strange mix of bewilderment, exuberance, amusement, and guilt. After all, I was a married man. Not to mention the guest of honor. It might not be good for me to be seen at an orgy. Yet we couldn't go back out into the hall, or else we risked being torn to pieces by Muggles and Orcs. I glanced around the room, looking for a place to hide, and spotted my old friend Tom Piccirilli. He was watching the action. A terrified expression haunted his cherubic face, and a thin line of drool dripped from the corner of his mouth.

"Sweet fucking Jesus, Joe," I shouted. "Pic is married, too. What the hell's he doing here?"

"Maybe he drank cough syrup again," Big Joe suggested. "Remember in Phoenix, when he chugged NyQuil and became convinced he was a bologna sandwich and wanted people to eat him?"

"Never mind that. We've got to get him out of here."

We managed to get Pic to his feet. He put his arms around our shoulders and mewled.

"Don't worry," I said. "We're here to help."

As we dragged the half-conscious Piccirilli toward the door, a woman stepped in front of us. She immediately caught my attention for three reasons:

1. She was strikingly attractive, and most of the other orgy participants looked like shaved wombats.

2. She was still clothed, unlike everyone else in the room.

3. She had a look in her eye that I immediately recognized—a

twinkle, a glimmer, the hint of mischief and mayhem, and the promise that she could give people bad days if she wanted to. I have the same look, or so I'm told.

"Mr. Keene isn't signing autographs," Big Joe told her. "Please step aside."

She smiled at him. "When I make my first million, you'll be the first one up against the fucking wall."

I thought perhaps I'd fallen in love.

"W-who are you?" I asked.

"Alethea. Alethea Kontis. And if you guys are leaving, take me with you. This party is boring."

So we did.

Now that there were more of us, the wizards and hobbits and the rest of the long-underwear crowd got out of our way. We escaped back to my room, where Big Joe had wisely kept some Corona and Miller Lite on ice. But soon, our serenity was shattered when some computer hackers from a party in the next room raided ours, offered to trade me a bottle of vodka for a bottle of whiskey, and then ranted at me about *Revenge of the Sith*. We gave them the rest of the beer and the key to the room, and told them they could have it if we could leave first. The hackers agreed.

We found another party on the fourth floor of the hotel. This was a more laid back affair. A small group of people with guitars were singing "Kumbaya" and various Pink Floyd and Neil Young songs. Big Joe clapped happily. Pic sank into a recliner and hummed along to "Heart of Gold." I pulled Alethea into the corner and got to know her better.

"So, you mentioned your first million earlier. Sounds to me like you're planning a revolution."

"Oh, yes," she said. "When I make my first million, I intend to kill all the redheads in the world by hiring hit men."

"You don't like redheads?"

"There's not a more wretched race of scum and villainy than redheads."

"And you're going to pay people to eradicate them?"

"Yes. Then I'll donate the rest of my money to charity."

I nodded, faking understanding. "It's good to have goals."

Suddenly, a very drunken old man named Ken, who, in convention circles, is apparently famous for nothing more than being a very drunken old man named Ken, leaned back on his chair and shouted in our general direction.

"Don't be stupid!"

"Is he talking to us?" Alethea whispered.

"Let's pretend he isn't," I said. "If we ignore him, maybe he'll sing another verse of 'Kumbaya.'"

"I heard what she said," Ken yelled. "Don't be stupid."

Alethea and I started giggling. Pic was laughing as well, but since his eyes were closed, I think he was more likely enjoying his own little joke.

Ken jumped out of his chair. "Don't be stupid you fucking Yankee."

I'd had enough. "Dude, chill the fuck out or I'll sic my bodyguard on you."

He responded by throwing a meatloaf at us. I don't know where it came from, nor did I know just how much an airborne meatloaf thrown at a high velocity could hurt when it smacks you in the head.

Then Alethea beat the shit out of him and we grabbed Pic and Big Joe and retreated back to my room, where she proceeded to do the same thing to the hackers. Turns out Alethea was trained in the secret ways of the ninja.

And the meatloaf tasted pretty good, too, in retrospect.

Alethea Kontis.

She's badass. And hot. Oh, and she writes books. Including this one: *Beauty and Dynamite.*

You should read it.

—Brian Keene
Heart of Darkness, Pennsylvania
September 2007

PART ONE

Destined for Greatness

To me it is to reach out, touch the mirror
And finally have my hand go through
To stand at a door and open it
On the other side of the world
To address my reflection in a still pond
And have it speak back
To see a star fall
At my feet
It is more than a man
It is more than a miracle
It is the hope of the impossible
It is the dream of the dream
Within the dreamer

-from *Intangible*, 1999

Casey A. Cothran says...

I know a lot of secrets about Alethea Kontis. Oh yes, indeed.

When I think of Alethea, I think of her at sixteen, in her black and white bathing suit, her long brown hair pulled up into a complicated bun that's held in place by chopsticks. She is sitting on the dock in her backyard, slathering her skin with baby oil and watching the clouds as they roll along over the lake.

But that's just a picture.

Let me see. I can expose some little known facts about the author. One: She knows the secret trick to making perfect baklava. Two: Her father can read the future in coffee grounds. Three: To date, I believe she's had her heart broken by three men. Four: She knows how to shoot a gun.

That's not enough either, is it?

Perhaps I can tell you a story.

Once upon a time, a girl with dark hair and dark eyes met a girl with light hair and light eyes. The two girls, for they were girls still, not almost-women like some of their classmates, were determined to devote their lives to magic. Consequently, they spent their free time reading books about dragons and writing stories about unicorns and talking with each other about the greatest magic of all–the dream of somehow eluding the cold claws of the real world.

The girl with dark hair and dark eyes was interested in portals. She formulated the theory that an average girl might develop the ability to shift out of concrete reality and move into a world of her own making.

As the evening crickets began to play their mournful songs, she used a green pen to describe an alternate world held together by a band of gold.

The girl with light hair and light eyes was interested in sight. Because she wore glasses, she knew that eyes could play tricks. This knowledge made her eager to see new things, and also to question the things that she saw. She used a pen as well, peeling up the gray rectangles of reality in search of hidden colors and secret patterns.

The two girls loved each other dearly, and spent the years of their youth talking about history, practicing their writing, and swimming in the magical space between the green-black bottom of the lake and the blue bowl of the sky. They got jobs at a movie theater so that they could be surrounded by storytelling. They spent their evenings popping popcorn, watching as hard orange kernels were transformed into something entirely new: weightless poufs of white and gold.

But the day came when the girls, women now, were asked to set out on their life quests, to leave the homes they had known as girls and to venture into the wilderness. So they set out. And they both learned a secret, but each in her own way.

The girl with dark hair and dark eyes found herself immersed in the study of science, but after many hours in white laboratories she discovered that science did not hold the key to shifting reality. Physics cannot show a woman how to walk through a rainstorm without getting wet–how to step between the drops, deftly avoiding the cold grief that pours down out of the sky. Only magic can do that. So the girl with dark hair and dark eyes took up her pen again and threw away her test tubes and Bunsen burners.

The girl with light hair and light eyes learned to climb towers. From the top of a tower, she could see so far, so wide! She climbed tower after tower, always in search of something new to see. But she soon learned that towers were lonely places, and she began to wonder if she could find other magics in common places on the ground. So she took up her pen again, but in a new way, and with new eyes.

And so in places far away, in rooms small or large, two pens continue to fly across sheets of paper. Fingers dance on keyboards, eyes rove over pages. The magic of girlhood faded away long ago, but the pens keep up their work. The girl with dark hair and dark eyes works on the chemical formula that will transform an amphibian into a man. The girl with light hair and light eyes makes tangles of lines and words and then straightens them out again. As pens move, queens rise and fall, legacies are begun and ended, mirrors are broken and then pieced back together. Perhaps one day the stringy old stallion, sassy with age, will grow wings and rise up from earthly fields of gold. With luck he may carry both women into the clouds, and all three will join the invisible war between angels and demons. And so it goes. Once upon a time, a girl with dark hair and dark eyes met a girl with light hair and light eyes.

Meeting Sherrilyn Kenyon

Rutherford Reader
March 6, 2003

If you're a bibliophile, you know there's almost nothing as wonderful as discovering an extraordinary author you've never read before. Except maybe finding out she lives only an hour away and getting to meet her right before she hits the big time.

My friend Nicole and I are great fans of the romance genre. Sure, anyone can be literary, but we appreciate the finer points of escapist fiction. Even better, we get to recommend things to each other and discuss them at length. Our own little book club of two. We stumbled on Sherrilyn Kenyon in a short story collection entitled *Tapestry*. Her novella, "Dragonswan," was a fun and unique mixture of fantasy and romance that made the other three stories in the book pale in comparison. Immediately, we set out on the internet to find out more, hoping this extremely talented woman had a ready backlist so we could gobble it up.

Not only did we find that Mrs. Kenyon had full-length novels under her belt, but we also came across a number of books she wrote under the pseudonym Kinley MacGregor. We ordered them all and took turns reading and discussing them. In less than two weeks we had made it through her entire list, and Mrs. Kenyon had become our new favorite author.

On her website, we were thrilled to find that she would be signing books at the Borders in Franklin the day before Valentine's Day. We were giddy for weeks, and made plans to meet up there.

Shame on Borders for not advertising the event more. If we hadn't checked the website, we never would have known about the event. As it was, upon entering the store, our first thought was that we had the wrong place. There wasn't even a flyer on the door. I was kind of disappointed at the turnout, but it was a bit of a double-edged sword. I was sad that such an excellent local author was still so relatively unknown, but Nicole and I were ridiculously grateful that we could unabashedly monopolize her time. Which, of course, we did.

Mrs. Kenyon is a delightful, petite redhead with a sparkling personality. And after talking to her for a bit, you realize that she's the sort of entertaining and honest girlfriend anyone would love to have. She lives in Spring Hill with her husband and three boys. I asked her if, as a romance author, her husband was ever jealous of her fictional leading men. "Oh, I always tell him they're really him," she answered with a lusty wink.

Her young sons manage to keep her on her toes. Ian, the youngest, manages to rat her out every time she's on the computer researching male models for her website. "For a three-year-old, he can manage to be awfully quiet," she said, laughing. Ian, no doubt, has a great future as a true Spy Kid.

As Kinley MacGregor, Mrs. Kenyon writes historical novels; two have a piratical story arc, the others are set in the Scottish Highlands and center around the men of clan MacAllister. Under her own name, Mrs. Kenyon penned last year's *Fantasy Lover*, a modern tale of mythical proportions. Her newest, *Night Pleasures*, is definitely for the *Buffy the Vampire Slayer* set (yes, the author is a fan). The hero, Kyrian, is a vampire, but don't worry—like Angel, he's one of the good guys. There are other Dark-Hunters, of course, and *Night Embrace*, which comes out in July, will continue this series.

Just don't try asking the author if she has a favorite. We did. "Just wait 'til you read about Zarek," she smiled, with an appreciative purr. "Or Ash. Ash is very tortured." Which only implies that the best is yet to come. Nicole and I certainly can't wait for them all.

Check out the "Upcoming Books" section on her website—she has tentative plot lines for both the MacAllister and Dark-Hunter series all the way up to 2005. Be prepared to spend some time, though, it's one of the most amazing sites I've ever been on. No surprise, I guess, as Mrs. Kenyon was once a web designer for Bookville. Apparently, she spends almost as much time working on her website as she does writing—a feat in itself.

Be sure to pick up *Night Pleasures* and become a fan. Nicole and I will join you in line at the next signing. I'm betting that with Mrs. Kenyon's growing popularity we won't have quite as much time to chat with her in the future!

Journal from Orson Scott Card's Boot Camp

July 2003

DAY 0

So I'm here. After almost nine stinkin' hours in the car, I'm here. The traffic through the mountains was terrible, and the weather increasingly worse. It is now officially a "dark and stormy night"—the perfect way to start a writing class, don't you think? After glancing at the list of the Boot Campers, I noticed that most were girls. In fact, all the names I caught were girl names. Not really sure what this means...but I think I would still feel more comfortable on the boys' side of the dormitory, talking geek stuff. I'm just not good with girls. Casey always did that. So far only one said "Hi" to me as I was bringing in a bunch of my junk. One saw me in the hall and completely ignored me. So be it, I guess. I may slink out to the lobby later and see if anyone shows up and wants to talk.

I have a "single," despite the fact that there are two of everything in this cell. The bed is like an army cot, the window only opens halfway, and I can reach up and touch the ceiling in the hallway on the way to the communal bathroom.

Oh, I guess if there are tons of girls I should think about shower time in the morning. I'll just conquer that one later, too.

I feel like I've regressed to being alone, back in my room at home. Only the technology is better.

Things will be more social tomorrow; I have faith.

There were two women at the desk when I came in, a young girl and an older woman with a foreign accent. The girl told me that Tuesday, Orson Scott Card will be asking for volunteers to complete their story early, and that I should keep that in mind. Should I be writing now? I don't really have anything original *now*.

Yeah, I'm nervous. Kind of wish I had brought a book, but kind of glad I didn't. I brought *Grimms' Fairy Tales*—I suppose I can read a couple of those and nudge inspiration along.

I'm very glad to be out of the car.

I'm very glad that I brought power bars and water in case I feel too agoraphobic.

I'm glad I don't feel bad about having the AC on and the window open.

I think the rain's stopped. Or slowed down, anyway. The sky is still grumbling. My forearms are killing me from all the yard work yesterday. But it looks good, and I get to appreciate it when I get home.

My sister said to get in the mood to write you had to first get out three pages of crap. Maybe Sami meant written crap. Typed crap seems to last a lot longer, and I don't really want to do this for two more pages. I don't really have anything else to talk about. The rain's started again.

Evanescence's *Fallen* is a good CD. I listened to it a lot on the way here. My head hurts. Maybe I'll have a precious power bar and a couple Excedrin.

I have to remember that the clock on the computer is an hour behind. I don't really feel like going in and changing it just for this week. I guess I will if it pisses me off or something. So it's 8:30 and not 7:30. Doesn't matter today anyway. Tonight. Whatever.

I hate being in the car that long. I feel like I smell. And I don't feel like experimenting with showers. Maybe I will in a bit. Then I won't have to mess with it in the morning, right? I have to remember, I didn't get here by being timid. I suppose if it's me that has to break the ice, so be it.

Man, why does it always have to be me? Why can't I go back to the old days of making Sami ask for ketchup at McDonald's?

What the hell am I going to write about? Maybe I'll be so inspired tomorrow, I'll write at every break and be one of the cool people to go first. I have a one-in-nine chance. I don't have to be first. But I probably will be, right?

Why couldn't this have been a more active floor? Why couldn't there have been an impromptu gathering planned in the lobby? Why the hell isn't everyone acting like they're on *Felicity*? I am so dormitory ignorant...which means I can get away with anything, right? Heehee...

I WANT TO DO SOMETHING!!!

<u>9:00 PM</u>

Well, I wandered downstairs. There were three people in the lobby—two on computers and an older woman on a couch with a notebook (a real one, not a computer). So I walked down and checked out the pool table (twenty-five cents, but only one cue stick had a tip on it, what good is that?) and the air hockey table, and the floor covered in dead...worms? Centipedes? And the nice covered back porch, where

I found out that if you shut the door you get locked out. Well, how was I going to find out if I didn't try? The front door stays open 'til 10:00pm, so I have a whole nother hour to get locked out.

When I came back in the front door, the older lady was gone. The girl and guy were still on the computers, silent as anything. Is there some rule where writers all have to be hapless introverts? Must have been on the memo I didn't get. I have the feeling I didn't get a lot of memos.

I said hi to one more girl as she left the bathroom. She's in 305. I'm in 304, across the hall. The stairs at the end are being worked on; the glue is on all the steps, but the rubber steps are not in place. There is, however, a plastic cup sitting in the glue on one of the steps. I can't help but wonder if that is now a permanent addition.

There's a bulletin board at the end of the hall. It has one thumbtack in it. I took out a piece of notebook paper and wrote in big black letters, "ARE WE HAVING FUN YET?"

Aren't writers supposed to have imaginations? Aren't they supposed to be curious? I went into the shower stall. Doesn't look too complicated. I think I might have a go. Some old sticker on the back of the door limits the shower taker to five minutes. I laughed out loud at that one. Hey, it's summer. I doubt the hot water's in jeopardy.

Okay. Plan of attack. Take a shower and go sit in the lobby with the damn book and attract some attention. Get some ideas. Write some stuff. Wish I had stolen Dave's headphones. Hey—if they want to break the silence and tell me to turn the music down, that's a step, isn't it?

Holy shit, I'm on page three, aren't I?

9:30 PM

Okay, braved the bathroom. It wasn't so bad. What am I saying? It's a bathroom. Aren't we supposed to be geniuses or something?

Maybe not. So I'm all nice & clean & smelling like coconut 'cause I ran out of mango body butter (why does that stuff have to cost a fortune?) and realizing that I have a billion skeeter bites on my legs from Patrick's house. Guess I should have put that questionable spray stuff on after all.

Well, at least the girls in the corner at the computers are talking. And laughing. So I guess we're not all lost causes. So I wasn't brave enough to breach their sanctum—I took the couches on the other side. I should go across the room and see what fun pictures are up on the wall.

I can't figure out what the etching on this table says. Some enterprising youth has carved something like "I love vicious Ed" or some nonsense on it. If anyone else comes over, I'll get their take on it.

Have I done three pages yet? I can't get comfortable on this stupid couch. Maybe it's 'cause I'm wearing shorts. I need to give the stinky car jeans a break, though.

I need to think of more things to write. I thought of a few things on the way down while I was stuck in traffic—Sami laughed at me for writing in traffic while other sane people would have been talking on the cell phone or something.

The girls have stopped talking. Some guy walked out and then in again. That makes two, I guess. Of course, I don't know how many more are sequestered here for the class, how many are for the Boot Camp, and how many are here for other things.

Did I mention this lasts until Saturday? I thought Friday was the last day, but after looking at the agenda again, it appears I was wrong. I don't know why I thought that. Oh, one more boy. What do you know? And he talks too. What a freaking miracle. I guess I could go check out the computers, but I don't want to be on the Internet. I just want to write. Isn't that what we're here for? Then again, what am I writing now? Just a bunch of crap. Am I supposed to be writing a story? Do you think anyone would have told me if I was? Why isn't there some outgoing person in here?

Am I done with the three pages of crap yet?

I guess after this I can work on a story. Or brainstorm some other crapola. One of the girls left. The other one sitting at the computer has hair about like mine, in a long braid. I don't want us to be cookie cutter writers. I want us to all be different. I want to be unique in the whole fairy tale/suburban fantasy thing. Of course, if that were *really* true, I wouldn't get a job anywhere. So I suppose others need to be out there. But that stupid "be the best" thing is still stuck in my head from where my parents put it there twenty years or so ago. I want to think that my name (albeit spelled "Althea") was first on the list because my story was a shoe-in and that the rest were debatable, and not because it begins with "A."

This is going to be fun.

This is going to be educational.

This is going to be tough because it's supposed to be.

I'll make a few friends.

I hope.

Oh, lookie there. Page four.

DAY 2

Well, shee-ite. I should have written six pages the first night I was here, 'cause I haven't been able to do anything since but classwork. We had *seven* writing assignments last night, and we got out of class at about 5:30 or 6:00. The first three assignments were to go to the library and research something you knew nothing about. (I uncovered some books about engraving, one involving the lost works of Victorian female engravers, and one about alchemical engravings which I didn't get too far into because the first was so amazing, and my partner was so antsy.) (We had to have partners.)

The second group of three was to go around and *look* at everything.

"See the world through the eyes of a writer," he said. To which I replied, "Like we don't already." And to which Orson Scott Card responded, "You'd be surprised how many people don't."

That reminds me of *Joe vs. the Volcano*, about how most of the world is asleep, and those of us who are awake live in a state of constant amazement. It's funny to think that there are writers in this room who don't sign a waiver at the doctor's office and then think up a scene to go along with that. Or look at the graffiti on the underside of the lid of a dumpster and don't imagine that's where a serial killer marked the bodies.

The last assignment was the interview. Yes, after going to the library for two hours and eating dinner, we had to walk up to a stranger (the reason we had partners) and ask them for an interview. After which we were supposed to make up a story based on elements of things they told us about their lives. Since my partner was from Greensboro, I took advantage of that. We went to a nice restaurant to eat (I had a huge hamburger because I felt I deserved it) and then I proclaimed that I wanted to go to Walmart to interview the greeter at the front door. This person usually has nothing more to do than say "Hello" and hand shopping carts out to walkers-in.

Ben went reluctantly—he decided that doing an interview wasn't for him. So be it. I'm going to squeeze as much out of this class as humanly possible. I planned on writing all six stories, too. But, as is always my problem, there aren't enough hours in the day.

Clara was the name of the lady offering the cart on our way in. She looked like a nice old lady who probably had a lot of stories under her belt. I introduced myself and said I was in a writing class, and asked her if she wouldn't mind being interviewed. Well, Clara told me she'd be glad, but that I should really interview "that lady over there." She pointed over her shoulder at a stout blonde woman wearing polka dots under her regulation Wally-blue vest. "She's from Germany," Clara whispered, as if it were a precious secret (see, I'm writing this story already!).

I waited until a young man pushed a caterpillar train of shopping carts into their station, and then introduced myself to Greta.

The first thing she told me was that she wasn't allowed to say anything about Walmart. I reassured her that that's not why I was there—I needed to know about her life. I started with some standard interview questions— what was her first name and where was she from. To the latter question she responded, "Germany." So I prompted her by asking what town. "Mannheim."

My next question was if she had any siblings. One sister, 13 years younger. How did she come to America? With her now ex-husband—she worked for the American library. She told me about Germany, and how when she goes back she travels back and forth on the train that goes 200 miles an hour, and she always takes Swiss Air.

And then she told me that she went to school in the Black Forest.

The floodgates opened.

Her school was in the French Zone, which was the most dangerous section to be in. It was the home of French Legionnaires, cutthroat men from Morocco and elsewhere in North Africa. They were given free rein over the region, which meant they took whatever they wanted and could rape women whenever they pleased. Greta and a friend had the luck of being escorted by two young lieutenants from the German army.

OH CRAP, FIVE 'TILL NINE.

Suppose I should stop. But I'll come back.

Okay…so I ended up being so busy during class that I never did come back. But I'll tell you a little more about Greta so as not to keep you in complete suspense. Also in the town where she lived were a bunch of chemical treatment plants that were always being bombed by the

Americans. She remembered taking the train to school, and wishing that the Americans would bomb the tracks so she wouldn't have to go.

She also told me about how, when she was a teenager, she and her girlfriend would go to the hospitals where the Dutch soldiers were recuperating and help out.

One of those trips was the day she met Hitler.

Of course, I would be the writer who went deep into the middle-of-nowhere North Carolina and introduced myself to the one person who had met Hitler.

But that's another story.

Scott M. Roberts says...

If you're ever called upon upon to face hordes of man-eating centipedes, there's no better person to have by your side than Lee Kontis.

Platinum Master Card

Rutherford Reader
November, 2006

Orson Scott Card's new hardcover, Empire*: $24.95*
A week at Uncle Orson's Literary Boot Camp: Priceless

It was the summer of 2003. I was in the car, journeying from Murfreesboro, Tennessee to the University of North Carolina, Greensboro. I had been accepted into the exclusive week-long Literary Boot Camp taught by Orson Scott Card, award-winning author of *Ender's Game* and one of my favorite writers of all time. I was armed with a laptop, a composition pad, and a box of breakfast bars.

Had I been wearing boots at the time, I'd have shaken in them.

I couldn't stop wondering about what the week ahead of me might bring. The first two days would be the workshop, which was open to anyone. After that, only the preselected eighteen of us would go on to the next stage: twenty-four hours to write a short story from beginning to end, and then three days of collaborative, exhaustive critique.

Each year, eighteen nobodies who desperately want to be somebodies are accepted to Scott Card's Literary Boot Camp. Three years ago, I was a nobody too. Discounting all the drivel I had penned in my school days, I had only gotten serious about writing six months before the class. Now I had twenty-four hours in which to complete a short story and an eight hour drive on which to become very, very scared.

The quiet dorms and that first dark, still-before-the-storm night didn't help the situation. Especially when, bright and early the next morning, I walked into a lecture room FULL of people. Talk about intimidating.

James Maxey, Boot Camp Class of 2001 and author of cult SF classic *Nobody Gets the Girl* and the upcoming *Bitterwood*, was also caught off guard. "I knew he was popular," says Maxey, "but until I walked into the auditorium and saw the hundreds of people who had shelled out big bucks for his two-day lecture, it hadn't dawned on me just how popular." His classmate Quinn Reid, author of *Talk the Talk: the Slang of 65 American Subcultures*, was more familiar with Scott and his work. "He was among my favorite writers at the time, and he still is," says Reid. "Turned out Scott is not only a gifted writer, but also a gifted teacher."

Edmund Schubert, who recently acquired the position of Editor at Scott's online SF magazine *Intergalactic Medicine Show*, was a graduate of the 2004 Boot Camp. "I was impressed that so many people had come all that way. There were people from all over the country." Schubert also had specific ideas about the writing workshop. "I had already read Scott's book *Characters & Viewpoint* twice, so my initial thought was, 'Let's get this writing class over with and get on to the Boot Camp.' But I ended up learning so much during the first two days of class that I was actually sorry when that part ended."

Those first two days were definitely not a "sit back and soak up Scott Card's wisdom for a few hours" kind of class. They were two long days of intense, dynamic, interactive lecture. I went through two mechanical pencils, flying through pages of my composition book as I frantically scrambled down notes. We *learned*, and we learned *fast*. "I remember toward the end of the first day, when he assigned us homework after almost twelve hours of lectures and Q&A. I thought Scott was insane," says Maxey.

Yes, you heard right: homework. The "Boot Camp" moniker wasn't just some clever labeling. The year I attended, the homework had seven parts. On three notecards, we were to write three complete story outlines based on research we did in the library. On the next three, we were to write three story outlines based on objects we encountered in the world around us. The last card was reserved for the interview. We broke into pairs, and were assigned to interview a perfect stranger about their life. From that interview, we were to write our seventh story synopsis.

The whole room froze when Scott said the word "interview." Interview a complete stranger? Did he realize what he was asking? After staring at the blank, frightened stares of over a hundred students, he laughed. "I know, I know. You're all introverts. Just trust me on this one. I've broken you into pairs for safety. Now I'm going to tell you how to start such an interview. And then I'm going to tell you how to end it. You'll be fine."

Like he had been so many times in the past twenty-four hours, Scott was right. My partner (who thankfully lived in Greensboro and had a car), drove us a good distance away and took me directly to the place where I suddenly had a burning desire to interview someone: Walmart.

I shocked the class the next day when I stood up in front of everyone and read my card about a woman who lived in the Black

Forest region of Germany during World War II and who, on a visit to a hospice as a young teen, met Hitler. An amazing, *amazing* encounter I would have never had without Scott's encouragement.

But mine was not the first such notable card. "One of my fellow Boot Campers took it too far and wrote the entire story on the index card," says Reid. "Scott was so impressed with the story that he immediately faxed it to an editor he knew. 'Wait, wait!' I thought. 'Hold the success train so I can jump on!'"

What Quinn Reid might not have noticed at the time was that she was already on that train. In the next few years she would go on to win the esteemed Writers of the Future contest, secure a book contract and, inspired by Scott's leadership, create an online writer's haven of her own: the Codex Writers Group. "I've made good friends, and they are still a daily influence on my life," says Reid.

Other Boot Camp graduates have gone on to become contest winners, novelists, essayists…even agents and editors. But before we flirted with fortune and fame, we were all subjected to the great equalizer: the twenty-four hour original short story based on one of the story cards we had done for homework.

For my story, I chose a card I had done based on library research about a Victorian Society of Lady Etchers. I called my best friend Casey—who just so happened to be a PhD in Victorian Literature and a professor at the College of William and Mary—and talked to her until 2 a.m., hashing out the details of the story. After a few hours of unsatisfying sleep on the lumpy bed in the centipede-infested dorm room, I sat up, pulled the laptop onto the pillow, and started writing. I did not eat, shower, get dressed, or even move until I found myself tripping over the last word roughly eight hours later.

When the story was critiqued, Scott spent a few minutes telling me how fantastic it was, right before pointing out the laundry list of common mistakes I had made and writing crutches I had unknowingly used. But that first bit of honest praise from a man I so respected and admired left me on cloud nine for weeks.

James Maxey had a similar experience. "We left class around 8 p.m. on Tuesday. I went home, lit up the tiki torches on my deck, hauled out my laptop, and cranked out my story, finishing around five in the morning." The story Maxey wrote that day, "Pentacle on His Forehead, Lizard on His Breath," later sold to the *Modern Magic* anthology at Fantasist Enterprise. "More than any particular thing Scott said in a lecture or a critique, simply forcing me to write a complete, marketable story in such a short window of time gave me a tremendous boost in confidence and changed my previously tentative, over-thought approach to writing. Momentum matters!"

Boot Camp was a simultaneous self-confidence boost and slap in the face. We were all good writers—as my mother likes to point out, she didn't need some *New York Times* bestselling author to tell *her* what friends and family had known for years. The bucket of cold water was realizing that the biggest obstacle between us and success was just sitting down and *doing* it. "Boot Camp transformed my attitude toward writing" says Reid, "from vague and nervous and occasional to obsessed and constant. I started getting a realistic idea of how much further I could take my writing if I was willing to slave away at it."

Teachers love little more than seeing their students take what they have learned and carry on, and Scott is no exception. If a student can catch him between projects, they can sometimes get his thoughts on a first chapter, or the first few pages of a story. But he has been known to drop everything in the middle of his overwhelming schedule to go over the terms of a former student's book contract. And, thanks to the Internet, many of the Boot Camp alumni still keep in touch through online writer's groups. We continue to challenge and inspire each other, ever striving to follow in the steps of our great leader.

Because momentum matters.

James Maxey says...

I first "met" Alethea via email. My novel *Nobody Gets the Girl* had just barely been released when I got an email with the header "Your Wonderful Book." At this point, I don't think even I had gotten a copy of the novel, so I just assumed it was spam, especially since the sender, Alethea Kontis, was unknown to me. But, as I was getting ready to delete it, some tiny voice in the back of my head told me to at least open the email.

I'm glad I did. Alethea had just returned from Orson Scott Card's Writers Boot Camp, which I had attended two years before. Scott had mentioned my book to the class and Alethea had gotten her hands on a copy and became, for all I know, the first person not employed by the publisher or sent a review copy to actually read the thing. It was the start of a terrific correspondence. Alethea has proven knowledgeable in so many areas of publishing that she's the first person I turn to when I have a question. Also, we often wind up at the same cons together and I can report she is an excellent companion to chat with at the bar. Her energy and enthusiasm for all things bookish are infectious.

I'm firmly convinced that the day will come when Alethea's name will command the same type of attention in the publishing industry as that of Ellen Datlow. She's already on her way, with a slew of books and writing gigs everywhere. Let us hope, when her time of power comes, she will use her abilities for good and not for evil. Although, should she choose the evil route, I, for one, plan to stay on her good side.

Miss Andre's Library

August 12, 2003

The only way you can tell Andre Norton's house apart from the others on Eventide Drive is that hers is the one with the biggest mailbox. You pull into the driveway and around to the back and park in front of a big three-car garage.

I came bearing gifts, flowers and cat toys. I gave them to Rose, Miss Andre's bubbly assistant, who greeted me at the back door. Rose escorted me down the ramp to the library, where Miss Andre (she never told me what to call her, so I defaulted to the southern expression) was sitting, cataloguing books.

What does it look like? Well, imagine a room the size of a three-car garage, completely gutted. Then imagine bookshelves all around the walls of the perimeter and back-to-back rows in between. But it's not institutional; it's homey. It's what I would do if I had that much space, and that many bookshelves.

On top of all the bookshelves are things ranging from foreign and limited edition statues to Harry Potter toys. (I imagine Rose as an older Tonks—both she and Miss Andre are fans of Harry Potter.) On the walls are things like framed, signed artwork and authentic witches' brooms. (There are a few pics at the High Hallack website.)

In my bag I had two books and the email Scott Card had sent me telling me how jealous he was that I was going to meet her. She was, of course, one of the authors who influenced him most, and he admitted to still having dreams about her work. But I never touched my bag the whole time I was there. It seemed tacky. I did mention that I had just come from Boot Camp, and that Scott was a huge fan of hers. She kept on talking like she never heard it.

David Drake told me once that she didn't realize what a huge influence she'd been on the genre. It took me until that minute to realize he was telling the truth.

Miss Andre is what, 81? She's a plump woman with red hair and a bridge around her bottom teeth that constantly slips while she's talking (not that it stops her at all). She's wonderful. We talked (she did most of the talking) for two and a half hours. I told her about some of the things I was writing, and she took me on an informal tour of the library. We scooted from section to section in desk chairs. The books are divided into sections that would be most advantageous to a researching fiction writer.

There's Archeology, Unexplained Phenomena, History (broken out into Ancient, by cultures, and then the wars), the Victorian period, the Regency period, Costumes...there's even a section for comics. And that's only half the library.

It was like spending a few hours with my grandmother, albeit a grandmother who admits upon introduction that she's just found a manuscript that was "lying around" that was part of a series she was planning to write on the five women Nathaniel Hawthorne most hated because they were more popular than he was. (One day I want to be so prolific that I come across a book I forgot I'd written!)

She told the greatest stories, and had fantastic ideas about subjects to brainstorm. When Rose came in about 1:00 pm to offer us something to drink, Miss Andre turned to me and said, "So, will you be coming to work in the library?"

Hello?!? People would *die* to work in that library. You have to *apply* to go there. I just happen to be lucky enough to live less than a mile away. Of course I said yes. All I have to do is call the day before I come. Mornings are best, so it looks like the weekends for me.

I'm going to Alabama with a friend this weekend, but next Saturday you can find me at High Hallack.

Strawberry

December 2003

How much of the world should we shield our kids from? The great academic, Bruno Bettelheim, was very much against censoring. He felt that it was a better learning experience for children to hear all the original fairy tales, however gruesome. Through these tales, children developed their sense of identity. For instance: a child would often change her mind about her "favorite" fairy tale—the current favorite was the one the child most identified with during that stage of her life. (What were your favorites as a child? This is a great late-night discussion—you'll get to know more about your friends than you ever thought you did!)

Bruno wrote *Uses of Enchantment* in 1976. By then, he would have seen the abridged version of *Snow White* and the bloodless version of *Cinderella*. It's a good thing he wasn't around long enough to see Disney's painless *The Little Mermaid*. (Though he was probably spinning in his grave as it was.)

Not that I loved *The Little Mermaid* or *Beauty and the Beast* any less. These were magnificent feats of storytelling. They made leaps and bounds in many areas of animation and raised the bar for the quality of dialogue and songs. But they just didn't have any evil. They had "menacing" and "frightening," but not plain old horrifying flat-out *evil.* Kids need evil. They need the bad to teach them what's good; they need the wrong to teach them what's right.

For some reason, that concept is foreign to today's entertainment industry. The more "advanced" we get, the more stuff for kids becomes as bland and harmless as vanilla pudding. Why is that? Kids are having sex younger, experimenting with drugs younger, killing each other younger—why are we protecting them from evil when they're going to have to recognize it pretty quickly in real life?

And when I say evil, I don't mean guns and death. I don't mean sex and nudity. I don't mean all those "bad" cable-television words that your kids know anyway.

I mean Strawberry Shortcake.

That's right, you heard me. Strawberry-friggin'-Shortcake. Just when you thought the world was safe. Who could take something as harmless (and slightly annoyingly so) as Strawberry Shortcake and give it a lobotomy? If you haven't seen this latest incarnation, you need to. Check out www.strawberryshortcake.com. But bring your barf bag.

Forget Straberryland as it was in the 80's—it now has all the feel of "Happy Tree Friends" (without the bittersweet bloodbath) and all the finesse of a politically correct Target commercial. Strawberry is still terminally happy, the sun always shines, her friends are all representatives from the United Colors of Benneton, and NOTHING BAD EVER HAPPENS. What's the point??

And where the hell is the Pieman?

The Pieman. You remember the Pieman. He was the best thing

about Strawberry Shortcake. He even had a theme song. 'Cause he was "The Peculiar Purple Pieman of Porcupine Peak...ya-ta-ta-ta-TA-ta...ta-TA-ta-TA." He had a big puffy purple chef's hat and a flock of blackbirds that followed him around and helped him make mischief. He was always trying to get the best of that naïve, do-gooder Shortcake kid. But Strawberry and her friends would always band together and triumph over his wickedness.

But if there's no Purple Pieman, what's the point? That's like having to watch "The Smurfs" without Gargamel or Azrael.

I know there are no new ideas, and that Hollywood's favorite pastime is taking our childhood memories and ripping them to shreds, but I would love to meet the executive whose bright idea it was to scrap the Pieman and give her a nice, fat bitchslap.

No wonder these kids are growing up on Teletubbies and Barney and then shooting up their classrooms and themselves. Maybe if they knew that Cinderella went to the ball three times before she was noticed by the prince, that the ugly stepsisters cut pieces of their feet off to fit inside the glass slipper, that the Little Mermaid killed herself because the prince married the girl he thought saved him, or that Sleeping Beauty was knocked up by the prince before he woke her, they might realize the responsibility they would have to take for their actions. Perhaps they would have a better idea of—and respect for—mortality.

I'm calling my band of renegades "Bruno's Bunch." Our mission is to read the untouched myths and shun the crap that's out there for kids today. Maybe years from now, the teenage pregnancy rate will drop, kids won't bring weapons to school, and there won't be so much hubbub about sex and violence in films because people will know the difference between reality and fantasy.

Blood, guts, Lemony Snicket, Gargamel, and the Pieman.

Amen.

Interlude

My blog didn't launch until October of 2004, but a lot more was happening in my personal life that wasn't exactly fodder for my review column in the *Rutherford Reader*. Several events were particularly notable:

January 2004

1.) I kicked a disappointing live-in boyfriend out of my house. From here on out, he is referred to as "the Ex."

2.) A handful of Boot Camp alumni and a handful of Writers of the Future alumni got together on an email chain (started by Quinn Reid) and decided it would be a good idea to create an online writing collective called the Codex Writers Group. For me, Codex wasn't just smart, it was life-changing. Its founders (including me, Quinn, James Maxey, Eric James Stone, Lawrence Schoen, Robert Defendi, and Max) instantly became my best friends in the world.

March 2004

Back in November 2003, I had woken up on the couch one morning with a great idea for a story about the alphabet, based on a conversation we'd had at Scott Card's Boot Camp. I wrote it down in about eight hours, typed it up, and sent it to a couple of friends of mine at Bookville to see what they thought. One of the women found it amusing and asked if she could, forward the story to a friend of hers who would enjoy it. I said of course, and didn't think much about it.

In March, I received a call at my desk at Bookville from Liz Bicknell, the head editor of Candlewick Press. Somehow the head of their art department had gotten a hold of my story, read it out loud to the entire department, and they were all cracking up—could they please, please publish it?

I said yes.

That story was called "The Telaphab from Z-A"...what later became *AlphaOops: The Day Z Went First.*

When we started Codex, I had felt like a big impostor again, with no published stories and nothing but an audition-only workshop under my belt. Within two months, it was like someone had waved a magic wand. Suddenly, I was legit. The best part is that I had friends with whom I could share my excitement...and my frustration over having a contract but not being published until 2007 (the original proposed pub date).

July 2004

My little sister and her boyfriend got a new apartment and invited us all to Charleston for an apartment-warming party. I drove down. Mom and Dad were there. And since I was still bummed out over the whole Ex business and confused about what to do with my life, I asked Mom if she would ride back to Tennessee with me and then fly home from there.

Mom and I solved all the world's problems on that eight-hour drive home. She told me that I needed to make a list of what I wanted in a guy and then use that list as a self-counselor. If the next guy I dated didn't have something on that list I felt was vital, It would essentially be *me* telling *myself* he wasn't good enough from the get-go.

Silly as it was, I made the list. Number one was "Foreign Duke." Number two was "Doesn't live with his mother."

August 2004

This is when I fell in love.

Max and I started rapid-fire emailing each only a few days after that fateful drive home with Mom. Our relationship quickly went from snowball to avalanche. He said the most amazing, romantic things and kind of checked off every single item on that list, with the exception of "Owns a Boat."

The universe didn't just click with me over Max…it *sang*.

I have never fallen for anyone like I fell for Max. This was *love*, real love, romantic love, the kind of love Shakespeare wrote about, the kind of love most people are lucky to even dream of having. I didn't eat or sleep for two straight weeks. We emailed and talked almost every minute of every waking hour, both on my side of the planet and his. I would print out his letters and take them with me everywhere I went and read them over and over again and marvel at the magical serendipity of the universe. I soaked up everything he loved like a sponge: authors, television shows, music. The world *glowed*. My body hummed. I randomly broke into screams of joy.

November 2004

I was positive that Max was my soulmate the angels had handed me on a silver platter. I called Mom and told her that I'd met the man

I was going to marry. Without so much as a pause, she asked if she should start planning a wedding. (That part made me break out in hives, because I never, *never* wanted a wedding.)

I told her that there was one small hiccup: I needed to actually meet him in person first. But that was okay, because we had decided to hook up in London right after Christmas. Me—the introverted, borderline agoraphobic, workaholic daughter who never wore skirts and never left home—was suddenly going to purchase an entire new wardrobe and fly halfway around the world to fall into the arms of some man she'd never met.

This time, Mom did pause. And when I asked for her help, she booked a ticket to fly up and stay with me for a couple of weeks at the beginning of December, so that we could sort out the details.

And with that, we now rejoin our story, already in progress…

The True Dead

November 11, 2004

Someone started a thread on Codex, asking what languages all our members speak. Man, not only are we international, we are a seriously diverse and educated group!

We're also a bunch of nutcases. After spoken language roll call, someone mentioned C++ and Fortran…it's only a matter of time before someone brings up the Language of Love.

Love has been referred to as "the unspoken language." But really…think about it. I bet you could turn to your significant other right now and spout a stream of seemingly unconnected words that would send you both into paroxysms of laughter and leave everyone else in the room incredibly puzzled. And not just words: names, songs, gestures, phrases. A wrinkle of the nose, a lift of the eyebrow—everything means something. It's a unique country with a population of two.

Writers are students of the world. We pay attention to things. And we have a love affair with words that normal people can't even begin to comprehend. Wanna know what made me cry the hardest after breaking up with my last boyfriend? I wasn't just losing a companion, I was losing a language. There were words that would not cross my lips again for as long as I lived. Made-up syllables that would never again be uttered into the ether. I was more connected to the words than I was to him. Forget Latin. Old Love is the true dead language.

And I mourned.

We throw ourselves on that bed of nails so that we can learn more about ourselves...and then get up and do it all over again. Painful lessons. But those who have not spent time on that dark side of the moon can't appreciate what it's like to see the sun. On the flip side of that orbit was my soulmate, the love of my life. (We'll call him Max, so I can talk about him and he won't get stalked.)

It's only been three months. Incredible. It seems like so long ago. I know the definition of every sigh. When I read his emails, I hear them in the inflection of his voice. Words like "ice cream" and "hobby" and "mayfly" have whole new meanings. And the first few beats of the theme to *Chariots of Fire* give me fits of giggles.

I would gladly give up all other languages to be what I am now—fluent in Max. And one of the happiest women in the world.

Real Isn't How You Are Made

November 30, 2004

"When a child loves you for a long, long time, not just to play with, but REALLY loves you, then you become Real."

"Does it hurt?" asked the Rabbit.

"Sometimes," said the Skin Horse, for he was always truthful. "When you are Real, you don't mind being hurt."

—The Velveteen Rabbit

Quinn had the Fantastic Four take personality tests today, so she could compare the actual results against what her genius mastermind had already decided we were. (Not surprisingly, she was pretty much correct.) Apparently, I am an "Idealist" of the INFP type.

I don't take a lot of stock in answers that computers spit out at me for filling in bubbles to multiple choice questions, but this was pretty much spot on. I live in two completely different worlds. I act like a normal functioning member of society, and then I go home and play with my stuffed animals.

I read *The Velveteen Rabbit* once. I never could read it again. It was too emotional. I saw the life that had been breathed into the stuffed rabbit, and I refused to believe that the same soul had transferred into a real-life bunny. It wasn't like Pinocchio, it was different. The little boy's best friend had died, and he was never coming back.

So does this—my mildly introverted self's penchant for a rich fantasy life—explain why I find The Invisible Ones irresistible?

It's a common enough thing in this e-day and age. People "meet" every day, all over the world, without ever really meeting. They become friends, share stories, talk and laugh together. Years go by. And you forget that one little trivial thing. You still haven't *actually* met.

In a way, it's a bit like stuffed animals, but backwards. We are given the essence of the person, and we fit them into the box of our imagination. What they look like, what their facial expressions might be, what they're wearing that day, what they had for lunch, what they really think of us. Four years and three days ago, I started my job at Bookville. Priscilla called me that day to welcome me there. We've been the internet equivalent of soul sisters ever since. And next weekend, four years and fourteen days from that first phone call, I will finally meet her.

Nadia always says she doesn't want to meet the people she knows only in an online capacity. Maybe she's afraid the real thing will blow her imaginary box to Kingdom Come. Me? Well, maybe I was scared at first. Okay, I *was* scared. When I saw Quinn for the first time, we met in a public place, and I brought half my family with me. It seems silly now, of course, but *then* it seemed like the logical thing to do. And then I met James. And Tom. The best thing about it? Each of them was more wonderful in real life than I could have ever imagined.

It made me absolutely giddy. Because there's one more person I have to meet. One more soulmate who in a week knew me inside and out and became one of my best friends in the whole wide world. And I need to stop worrying—worrying about all the things that don't matter, worrying about me being Real for him.

"It doesn't happen all at once," said the Skin Horse. "You become. It takes a long time. That's why it doesn't often happen to people who break easily, or have sharp edges, or have to be carefully kept. Generally, by the time you are Real, most of your hair has been loved off, and your eyes drop out, and you get loose in the joints and very shabby. But these things don't matter at all, because once you are Real you can't be ugly, except to people who don't understand."

Impossible Things Before Breakfast

December 2, 2004

Don't you hate people who are negative? People who say horrid and untrue things about themselves, so you can reply, "Oh, come on, you're not like that at all, you're wonderful!" just to have them smile and not believe you?

Yeah. I'm one of those. It even gets on *my* nerves.

The other day, I woke up and decided I wasn't going to get out of bed until I could think of something nice about myself. (Something nice that wasn't "smart" or "really great hair," 'cause those are way past tired at this point.) I couldn't think of anything. (I got up anyway.) I've thought about this for two days now, and wondered why it's so frustrating. This really shouldn't be that hard. I really am not that bad a person. Everyone *else* seems to like me just fine—leave it to me to be difficult and different.

It was something Max said to me that broke through the semi-conscious pea-soup fog in my stubborn brain. My wonderful, talented, romantic, amazing boyfriend. I so don't deserve him.

That's when I caught myself. Right there.

Because I *do* deserve him—him and all the best and all the mess that come with him. I am a great and beautiful woman, and I deserve lots of wonderful things. Like Quinn says, it's awfully satisfying to wish for things you already have. So. Every morning, I will think of at least three things I deserve. Here are my three things for today:

1.) I deserve to have friends who care about me so much, they're always giving me advice. (It's nice that those friends are so incredibly brilliant that their advice is actually *helpful.*)

2.) I deserve to have a mom who loves me so much she will fly to my rescue when I am too much of a mess to sort myself out. (Which I will really do my best to try and keep down to twice a year.)

3.) I deserve to have a boyfriend who will go halfway across town on his late morning just so he can talk to me for fifteen precious minutes before he has to go in to work. Because you're right, Duckie, I am worth a $25 cab ride.

My…I feel better already.

Swallowing the Worm

December 3, 2004

The Caterpillar once asked me who I was. I told him I was a writer. It was probably the first time I had ever been honest with myself. But while the Caterpillar may set you on your path, the wisdom is in the worm.

Mom and I went out for dinner last night. Deep into her second margarita, she sprung on me a diatribe that I never would have suspected she had flown seven hundred miles to impart. I was going on again about how badly I wanted to place in Writers of the Future, especially now that my fellow Boot Camp members Eric James Stone and Scott Roberts have both placed in quarters for 2004.

"Alethea," she said, swirling the ice around with her straw, "I need to tell you something. Are you going to listen?"

"Yes," I said. Of course I said yes. If your mother ever poses that question, "Yes" is always the correct answer.

"You have to stop this," she said. "You know exactly what you need to do to win that dumb contest. And you can do it if you want to."

"But I don't write what K.D. likes, Mom, and—"

"Ahh!" She aimed her straw at me. "Don't interrupt! Jesus, now I know what your father goes through when he's talking to me, 'cause I do the same thing." She took a sip of the fluorescent green liquid. Margaritas always look like a nifty crossbreed of lemonade and toxic waste. Me, I prefer water. "You can do it, and you know you can. You just don't *want* to. Because you know you would have to conform."

I didn't say anything, but we talented writers have ways of expressing ourselves without words. Mom laughed. "I wish I had a picture of your face," she said. "You've been making that face since you were four years old."

I thought about it. She was right. (She usually is, as she is constantly wont to remind me.) I knew exactly how to describe that face. Petulant. Incorrigible. In simpler Mom terms: ugly. Because "ugly" in our family was never about how you looked, it was about how you acted. And man, I was one ugly, cherub-faced brat. Still am.

Mom licked the huge salt crystals from the side of the glass. "It's why you almost failed English in school. You never wanted to write what they wanted, the way they wanted it. It's why you never would have been able to major in journalism. It's why you were never able to take criticism—at least, before Orson Scott Card."

"But Casey—" Oops. That was out loud.

"Casey doesn't count," she scolded. "She's the only one of us who ever *could* say anything, through that special best friend link she has to you. When you told me you were going to that Boot Camp, I was scared to death for you. But you came out just fine. You grew up. And you realized that you *are* talented, like we've been telling you all along."

I smiled. She was still mad that I hadn't believed that bit until I heard it from "some total stranger." Helped, though, that the total stranger in question was one of my heroes.

She took another sip. "The way I see it, you can do one of two things. You can suck it up and *conform*..." She eyed me. I had made the face again. What is it about that word? "...and sell your writing. Or you can write anything you want, not care about what people say and maybe get lucky, or maybe be famous after you're dead."

Okay, this time I *was* dumbstruck. Her talent for getting to the heart of the matter has gotten much better over time. Exactly how long had she been nursing *that* little gem?

She sucked the last of the margarita through the straw. "*Give up*," she said. "*Do* it. Or *don't* do it. You're going to be great either way. But for God's sake, stop worrying about it."

I stared at her empty glass. I had asked her to come sort me out. I figured we'd clean up my house, get the rest of the London details settled, and maybe do a bit of shopping. We'd talk and joke and relax, make cookies and watch movies and put up Christmas lights. But somewhere between the mellow restaurant light, the tequila and the toxic green, my mother had turned into Yoda.

They say by the time you get to the bottom of the bottle, you're so drunk you can't taste the worm. Mom had only had two shots.

But she wasn't the one who had to swallow it.

Stories are a Girl's Best Friend

December 4, 2004

There are twenty-two drawers in this house. Ten are in two organizers full of office supplies. Three are in an organizer in the bathroom. Four are in the kitchen. Five are in my bedroom. And at the back of the fourth drawer down, behind the black slip I wore once, my movie popcorn socks, the boxes of check carbons and an unopened bottle of thirteen-year-old perfume, I found a diamond.

Max told me this incident says a lot about me. I'm still trying to decide if what it says is a *good* thing, or a *bad* thing. Either way, he's right—it's definitely an Alethea thing.

What bothered me though was not the fact that I had shoved a box with one diamond earring in the back of a drawer, it was that I didn't know *why* I had done such a thing. I couldn't even remember where the box had come from. I had a feeling it was from my dad, but I couldn't remember. Luckily, I just so happened to have a family member around who might have known.

Mom examined the contents of the box and shrugged. "No idea," she said.

Great. I could hear it now:

"Gee, nice diamond earring, Alethea. How come you only have one?"

"No idea."

Oh, huh-uh. Since when has a writer ever answered a classic "tell me a story" line like this one with a two word answer? (Prediction: if Eric or Quinn is reading this now, each is trying their darndest to come up with an answer to this question. And they will.)

I had half a mind to shove the dumb thing back into the dark bowels from whence it came. What good is wearing a diamond if you have no idea why you have it in the first place?

Also in my house is a statue of an angel that I refused to leave Greece without twelve years ago. She's holding a seashell. In the seashell are a couple of pieces of fool's gold, some cool bits of painted granite, an evil eye, and a diamond ring. I dug the ring out and held it under Mom's nose.

"And whose was this one?"

"Ah." She smiled. "That's your Nana's engagement ring."

I liked that smile. I liked it because behind it, there was a story. "So why do I have it?"

"Oh, I think I was getting rid of some stuff and giving it to you girls. Cherie wanted the big diamond (Cherie wants more diamonds than Liz Taylor), Sami got my wedding band with the Greek key engraved in it, and you got that one."

I really don't remember this. "And *why* did I get this one?"

Mom shrugged. "Probably because it fit." I hate shrugs. They historically proceed a crap answer. But if you wait a few beats, sometimes… "She gave that ring back to him, you know."

"What?!?"

Mom smiled again. "When your grandfather gave Nana that ring, she took one look at it and said, 'Oh, no. This will never do.' And she gave it back. So he got her a bigger one."

I about died laughing. In order to appreciate this, you have to know my Nana. Being the true immortal that she is, my father's mother never wanted to be called "Yiayia," the Greek term for grandmother. (Being the true anglophile that she is, she settled on something a bit more proper.) She's a globetrotting wunderkind who works at a beauty counter in a mall in Florida and is often accused of being my father's sister. When Sami and I were little, she bought us Easter dresses every year. She taught us how to take our tea and how to "eat eggs with the queen," either because she was convinced that someday we would, or because at some point in the past she actually *had*. Nana is forever, and I hope I grow up to be even half as amazing as she is.

I looked at the ring again with new eyes. I even slipped it on once for good measure. And then I took it right back off again and returned it to the angel's bowl. What can I say? I'm just one of those girls who's more comfortable adorned with a Cracker Jack prize.

"You should wear it," Mom said. "It's not worth that much." But to me it wasn't about diamonds and carats or size and setting. It was the story that was priceless.

Then Mom told me the story of her own engagement ring—the really cheap one she wanted and never got, and the more expensive sapphire she and Dad picked out years later. "When I die, Cherie's got dibs on all the stuff she wants and Sami doesn't really have my taste," she said finally. "Do you want the sapphire?"

"No." I kissed her on the cheek. "I want the story."

Bibbidy Bobbity Byes

December 8, 2004

I dropped Mom off at the airport this morning. On the long, lonely drive back to work, I tried to think of other things in an effort to distract myself from being emotional. After covering traffic and other people who hate goodbyes, my brain settled on Cinderella.

I've always favored the Grimms' telling of *Cinderella* over the Perrault or Disney versions. Some may find that surprising, seeing as I'm a bit of a Fairy Godmother In Training—the Grimms' tale hadn't a fairy godmother in sight. (Not to despair, Briar Rose still had them to sort out that whole curse thing, so my future career choice is still justified.)

No, the less popular—and much darker—tale had Cinderella weeping over the grave of her mother. Birds in the tree planted on the grave spoke to her on her mother's behalf and helped her out in her times of need. They came to her aid when the evil stepmother gave Cinderella impossible tasks to accomplish. She didn't go to the ball once but three times, in dresses thrown to her from the birds. When the Prince came around to the house bearing the slipper, the stepsisters maimed themselves in their avarice, slicing off pieces of their feet in order to fit in the shoe. The Prince rode away with the wrong woman twice, and twice the birds warned him of the blood in the shoe and sent him back for the proper girl.

Being caught inside the whirlwind that my life has been lately had me thinking about Cinderella. Empathizing, asking questions, and coming to realizations. Somehow, Cinderella *must* have met the Prince prior to the ball. I'm not quite sure how she pulled it off, but there's no way she would have done all that stuff for him without being completely in love with him first. Big Love, capital letters and all, not just a crush on a pretty face and a castle. Showing up at a ball in a nice dress hoping to snare a man reeks of pettiness. I have to believe that Cinderella was much better than that. Picking a girl out of a crowd and marrying her solely based on her looks is equally as shallow. I have to believe that the Prince was much more than that too.

Cinderella was an introvert, my brain rationalized.

It's pretty obvious, isn't it? She kept her head low and kowtowed to the evil women who took over her house and took away her life. There is no way on Earth she would have gone through the trials she did and forced herself to be the center of attention three times for anything less than Big Love. My guess is, attending those balls was the most brave, scary, nervewracking thing she had ever done in her life. I'm betting she had more than a few panic attacks. But she still did it.

Then there's the issue of the Prince—who knew darn well what his True Love looked like, but his integrity still forced him to stay true to his word and ride away with the wrong woman. Can a man with a code of honor like that marry a virtual stranger? Well, the proclamation did say that his bride would be the one who fit the shoe… Good thing those birds were there to give him a suitable out-clause.

It certainly gives the tale more depth when you consider that Cinderella was probably a borderline basketcase coming out of her shell; the Prince, a tormented knight in shining armor with an annoying amount of moral fiber.

But the story is really about a mother's love for her daughter—a love so pure and strong it reaches from beyond the grave. Her birds don't exactly tell either of the lovers what to do, only nudge them a bit to help them down their paths. And so, Cinderella and her Prince lived Happily Ever After.

The moral of the story: Mom *is* always right.

Love you, Mom.

Tom Pendergrass says...

I remember clearly the first day I met her. Of course I didn't know her name then. It's better that way—don't get too attached to the clients.

I had been given the assignment, typical invisible ink on dissolving paper routine—nothing to let me know that this was out of the ordinary. I packed my rucksack with the essentials: bandages, morphine, speed clips, grenades, and piano wire. You never knew what you would face on a mission, but whatever it was, it would be deadly. I was okay with that: it was my job, and I was good at it.

I was to meet my contact on the outside of town, some Greek chick they said. Hell, I've been to Greece, I figured I could handle her. Just get in, get the job done, get back out—home in time to shoot ouzo with the guys.

I watched the convenience store from across the street until I saw her, all pigtails and teeth, munching on slim jims and trying to look inconspicuous. Amateur, I thought. I didn't care, as long as she did what I said. She needed to know who the boss was and everything would be okay.

I moved up behind her like a cat. She never heard me. I placed my hand across her mouth so she wouldn't scream.

"Do you know where I can get good souvlaki?" I asked. It was the recognition phrase. I uncovered her mouth and waited for her countersign. She stumbled around a bit as if she was trying to remember something she had rehearsed in the car on the way over.

"No, but I know the best place to get tzatziki." She said it like some kind of drone. I guess with that dialog though, the delivery didn't matter. I don't know who in HQ wrote the crap, but he had been watching too many bad spy movies.

"This way." I turned and left. She hesitated, then followed.

"I thought I was driving."

"You know how to do a bootlegger's turn?" Petulant silence. "It's all right—I've got a good ride."

I had parked my S2000 by the dumpster. Fire engine red and the top down—sometimes the best way to hide is to be so obvious that nobody thinks you're up to something. And the baby could scoot. I could tell by the way her eyes opened that the girl appreciated the car as well.

"Where we headed?" I asked.

"Bad situation in the countryside. They've been holed up for weeks."

"Show me the way."

We headed out of town until the pavement ended.

"We're almost there. It's just over that hill."

"You just hang back. I'll take care of it. In and out—keep the car running."

"I'm going," she said.

I failed to suppress a laugh. "You're kidding."

She opened her purse and pulled out a Glock 9mm. holding it gingerly by the stock with her thumb and forefinger.

"What'd you do, kill a cop? I don't need some girl in pigtails screwing things up. Stay here."

I serpentined up the back side of the hill, coming up in the shade of an enormous oak tree. I looked downslope into the most pitiable shack I had ever seen. It was the kind of rural abode that gives the state a bad name—the tin roof was rusted through and the front porch had collapsed, no doubt killing a dozen hounds in the process. One thing about a place like this—it was a sure thing that the residents were armed.

I heard the crack of gunfire and the *pfft* of a hollow-point as it cut through the air inches from my head. I jumped to the ground. These people weren't kidding.

I pulled off the knapsack and dug around for what I needed. A couple of smoke grenades to cover my advance. Get in, get the goods, get out. No need to hurt anybody more than was absolutely necessary.

Things always go according to plan until they don't, as my father always said. I had gotten to the shack, butt-stroked the occupant until his few remaining teeth had popped, and was searching the fetid property for the goods when I felt an enormous presence behind me.

"Mister," a booming voice said, "I apologize for what I'm about to do." An enormous hand closed about my throat from behind and lifted me all the way to the ceiling. He tossed me across the room into a pile of old coffee cans filled with tobacco spittle. The homer I had knocked out was getting to his feet now.

"Who the hell are you?" he asked through bleeding gums.

It's against my personal code of ethics to answer any questions of identity. I didn't have to. The Greek girl popped through the smoke, holding the Glock in front of her like some kind of dead rodent.

"Smyrna Public Library," she said, her voice getting stronger the more she talked. "You're overdue."

Bubba, the human Frigidaire, started giggling. Toothless Joe went to the sideboard and picked up a worn book.

"What you gonna do, shoot me?"

I tried to gain my feet, but the fall had shattered my ankle. My knapsack full of weapons was on the other side of the room.

The toothless one held the book in front of him while the girl shook like the ninth ward in a hurricane. He slowly ripped the cover from the book. Never have I seen such a transformation in a woman's face. It was as if she channeled the ghost of Boadicea. The Glock struck twice, two bullets in the brainpan, and the rednecks dropped like sacks of grits.

"Nobody defaces my books." She turned to me. "You all right?"

"Fine," I said through clenched teeth. The pain from my shattered ankle was hammering at me without cease. "I have morphine in my backpack."

She walked over, took the backpack and pulled out my two emergency pills. She made a face and swallowed them dry. "Thanks."

And that was how it all started.

Getting Used to It

December 10, 2004

Like most writers, I am an introvert. I make these little fantasy worlds in my head because they're ever so much more adventurous than living in the real one. The sum of my "dressing up" boils down to Halloween and the odd convention, where I comfortably become one with the world of Trekkies and vampires and fairies and geeks wearing T-shirts they made yesterday. I have a standing date with my urban family every other Friday night in order to thwart the inevitable slippage into agoraphobia (between DVD boxed sets, my computer, and Chinese take-out, I could happily stay home for months on end), and my mother comes to visit me two or three times a year when I've made so much of a mess of myself I can't think straight. It's a pretty sweet deal.

And then I had to go and get a book contract.

Luckily, *The Telaphab* won't be out until 2007. So I have two full years to crawl out of this chrysalis and be a butterfly. In the movie of my life, this would be a three-minute montage cut to the snappy beat of 311's "Come Original" (or something equally as easy to have stuck in your head). At the end, I would emerge from the back of a stretch limo and stride down the red carpet, the perfect picture of a beautiful and talented woman ready to soak up the spotlight.

We'd just skip over all those little episodes like panic attacks in the mall, being honked at by truckers, being hit on by strange restaurant managers, and all that silly hiding in the bathroom. (Yet another reason editors are priceless.)

My friend Robin took me out on her smoke break one afternoon when I was shaking so badly I couldn't type. She listened to me rant for a while.

"You know what?" she asked finally, dropping her butt into the container. "Get used to it."

Get used to it. It's what Sherrilyn Kenyon told me when she asked me to sign a copy of an interview I had done with her. It was my first writing-related autograph ever.

Where did I sign?

Wherever there was the most white space.

Did she want it personalized?

Yes.

I sighed and sat back on my heels.

"I have no idea what to say," I admitted.

"Get used to it," she said.

Get used to it. Right. I'm wondering how long that's gonna take, exactly. I'm sort of hoping that eventually I'll just learn to fake being used to it so well, no one will know the difference.

In the meantime, the Princess of Geekdom is off to Philcon. She will stand between Klingons and people with IQs too big for their britches and breathe deeply in the comfortable air of her demesne.

Remind me to schedule some more of these.

Strange Angels

December, 10 2004

The angels are still with me.

Stranded with me in Chicago, en route to Philadelphia, were two young and beautiful violin virtuosos. They took advantage of the hours in purgatory to practice—much to my delight. The violin is a beautiful instrument, a sort of old world soprano who at the same time can be both light and haunting.

I love the violin.

I have always loved music.

I can't imagine a world without it. In some ways, I wish I had had the patience to learn to play an instrument, but (as everyone keeps reminding me) I have enough outlets for my creativity without trying to take over everyone else's. So I limit my ear for perfect pitch to a pure and simple appreciation for the art form, harboring only the slight delusion that I can sing…and knowing full well that I would never attempt *Ave Maria* without proper lessons.

Words are an easy road to fantasy, but music also opens a window through which our zombified hearts can escape. I am trapped here in this airport in a city I've never been—it could be any city in the world, really, it doesn't matter.

I sit in a chair, one of the ranks of the Army of the Grounded Indefinitely, surrounded by leagues of passengers who are constantly departing and deftly avoiding the evil and jealous glares of my comrades. And yet if I closed my eyes, my claustrophobic mind would be able to fly away on the soft wings of *Silent Night* (and other classical pieces I never studied enough to know the names of). Words didn't matter.

And there lay my escape.

In this moment, words didn't matter.

That small slice of blissful solitude was better than any literary drug.

Thanks, ladies.

We Will Pay the Price

December 15, 2004

I have one of those squeezey stress balls on my desk—a tchotchke given to me from the folks at World Almanac. It's a tennis-ball sized image of the globe. Sometimes I look at it and wonder what I would have put on it if I was God.

I start with all the good things, of course—the things Nana told me to think about before I fell asleep every night. World Peace. Love. Flowers. Blue skies. Happiness. Laughter. Blueberry pancakes—the kind Mom makes that have more berries than batter. Blue jeans. Violins. Only good things. Wouldn't that be nice?

Probably not. It would probably, in fact, be boring as dirt. You can't have good without evil. You can't have life without death. You can't have rainbows without rain. There needs to be darkness in the world for us to appreciate light. There is no adventure if the world is all peachy and Strawberryland.

Besides—I *like* my darkness. I like my rain. My solitude, my pain, my tears. I like living life—every perfect, blissful moment.

So this world…the tiny thing I hold in my hand…if I had to remake it…I'd probably just end up making it the exact same way. Mullets, white spandex, Britney Spears and all. Besides, I could never be God. Who would believe in me? I barely have enough faith to believe in myself.

Living is hard. But you know what? It's worth it. It's all worth it.

Reflection

December 21, 2004

"I've looked into the abyss, the abyss has looked back, and we've both grinned."
–James Maxey

Spark

Shortest day
Longest night
Point of orbit on the dark side of the moon
loss of signal, radio silence
sailing where brilliant stars scatter across a Land Without Sun
Breadcrumbs along the path to infinity
Christmas lights in cold windows
Glitter on painted nails
Crystals of freefalling snow
perfect, unique, alone
sadness so small
little leftover
pieces of me
in that deep dark space
tiny, bright, beautiful
significant

Faith

December 22, 2004

I took my time in bed this morning. It's a short week, the boss is on vacation, and I had a brain full of things to think about. Somewhere around the fifth scream of the alarm clock monster, I threw back the covers and got up. I walked into the bathroom to put my contacts in and peeked through the blinds at the dawn.

"Welcome back," I said to the sun. And then I went to check my email.

I don't know if my hyperawareness of light and dark began before or after the adoption of all my Pagan friends. I suppose it's always been there somewhere, just like it is in all of us. Last night was Yule, the Winter Solstice, the longest night. Now the days start taking over again and getting brighter—like the world waking up. In some way, I suppose this is the marker of a New Year. It seemed only fitting to extend a greeting to our star after such a long absence. But the sun will still rise and set, I reminded myself. It did before you came, and it will after you're gone.

On the way to the car I remembered a time when the sun coming up again wasn't something I looked forward to. The thought that another day of hell waited after this one and another day after that, in perpetuity, only added to my downward spiral. Didn't matter that it was a hell of my own making. Nothing mattered. So, the fact that I was glad it was a new day made me feel rather nice.

When I turned on to the main road, I gasped. Shooting straight up into the sky, like a multicolored spotlight, was a rainbow. It only went up a little ways before it faded but there it was, in all its Technicolor glory. Sure, it had rained during the night, but it had rained lots of nights before and I had never seen a rainbow in the morning.

When I moved to Tennessee six years ago, I remember being struck by how many rainbows greeted my arrival. Coupled with the occasional feeling like I was in Vermont—my real home, my soul's home—I decided that it was the world telling me that my move from South Carolina had been a good thing. It was trying to set my mind at ease by making Tennessee welcoming and comfortable. *This* was where I was supposed to be, no question about it.

I kept shooting glances at the rainbow out of the corner of my eye. It was growing. I watched it until it spanned half the sky.

Mom and I went through the Arizona desert once at night. I spent more time looking up at the stars than I did looking at the road. Mom finally made me pull over and let her drive.

I suppose I could have pulled over. But as beautiful and magical as it seemed, it was just a rainbow…and I was late for work. At the next break in the trees, right before I got onto the interstate, I looked over again. It wasn't just a rainbow.

There were two.

The first rainbow got even brighter, the other end of it slamming into the world on the other side of the horizon. The second one was wider and fainter, but it stuck right beside its brilliant counterpart all the way to the other end.

People were now stopping on the side of the road to look up at the sky. I drove on, holding the steering wheel in a white-knuckled grip and sobbing like an idiot at the beauty of the world. I had written an email to a friend this morning about being nervous—how we constantly worry that things might go wrong, and how infinitely scarier the thought is that they might actually go *right.* People say they want the book, the dream, the fairy tale, but what if they actually got it? Could they accept it and live a life other people only watch in movies? Or would their disbelief, seeded in them by huge doses of jaded reality, pound it back into nonexistence?

I have always believed in magic. I followed the path of a scientist and realized there was rationally no such thing, but I never could kill the hope that somehow, someway, magic would suddenly show up in my world. I became two people—the woman who grew up and settled for her life, and the little girl inside her who wrote fantasy stories. When the woman had finally been through enough torture, the little girl asked her why she bothered. What was the harm in having unattainable standards and wishing on stars? Even if it doesn't exist, the fairy tale is much preferable to pain. She had a point.

So I went back to square one. And you know what? Magic *does* exist. That perfect synchronicity? It's out there. The happy ending? It's just another beginning in a series of beginnings, each one more exciting than the next. Maybe the world was trying to tell me something this morning. Maybe it was just a freak of nature on top of a bunch of unbelievable coincidences—a double rainbow on the day I drive in late to work on *this* morning, the morning after the longest night, a morning in the midst of a time in my life I never let myself dream of experiencing, a morning where 4500 miles behind that sunrise is a person who can see this through my eyes and know how much it means.

Occam's Razor has me believing the former. But don't you see? That's just it.

I *believe.*

By the time I pulled into the driveway, the concentric ribbons of color had faded into the dark gray clouds. I walked slowly into the building, letting the rain kiss my face stiff with tears, my cheeks aching from smiling.

I have just had the most incredible morning of my whole entire life. Whatever else happens today is just a bonus. Whatever happens a week from now is a dream. Whatever happens after that is just part of the fairy tale.

Surf's Up

December 29, 2004

Well, I'm officially useless. My journey to London begins in less than two hours, and I'm so tired I can't concentrate. So I thought I'd drop a post in to say I love you guys—I hope you all have a safe and wonderful New Year. I'll be sure to fill everybody in on how the movie ends…

PART TWO

The Story Magnet

Tell me of sunlight
Tell me of moonbeams
Tell me you'll buy me
the stars as a gift
Tell me of rainbows,
Sweet songs and summertime
Tell me you'll love me
as long as you live.

~*Declaration*, 1992

Back to the Future

10 January 2005, 5:00pm GMT
London, England

The sun is setting now and turning the underside of the rainclouds pink.

Somewhere in London is a hotel room overlooking Hyde Park that has in it the most uncomfortable bed in the world.

Somewhere along Bayswater Road is a white hat we were too tired to go back and look for, but which I promised to buy a duplicate of when I get home.

Somewhere on the steps of the Corus Hotel are seed beads from my mati bracelet, whose help the world decided I just didn't need anymore.

Somewhere in the fountain in Trafalgar Square is a lucky penny with two wishes on it.

And somewhere at another airport, on a plane headed in the

opposite direction, the man who keeps my heart is flying back home.

Me and my lovely memories are going to bed now…nighty night, all.

And happy birthday to me.

Birthday Blog

January 11, 2005

Dinner was really fun. I was running on fumes and adrenaline. Ellen had to bow out, but she had invited Gail to go in her place. I love Gail. She's so smart and witty and always seems to say the right thing, however blunt. I want to be just like her in twenty years.

So I sat down right across from Gail, because I knew I could feed off her energy and not pass out at the table, like I really wanted to do. Plus, having her there raised the bar of the conversation, and I didn't feel like I had to hide in the corner and say nothing. Which means I was *me*, and I talked *way* too much, and was *way* too energetic.

There were ten of us. I was on one end between Mordecai Gerstein and Christine. Simon (the head of Roaring Brook Press) was on the other far end. It always stinks when there are too many people at a table because there are inevitably two conversations, one on either end, and you're always missing something. I was afraid I would never get to know Simon at all, but right before dessert he asked Christine if he could switch places with her. Coolness.

He asked me a little about my book and I just kept telling stories: the "how I got published" story and the Nazi Lady story, and seeing as Simon's a Brit (did I mention that he signed *The Golden Compass* while he was at Knopf?) we talked about London and where Max and I had gone and what we did.

Gail was amazingly nice and kept saying things like: "We missed you so much because it was so quiet." And since I had heard variations of that same thing all day long, I asked her why people kept saying that. She went on this long diatribe about how I inspire everyone in the office, and how they all live vicariously through me, and how it's just not as bright when I'm not there. I was halfway touched and halfway embarrassed.

Simon turned to me and said, "Is this true?"

I shrugged. "I don't know. I'm never around when I'm not there."

More of Gail's enthusiasm inevitably brought out more of the story that is my life, and the inference of Max, whom I couldn't even think about without that damn smile plaguing me that makes people ask questions.

Finally, Mordecai, who had been conversing with the other end of the table, turned to me and said (in that way we writers have of getting straight to the nitty-gritty), "Okay, *how* did you meet this guy?"

At which point I was obligated to tell him a condensed version of the story.

Mordecai's a pretty reserved kind of guy. Even though we sat next to each other, he didn't say much to me the whole meal. But after I gave the gist of the story, he asked, "So, how did it end up?"

"Well," I told him, "kind of like the end of *Sleepless in Seattle*."

He gave me this exceptionally huge smile and said, "Oh, that's wonderful."

Gail is of the opinion that Max and I should pick up everything, choose a country to live in, and just go while we're young. I brought up the fact that money was still an issue, as well as the whole "me not having a European passport" thing, and the fact that I probably couldn't get a job anywhere. She thought differently, and was quite adamant about it. I reminded her that we were both still on the verge of great careers and we could go anywhere when we're both famous and financially independent. Gail actually scoffed at me. I reminded her that I had friends here and my house, and my job, but she wasn't having any of it.

Mordecai said, "But you can write anywhere."

I patted him on the shoulder. "Please tell that to my mother."

For dessert there was a candle in my crème brulée and they sang "Happy Birthday" to me, which was also very nice. I stared at the candle and looked up at Gail.

"What do I wish for?" I asked her.

"I don't know," she said. "All your dreams have already come true."

"Okay then," I said. "So here's to the next chapter."

I blew it out, and everybody clapped. (Shortly after, Mordecai was talking about the Caldecott, and I threw my hands up in the air. "*That's* what I should have wished for!" I spouted. Mordecai laughed. "That's okay," said Gail. "You still have time. Wish for it next year.")

Mordecai wrote "Happy Birthday!" in the inscription on my galley for *The Old Country*, and he drew a picture of a fox. In the meantime, across town at the Borders in Franklin, Sherrilyn Kenyon was scolding Nicole for not bringing a *Telaphab* bracelet to her book signing. (They were the hit of work yesterday—everyone was wearing one. It was the best birthday present.)

The whole day was just surreal. It seemed odd and detached while I was living it, but as I look back I realize how amazing it really was. The only thing that would have made it more perfect would have been coming home to Max and telling him all about it.

"HEY, BABY, WHAT'S YOUR SIGN?"

March 9, 2005

I forget how old I was…twelve? fifteen?…but I remember it as clearly as if it had happened yesterday. I was passing my mother on the stairs and I asked her, "Mom, am I weird?"

"No, honey," she replied. "You're normal."

I immediately went up to my room and cried.

To me—a girl who collected misfits, and teddy bears with crooked noses, and loved nothing without flaws—"weird" was the epitome of imperfect perfection. To be normal was…well, it was nothing. It was everyday, apple pie, vanilla pudding. That thought seriously depressed me for much longer than it should have.

Many, many years later I related this story to my mother. She laughed so hard tears came to her eyes.

"Oh, Alethea," she gasped. "I meant normal for *you*."

I've recently become obsessed with Jonathan Carroll. It's unsettling to find an author you've never read before who seems to have been put on this earth to write words that speak directly to you. Even better—he started doing this twenty-five years ago, so I have his entire backlist to gobble up.

The best part about Carroll is that he can write women. He can write relationships and feelings in a way that most men are unable…or afraid…to. It's an awesome and powerful talent for a male author to have, and I have encountered few to date that can do it with such stunning accuracy.

I think the secret behind the authors' magic is simple—he is a lover. And I don't mean lovers in the big-sweeping-cheesy-Nicholas-Sparks definition of the word. I mean that this author *loves* women…physically, mentally, and down to every last tiny idiosyncrasy. His heroines are beautiful…and quirky. They have flaws. They're usually a little secretive, a little unstable, a little out of reach. A little crazy. A little weird. And they make the reader fall in love with every last nutso bit of them.

This imperfect, slightly-crazy, off-the-cuff woman has become the uberheroine in other incarnations as well. She's the down-to-Earth, girl-next-door with a twist. Jaye in *Wonderfalls*. Dharma in *Dharma & Greg*. Sandra Bullock in *Speed*. They're the curry, the cinnamon, the cayenne that make life spicy. They're normal…for them. They are the perfect counterpart to the Everyman. And we love every last nutso bit of them.

So why is it that in *real* life—this life we continually say is so different from movies and television and books when all those art forms try to do is recreate it—men only *think* they want the weird girl? Oh sure, they'll fall in love with her. They'll have loads of fun. They'll laugh at all the crazy things she does and the crazy things she says. They'll ride the wave of her energy, and they'll have a blast doing it.

But a month down the road…a year…two years…and he will

inevitably turn to this woman and say, "Have you ever considered therapy?" or "You know, my life was a lot simpler without you." (That one's for you, Kitti dearest.)

Gentlemen, I have a request. If you're thinking about falling for a woman who is a handful, a verbal fanaticist, a mental genius, a roller coaster of energy and emotion, a dreamer of impossible worlds, an incredible whirlwind of beauty and dynamite...admit this to yourself right up front. You're not going to change her, and you'd be foolish to try. If you're not brave enough, big enough, strong enough, and clever enough to step up to the plate and look her dead in the eye, then stand down and admit defeat. Carroll, a true lover of women knows what sort is worth fighting for. But he is also aware that there will be a fight, and that she will be worth it. Every last nutso bit of her.

There's a Native American legend told in a variety of forms about a scorpion who asks a frog to help him across a river. The frog is wary. The scorpion does not excuse himself for what he is, but he still asks the frog to carry him across the water. The frog does, and right before he gets to the other side, the scorpion stings him...effectively killing them both. Before they drown, the frog asks the scorpion why he did it and the scorpion says, "You knew what I was when you picked me up."

This fable has been used as a metaphor for all sorts of things: drugs, alcohol, the current vice du jour. But you guys remember this story the next time you believe yourself to be "burdened" with a "crazy" woman. You must choose. Step up or stand down.

'Cause you knew what she was when you picked her up.

Look, Ma!

March 13, 2005

I'm writing. I really am.

In the last week I've had two friends threaten me within an inch of my life (one of them being an ex-CIA agent). I've had a rather nasty message left on my answering machine by another friend. And my mother called today, informing me that if I didn't finish *Haven* by the end of the day, she and Quinn were both going to kick my butt when we got to Vermont for Easter. There was also a lot of screaming involved.

Sigh.

I should probably stop letting people read my Works in Progress. But I would totally be lying if I said this didn't make the ego rather happy.

I'm writing, Mom. I won't have the book done by the end of the day, but I'm writing…

By Popular Demand

March 14, 2005

I've had a request to post the abridged (and censored) conversation I had with my mother that kicked my butt out of the writing wasteland I have termed the "Seventh-Inning Stretch." (Thanks, Mom!)

[Disclaimer: unless you all have very strong constitutions, or very good relationships with your mother, I don't necessarily advise sending your own mothers an unfinished manuscript.]

[answering machine clicks on]

"No one is available to–"

(audible sigh of exasperation)

"–take your call, please–"

"ALEEEEEEEEEEEEEEETHEAAAAAA!!" Mom cries over the

computerized voice of my message.

(Alethea picks up the phone) "Yeah? Hi."

"What's the biggest lie she ever told?!?" Mom asks.

"Huh?"

"It ends with 'the biggest lie she ever told.' So what's the lie?"

It dawns on me. *Haven*. That's the last line of Chapter 15. Oh crap. "Oh, um…wasn't there something in the line before it…something she told herself?"

"'Tomorrow night, everything will be back to normal and I will be able to sleep in peace.' That?" she asks. She's got the friggin' manuscript in front of her. Great.

"Yeah, that."

"Oh. Okay," she says. "So she's lying to herself."

"You finished all of it already? God, I knew it was too short…"

"Well, I had to keep putting it down because your father wanted to go someplace…and then he wanted to work on taxes…so I had to read it a little at a time, but I never forgot what was going on. I told him to stop bothering me because I had your new book. He said, 'Oh, is it the one I read?' [Laney's story] and when I told him it was a different one, his face kind of fell."

"Yeah, I've been thinking about that one. I think I've figured out how to make it better. See, I need to put Laney's sister in from the beginning—"

"Whatever. Don't worry about that one right now," she says. "What are you doing?"

"Well," I say. "I'm about to finish a book, and then later this afternoon I'm going to the movies with the girls."

"A book. As in, a book you're reading?" she asks innocently.

"Well, yeah."

"THROW IT IN THE GARBAGE!" She screams into the phone. "Sit your butt down and write until you have to go to the movies. And before you go to the movies, click 'send' so I can find out what happens!!"

(At this point I am rolling on the bed cracking up, laughing so hard I can't reply.)

"IF YOU DON'T FINISH THIS BOOK, LUC AND I ARE BOTH GOING TO KICK YOUR ASS WHEN WE GET TO VERMONT!!!"

(more laughing)

"*Haven*…is this the one Orson Scott Card said would be a great series of books?" she asks.

"No," I sigh. "That was 'Small Magics.' The one everybody *else* is on my case about writing." I explain to her a little bit about it, but I'm pretty sure she's never read it.

There is silence on the line. And then: "Jeeeezus, Alethea…"

Caution

March 15, 2005

Kitti had to reprimand Lia last night for hurting their dog without thinking. I understand that kids need discipline, but I hate seeing it. I'm too emotional and too empathic. It's why I don't like watching movies where people hurt other people—be it slasher movies or *Saving Private Ryan*. I also don't like to watch movies where people are embarrassed. I skip over those "What's the Most Embarrassing Thing You Ever Did?" pages in teen magazines. I don't even read the do-it-yourself mishap columns in *Handyman*. I don't see the humor in it. Being embarrassed feels awful. Watching someone else be embarrassed is worse.

I patted Lia on the head and wiped away a teardrop. "It's okay," I said. "I did something really dumb today and cried on your mommy's shoulder too."

I wasn't lying. I was having a great day yesterday…until I did one of the possibly stupidest things I've ever done in my life.

In a nutshell: Max sent me the first chapter of a novel he's working on, and forwarded his editor's comments to me. I was in the middle of something and didn't really have the time to look at it, but I couldn't resist. I replied with my comments in brief: things I agreed with, things I didn't. She suggested taking out my favorite part. I thought she was nuts. The last line of my email was: "You're brave, baby. I think halfway through this process I'd want to kill her." and I hit send.

In less than a second, my blood froze. I hadn't responded to Max's email. I had responded to the *forwarded* email. My blunt, unabashed comments went straight to his editor's inbox.

I immediately broke out in hives. I recalled the message (which you know never really works) and then hunted down our Computer Tech Guru to ask if we could recall emails sent outside the company. Nope. So then I wrote a frantic "oh my god i feel awful and i am so sorry" email to Max's editor. I wrote Quinn, half in tears, telling her what a horrible person I was.

I had to confess to Max. I *warned* him long ago about the repercussions of falling in love with a crazy woman. You have to live with her insanity, but you'll never run out of stories to tell. I think maybe for a second he was horrified. Half a second. He wrote his own apology to his editor on my behalf.

And then he started laughing. He started laughing and telling everyone he knew what an incredibly mixed-up kid his girlfriend was. (Miserable writers…) They laughed. I told some of my friends, especially ones who knew his editor, asking them if she had a sense of humor about things and wouldn't fire Max just for having a horrid girlfriend. *They* laughed. The red splotches on my face spread down to my chest.

I went to the gym to do penance. I normally run four or five miles on the weekdays…sometimes six…whatever fills up an hour.

I ran eight.

When my feet started to hurt, I switched to the bike. I knew that no matter how much I exhausted myself, I still wouldn't be able to sleep, but I had to try.

There's a warning on the display panel of the bike: **CAUTION: STOP PEDALING IF YOU DON'T FEEL WELL.**

Well. That's relative, isn't it? I mean, think about it. It should be a little more specific. Stop pedaling if you develop a leg cramp. Stop pedaling if you have a twinge in your knee. Stop pedaling if you feel faint. What it doesn't say is: stop pedaling if you're feeling really sorry for yourself, or if your heart is breaking into a million pieces. Stop pedaling if you've just disappointed your best friend. Stop pedaling if you wish the Earth would open up and swallow you whole.

Winston Churchill said: "If you are going through Hell, keep going." So I kept going. But I didn't feel better. I didn't feel better until I had a tear-stained five-year-old in my arms and I teased them for making sniffly-snot noises into my shoulder right before I reciprocated. Soon we were both giggling like the silly children we were.

Max's editor wrote me back this morning. "Wow. Well, bit more than I was expecting on a Tuesday morning. Nice to meet you, Alethea."

Never let it be said that I don't know how to make a first impression. I still feel like a miserable human being. Max says we're all miserable human beings. I know I'm supposed to laugh at myself, it's just hard. But then I think of Lia's giggles. There is no sound on Earth better than the laughter of a child. And slowly, ever so slowly, the world gets a little bit brighter.

Like a Box of Chocolates

March 18, 2005

I think just about everybody has to agree...this has been one hell of a week.

I went to see my friend Chris last night. I wanted to tell him about my crazy week, but I hadn't seen him in so long that I had to start at the beginning. First I had to find out where the beginning was.

"Okay, where did I last leave off with you?" I asked him.

"Last time I saw you, you were with the Ex," he said.

My mouth dropped open. "So...you don't know *anything* about Max?"

Chris shook his head.

"Um...maybe you should tell me what's been going on with you first," I said. Because the beginning of my story wasn't this past Monday. It was this past July.

Five hours and dinner later, I left Chris's apartment. He was all caught up. I was almost completely hoarse. He gave me a big hug and told me what they all say: "When any of these things you told me about comes to pass, don't wait so long before telling me again." Which is part of the reason I have this blog. I've got a great big mouth and I can tell stories with the best of them, but I have so many friends it'll be lifetimes before I get them all caught up.

I walked to my car berating myself for the excessive display of verbal diarrhea I always seem to find myself getting into once I'm on a roll. Chris had gotten a few stories in edgewise…but not many. And I hoped, like I always do after episodes like that, that he wasn't leaning against the door in a slump, rolling his eyes and muttering to himself, "My God, that girl never shuts up!" I suddenly felt the overwhelming desire to go home, shut my door, and not come out for the entire weekend. A bad thing? Not at all. A slightly overdramatic agoraphobic reaction? Probably.

But maybe that's just what writers do.

The day I met Andre Norton, she did most of the talking.

David Drake had told me to get in touch with her because "she has no idea what she means to the science fiction community." I thought he was full of beans. How could a woman as huge and prolific and groundbreaking as Andre Norton not know that?

So I got over my fear and wrote her a messy letter on plain white paper and included a picture of me, David, John Ringo, David Coe, and my friends Leigh and Kristi at the 2002 Southern Festival of Books. It wasn't a gushy fan letter, it was more like a letter I would write to my grandmother. I told her what was going on with me and who I was…that I heard she had a library in town, and I thought that was wonderful. She had been sick so I wished her well. I don't even remember the rest of what I rambled on about.

She wrote me a card back, inviting me to come see the library, High Hallack, after the holidays. I still remember staring at the envelope, at my address in what I assumed was Miss Andre's handwriting. At her cute return address label sticker. Normal handwriting, normal sticker…just like every human being on the planet.

But I didn't go.

I drove by the house. It was less than two miles from where I lived. It looked like every other house on the street, except that it had a big, black, oversized mailbox. I would try to drum up the courage to call or write…but who was I? Sure, I called myself a writer, but I hadn't ever published anything. You had to *apply* to go to High Hallack. You had to *prove* you were working on something. Even with an invitation, I was an impostor. I was a book buyer with a Chemistry degree and delusions of grandeur. She'd see right through me.

So I didn't go.

That January I decided I was going to get serious about writing. I was a writer, but what was I doing? A writer writes. Didn't matter if it was just for me. I had to write. I *needed* to write.

By the end of January, I had a bi-monthly book review column in the local free press and I had written a television pilot. I wanted to try to write short stories again, and I wanted to start a novel. I wrote a story that spring…my first story in almost ten years. It was 17,000 words, and it took me four days to write it.

That July, I went to Orson Scott Card's Literary Boot Camp and had one of the most life-altering weeks of my entire life. Sitting at a table with Scott Card and eighteen of the most amazingly talented people on the planet, I came to the realization that my delusions of grandeur weren't delusions at all. They were possibilities. These people—these amazing people who mattered—were my peers. We were writers. When I got home, I called Miss Andre and set up an appointment to visit the library. Scott Card told me he was jealous.

I don't have any books signed by her. I don't have any pictures of us together. But I have her letters. I have her Christmas cards. I have the books I bought from the sale of High Hallack right before she moved, the proceeds of which went to fund the Andre Norton Nebula Award for Young Adult Science Fiction and Fantasy.

More importantly, I have the memories. I can look back on the totally surreal and unique experience of having the Grand Dame of Science Fiction all to myself for a few hours. I smile at the image of us scooting around High Hallack in desk chairs as she gave me the grand tour. I remember her sparkly voice as she read to me passages from a humorous book of ridiculous and true answers to actual test questions. I remember the complete shock and honor I felt when she asked me if I planned on coming back to work in the library.

Max hated the day he found out they had sent her home from the hospital and placed her in hospice care. He hadn't wanted to tell me, but he knew he would never forgive himself if I didn't manage to write her one last letter. She had just written me to wish me luck on *Elemental* and thank me for some book trade magazines I had sent her. I had opened the card with a smile. It never occurred to me that it would be the last.

I was fine until I was staring at my envelope—sealed, addressed and stamped—waiting patiently on the giant candle by the door for me to take it to the post office. Because that was it. That letter would be the last of our correspondence. I hoped she would live long enough to read it. It wasn't full of sappy sentiments or anything…it was just a typical letter. I wished her a belated happy birthday and drew her a picture of a cake. I told her what was going on with me and the anthology, and I thanked her for her kind words. I told her Max and I were thinking of her, and that we sent our love. It wasn't anything earth-shattering or remarkable. It was just me. And I just wanted her to know.

She held on for three more weeks. I'm sure she was flooded with letters. I tell myself it was enough time for her to have read mine.

I was helping an author sign books at a publisher expo on Thursday, so I didn't even know about her death until a friend mentioned it right before the show was over. I was so keyed up from the show, so high on adrenaline, that it took a little while for it to sink in.

And then I started crying.

I cried all the way home, and in the shower. I cried when I woke up in the middle of the night, and I cried in my dreams. I cried in the morning, when I opened the windows and smiled at the sun…that damned sun that keeps rising and setting without a care in the world.

Why did Miss Andre's passing upset me so much? Who was I? I wasn't a family member or a friend she had known all her life. I was just some tiny little person who met her a handful of times and sent her catalogues. I held no claim on her soul. So why did it tear me apart like it did? She was a famous woman loved by millions of people. She was a Great Lady and a Grand Dame and a thousand other things I could only hope to be. But she was also a nice woman, an incredibly humble person, an ex-librarian, and a lover of books.

And she was my friend.

Robin read my palm before she knew me very well. She told me I didn't have many acquaintances. I was shocked, because I pride myself on the massive number of people I call friends. "No," she clarified. "What it means is that you either *love* people, or you don't know them. There aren't many in between."

The nicest thing my Ex ever said about me was that if Armageddon happened and he somehow got to choose the ten people left on the planet, he would pick me to be one of them. "So you could love everybody," he said.

Death hurts by not hurting. It is numbness, the absence of feeling, the opposite of every wild, spontaneous impulse that makes life what it is. I realized, while I was kneeling in the bathtub, wishing the water was ten times hotter than it was, that by having all these friends I was only setting myself up for disaster. Was it worth it? I hadn't even finished asking myself the question before I had the answer.

Yes.

Of course it's worth it.

I love having friends. I want as many as my heart can hold. I want them all. Even if it means that eventually and painfully I'll have to lose every single one. The minutes and hours and years on the roller coaster of happiness and sadness with them are worth every second of gray numbness.

Max's editor got my guilt present yesterday—a huge box of chocolates delivered to her office from "that awful picture book writer with the big mouth." I heard from Max that they went over extremely well. She gushed about them and they laughed about what had happened...and then she offered him another contract.

It wasn't the way I would have liked to do it, but I think I've made another friend. I certainly hope so.

'Cause when I get to heaven, I want there to be a heck of a lot more than five people waiting.

I just hope they all bear with me while I catch them up.

The Triplets of Morrisville

March 28, 2005

It's Monday morning and I'm awake before the rest of the house. Or I've found that tiny window of the day when the kids have gone off to school and the adults are still too wiped from the last three days to function at 6:45 in the am. Either way, I'm alone in the kitchen and everything is unnaturally quiet. Now that I'm so used to being alone, the quiet holds a special sereneness, a sort of sanctuary, a time when I can actually hear myself think.

My plane leaves in twelve hours. In eighteen hours, I will be alone again. But it won't be the same.

For one, I won't be sitting in the kitchen. There *is* nowhere to sit in the kitchen at my little house. I won't live on linoleum, or be within ten feet of the refrigerator at any given point in the day. If my countertops have on them the remnants of the night before, they come in the form of a dirty plate or ball of foil.

The flat surfaces in my sister Cherie's kitchen tell the epic story of our Easter weekend. There are plastic cups, paper cups, and soda cans everywhere. Wine glasses and tumblers and empty juice bottles. There's a dirty demitasse beside the sink; I can see the trails of dried coffee grounds from here, streaking their way down the insides in strange, prophetic patterns.

I think that was my nephew Josh's cup. Dad told Josh he was going to have a ton of girls after him and a very lucky year. Dad saw a lucky year in all of our cups. He said he's never seen more symbols of good luck in his whole life. You can imagine his smile as he said it.

Unfortunately that luck didn't come last night…evidenced by the scraps of lottery tickets and bum scratch-offs strewn about. Close, but no cigar. Mom still has hope.

The plates and bowls here next to me are filled with peanut and pistachio shells, gum wrappers and candy foil, a blood-red colored real egg and an orange plastic one. The orange one had the candy in it. The red one's shell is broken on both ends, marking it a loser of last night's egg-cracking tournament.

This may be the French branch of the tree, but in our family, everyone is Greek.

There's a camera bag over by the cookie jar and a camera on the other side of the room beside the last of the blueberry muffins. They don't belong to each other, but they hold inside them digital photos and rolls of film full of memories that Cherie will collect and stick in her photo album. We'll write funny captions beside them next year.

Next year. The clock on the wall in the living room ticks so loudly I can hear every second. I wonder how many seconds it will be until we're here again, but it's a rhetorical question. I don't really want to know. I am happy enough with the knowledge that everyone keeps saying "next year" like it's the definition of Easter and always has been. Last year, all of us showing up in Morrisville, Vermont was a surprise for Cherie. This year, it's tradition.

One of the dogs is growling, so someone must be stirring. There are no dogs in my little house in Tennessee, but Cherie's poodles are so gentle and well-behaved they've almost made me change my mind. I would never have three, though. And now there are six.

Bijou had her puppies last night. I have never seen such a thing in my life. "It's what you get for not growing up on a farm," my father said, as if every child in America born prior to 1970 grew up on a farm, and I simply missed out due to the unfortunate timing of my birth. It was amazing. And weird and gross and strange and cool and awesome. Just when you think you've got a handle on things, you find out that there is so much left to learn.

I looked at them and at us—Cherie and West and Sami and me—the cadre of siblings huddled around the dog bed swapping stories and sharing memories. We are the core, the middle of the generations, the glue that the family will depend on to hold together through the years. Time and distance may keep us apart, but we will always have this. We will always have us. We are my mother's miracles.

Bijou's litter wasn't the only Mommy's Easter present…Casey had her beautiful little daughter Sunday morning. She's already got a ton of dark hair, a wicked gleam in her eye, and a fairy godmother ready to corrupt her. Promising.

I'm pausing every few minutes to look out the window. My windows back home don't frame snow-covered mountains. I had to wait until spring to see snow, but it was worth it. Tomorrow it will be seventy degrees in Tennessee and boy, will I appreciate it.

I can't believe it only took a day to see my grandmother. Only an afternoon to see Quinn. Only a few days with my humongous family. Right when we're all getting used to each other, we have to leave again. We'll make promises to get together…we'll try to keep them…but even if we don't we'll have next year. Next snow. Next

Kitchen Summit. Next Easter.

As much as I miss the people here I will miss all the things, these things that tell the stories of our lives. Men's cologne. Bubblegum toothpaste. Burned candles. Empty liquor bottles. Papers with doodles on them. A bowl of fortune cookies.

In the next room is a little boy who will ask me if I would like to play Harry Potter with him. If I do, I get to be Hermione. Once upon a time I came to Vermont and played Princess Leia. Some things change, and some things stay the same.

In some ways, I look forward to being home. But home is a place where there is no clock ticking, no puppies, no kids waking up and getting ready for school, no groggy adults wandering in craving caffeine and nicotine. Nothing but my precious silence and all that thinking…all those thoughts running through the hallways and slamming the doors of my brain so loudly I can't sleep.

And yet somehow all the noise from this weekend—the voices of five generations—distracted me from my thoughts long enough for three straight days of uninterrupted, almost dreamless sleep. So I will return well-rested, heart full, and soul at peace.

They say Easter is full of miracles.

They would be right.

The Story Magnet

March 28, 2005

I've been reading a lot of of material lately on dreams. I get a lot of great ideas from my dreams. Some people think they don't dream. Not true. Everybody dreams, just not everybody remembers. Apparently, you can teach yourself to remember your dreams. Different sources suggest various methods for doing it, but they all seem to agree—once you learn how to remember a few, you find yourself remembering more and more.

This, of course, sets the idle mind of an ex-scientist/writer a-wondering. Surely remembering dreams can't just be like flipping a switch. Heisenberg Uncertainty Principle. Just the process of remembering has to influence what you're dreaming. Would you dream more if your subconscious wanted attention? Would your dreams be crazier if you're an inner show-off? Through the simple act of paying attention, do you turn yourself into a dream attractor?

In 2004, I launched my website: www.aletheakontis.com. My best friend/web designer was too busy to set it up all the way, but he suggested I start a blog there just to have something for people to find. I've kept diaries my whole life, but I've never gotten into the whole blogging thing. Who on Earth would care about anything I had to say? But Kit was offering, and I couldn't leave my website bare, so I shrugged and started making stuff up.

The entries were short, few, and far between. It wasn't like I didn't have other things to do…or other things to write. In between novel chapters and book reviews, I would find myself lying in bed, wracking my brain to try to think of something to say on my blog before it got neglected. I would examine every part of my life, every moment of my day, combing the seconds for poetic fragments I could share with the electronic world, my fan base of invisible millions. (According to the comments posted at the time, my site was frequented by two friends and my mother.)

And then the strangest things started happening to me. Of course, weird and crazy things happen to me all the time…but this was different. It didn't take much digging to find perfectly structured little capsules of time to show off. And then it didn't take any digging at all. Joy and sadness and pain and frustration…it got to the point where I could barely walk out my front door without stepping in a story that had come begging on my stoop.

But was this phenomenon occurring because I was simply now able to recognize stories in the ether? Or, because I was paying attention, did they pop up and *purposely* mess up my life? Had word spread through the story community that my life was suddenly a halfway house for vagrant plot lines?

I centered my novel around a fictional town in Kansas that I later discovered *actually existed.* I made a wish for a boy, and he came true. Three months ago, we met for the first time. Two days ago, I made contact with a long lost friend that I'd been trying to find for seven years. Last month, I embarrassed myself in a situation that put every episode of *Seinfeld* to shame. Five minutes ago, I was officially passed over for a job in Marketing because I was too overqualified. (I've never had a marketing job in my entire life.) On Monday, I had lunch with Codex's esteemed founder, Quinn Reid.

I was in Morrisville, Vermont, visiting my family for the Easter holiday. Quinn suggested that we get together for lunch in Montpelier, only about forty minutes away. She would meet me at noon on the corner of Main and Elm. I said sure (and hoped I could be heard over the cacophony of cousins wrestling in the background). My dad could drive me there and drop me off. Everything was fine…for about fifteen minutes.

Why should Dad take me? I could just drive my sister Cherie's humongous minivan. It wasn't raining that badly. I knew how to get to Montpelier, didn't I? (Drive through Stowe and go two exits down 89. Easy.) But I should really have a cell phone. Cherie can't find her phone and Bill's is low on juice…here, take Dad's. (Only first, Dad had to program in all the numbers I would need, because they were all going to go to the movies. If I needed anything, I could call them there. Fine.) Oh…and Lee? Since you're going in that direction, can you drop Caleb off at school? Please?

I looked at the clock in the dashboard. I felt bad. At the rate I was going, by the time I got to Montpelier, Quinn would have been standing in the rain for fifteen minutes.

And all of this happened before I hit a deer on the highway (the humongous boat of a van was fine; I don't know what happened to the deer), showed up in Montpelier and walked at least two miles—in the rain—all the way up Elm Street. When I found myself surrounded by snow-covered hills I backtracked, found a cross street, and walked all the way down Main.

At no point did they intersect.

When I got back to the van, I cranked up the heater. I finally got in touch with Bill at the theater and had him drive back to the house to get Quinn's number at work. (I hadn't brought it with me 'cause I figured she'd be standing outside...why would I need it?) An hour after we were supposed to meet, I called her office.

"You know I can't do anything right, don't you?" I asked without preamble.

"I think I told you the wrong thing," she apologized. "It's the corner of State and Elm. Main and Elm don't meet anywhere."

I laughed. "Yeah. I got that."

"Are you at least someplace warm?" she asked.

I glanced at myself in the rear view mirror. My hair hung in a long, sopping, wavy mess. My face and neck were beet red—from windburn or early onset hypothermia (or both). My lips were a nice, expensive-lipstick shade of blue.

"I am now," I replied.

Quinn bought me lunch, and we did the geeky writer thing for an hour over sandwiches and designer desserts. She got a kick out of my story, but Quinn's a great audience. She gets a kick out of all my stories.

"Are you going to put this in your blog?" she asked.

I smiled. Humphrey Bogart spoke up in the back of my head. *Maybe not today, maybe not tomorrow, but soon, and for the rest of my life.*

It kind of feels like cheating, plagiarizing my dreams and my life the way I do. But with material like this, what kind of writer would I be if I passed it up?

The Love of My Seven Minutes

April 30, 2005

There's just something about the first day you feel better after being really really sick. Like a starving man at an all-you-can-eat buffet—life suddenly seems worth living again. You can laugh without parts of your body screaming. You can listen to music without your ears burning; you can dance without your brain wishing it would fall out of your head. You can taste excitement and love and inspiration like snowflakes on your tongue and it feels...happy.

Being sick—painfully sick—breaks everything down to simple. The world happens one slow, excruciating step at a time. As a result, all that extraneous worrying takes the day off. And when you come back to your life, you get the bonus of waking up in that simple world.

So what if the sun is not shining? It's out there somewhere. So what if the flowers aren't blooming yet? They will soon enough. So what if my family is leaving after only one night? They were here. I was unconditionally loved for twenty-four hours and I now have the most beautiful door on my street. So what if I don't write a billion wonderful words today? I will write some, and whatever that is will be enough.

So what if I only have seven minutes to talk to Max? It's seven minutes of happiness to enjoy. Seven minutes of remembering I am not alone. Seven minutes of smiles and laughter. Seven minutes of a heart that soars. Seven minutes of blissful death, destruction and mayhem. Seven minutes closer to July.

My nose is still stuffy and my singing voice is flat. I still laugh like a crow and dance like a spaz. But somewhere, the sun is shining. God, it feels good to feel better.

Tuxedo Girl

May 5, 2005

"A sweet Tuxedo girl you see,
Queen of swell society,
Fond of fun as fun can be,
When it's on the strict Q. T.
I'm not too young, I'm not too old,
Not too timid, not too bold,
Just the kind of sport I'm told -
Ta-ra-ra-boom-de-ay…"

–Lottie Collins, *On the Q. T.*

You know what's worse than not knowing what to write about? Knowing *exactly* what you want to write about, but not being able to do it.

Sigh.

What *can* I say…let's see…a big project I've been working on has been greenlit by a major NY publisher, and if the manuscript gets finished by the end of this month, it could see an April 2006 publication. A whole year before *The Telaphab*…can you imagine?

The other thing…and I don't want to jinx myself—or as Dad and the Greeks say, "Put the Mouth on it"—is that Candlewick has asked to have a look at *Haven*. (Can you say "AAAAAHHHHHHH!" boys and girls?)

Of course, it's one thing to have it read; it's another to have the contract in your grubby little hands. So I will finish up my edits this week and have it in the post by next week…

Just wish me luck, you guys. (You may not think I need it, but I do.) Thanks!

More to come…like the whole matter of the pink Cadillac…

**For reference: The project that was officially greenlit was* Elemental. *Candlewick did not pick up* Haven. *And I really do love all of my Dad's Greek sayings.*

Desperate Housegirl

May 7, 2005

I am listening giddily to the melodious sound of a weed whacker. I know, I know...it seems ridiculous. But one of the things I have wanted my whole life is a handyman. I don't *mind* mowing the lawn, or working outside once in a while...like Dad says, it's one of the responsibilities of being a homeowner.

But after the contracts—and all the writing and editing I have to do—and after being struck down by the allergy monster so hard this last time I'm actually *afraid* to go outside (and I really didn't want that to happen again), I prayed for someone to leave a flyer on my mailbox.

Finally someone did. His name was Jeff. The flyer was green. And I was so desperate, I even managed to pick up the phone (friends and family who know me are now gasping in shock) and give him a call. I left a message on his cell phone. He even called me back.

He's a nice, older gentleman (I had to specify this for Max, who got a little jealous I think because I was so excited about the whole thing). He wrote my information down in this nice, professional book and offered to mow and weed my lawn for $30/week. He even offered to modify my fence so he could get his riding lawnmower through my back gate. He charged me $15. It's already done.

I peeked through the blinds at him as he sped around my front yard on his lawnmower, and I smiled and giggled like a schoolgirl. I just never treat myself like this. Ever. I'm not a girlie girl. Sure…once in a great while I'll curl my hair or paint my nails blue, but that's about it.

But this is so much more than being a girlie girl. This is the freedom to go to conventions any weekend I want without having to worry about when I'm going to mow. This is the time I get to spend working on my *other* job, the one I love, the one that hopefully will pay my bills one day. This is the asthma I don't develop from exposure to Tennessee in the spring. This is the knowledge that, for the price of six cups of Starbucks coffee, my lawn will be *done* and done fast, and done well.

My neighbors will not be disappointed in me. The guy across the street won't have to come over and mow my front lawn while I'm at work and embarrass the heck out of me, like he did that one time last year after Mom and I were in a car wreck and I sprained my wrist.

Tonight, I plan on going out onto my deck, while the pollen is in bed for the night. I will look out at my beautiful yard - because I do have a beautiful yard. I will light some candles and turn on the lights around my pavilion, and I will smile at the present I have given myself.

And, if I so desire, Jeff also does gutters and painting and remodeling…it says so right there in green.

I think this is the beginning of a beautiful friendship.

St. George and the Cockroach

May 11, 2005

There are little pieces of your life that never go away—tiny memories that burrow themselves deep into your brain only to reemerge at random times days, months—even years—later.

The most annoying thing, other than the fact that these memories exist at all, is that they're stupid. The toilet you used at a bar that didn't flush. The chair at your aunt's house that broke when you sat on it. A stranger's offhanded condescension. The test you didn't study for in high school. The tone of voice your boss used to criticize you.

They aren't battles won or loves lost; they just are what they are. Subconscious insects. Emotional pests. Immortal cockroaches.

I am a loud woman; I make no excuses or claim to be otherwise. I come from an even louder family. We tell amazing stories. We project. We make fantastic performers and public speakers and friends. It's a simple enough affliction to comprehend—our personal volume increases in direct proportion to our excitement. As an added bonus, our voices have the special ability to ride a certain wavelength that, even at a whisper, can include the whole room.

If we are quiet for any reason we are either sick, extremely upset, or dead.

Of course, all of this is based on the assumption that everybody in the room wants to be part of our audience, and that each and every one of them is paying rapt attention.

And why wouldn't they be?

Over Easter, Mom, Dad, Sami and I all met up in the Dulles airport and flew on to Vermont together. I hadn't seen my mother since December, my father since August, and my sister and her boyfriend since July. What with all that had gone on in my life since those times, you can imagine how eager I was to catch up and how many wonderful stories I had to tell.

Don't ask me how we got on the subject because I can't remember—but prior to take off I became wrapped up in relating the experience of watching my first football (soccer) game in a London pub.

Murphy knew I was watching…so of course it had been no normal game.

Any of you who happened to be following football that first week in January will remember the Tottenham Spurs' uncounted point against Manchester United. A Spurs player kicked the ball over halfway across the field. The Man U keeper caught it, bobbled it, and dropped it behind him. It landed about three feet inside the goal.

And no one saw it, so it didn't count.

No one saw it except half the stadium, thousands of folks in pubs and living rooms around the world, and all the cameras at the game that had it plastered on the back page of every newspaper in the city the next day.

This was my first football-watching experience. Admit it! It's a good story! My parents (sitting behind me) were hanging on every word. (Sami was buried in the latest issue of Vanity Fair, but I knew she was listening.)

However, the guy three seats behind Sami was apparently an overtired football hater in a foul mood. He sat up in his seat, scowled at me, and did that whack-a-mole thing with the flat of his hand. I imagine the caption that was meant to go with the sign language was: "Pipe down!"

As I write this, I wonder why the guy didn't just say as much…but it doesn't matter.

The damage was done.

I instantly turned red and embarrassed down to my toes. I actually said out loud, "Oh, come on—I haven't seen these people in almost a year. I'm excited." And then I sank down into my seat.

My family, having not witnessed the visual part of the exchange, immediately wanted to know what had happened. I all but whispered it to them. They couldn't believe the man's gall. They saw how freaked out he had made me and they tried to make me feel better. (Just wait!" said Dad. "In a few years he'll realize who you are and tell someone, 'Oh my God, can you believe I once told *Alethea Kontis* to be quiet?'")

I laughed, but it still hurt. It always does.

My Ex was extremely fond of saying, "Alethea, you're at an Eleven. I need you at about a Four." I never found it cute or clever. My saving graces at my job in a sea of cubicles are that I am very enthusiastic, have a great laugh, and tell really interesting stories. That…and the fabulous woman who hired me is even louder than I am.

Max earned a billion cool points after London when I realized that not once for the whole entire trip had he told me to shut up. My mother thought that was both amazing and rare, and she said so.

"I never tell you to shut up," Dad said to Mom. "I just ask you to lower your voice sometimes."

"Same thing," Mom and I said in unison.

The worst part about the experience was that this guy—this ridiculous nobody cockroach of a man who slept the entire time once the noise of the plane drowned out everything else—haunted me for the rest of the trip.

Two days later, Sami's boyfriend was sitting next to me in Cherie's kitchen. "Are you okay?" he asked me. "You've been quiet this whole weekend. I don't think I've ever seen you this quiet."

I shrugged and said something like, "I'm just soaking it all in." Which was true. But I failed to mention that that stupid guy was in the back of my head every time I opened my mouth, motioning for me to pipe down.

Yesterday, my computer at work screwed up and I was without iTunes for the entire morning. [*Gasp*] Since I can't possibly go about my day without a soundtrack, I popped in my Lightning Seeds "Best Of" CD and ran it through Windows Media. The last track on the disc is "Three Lions," a song about English football. And I kid you not, that jerk was there in the back of my head again, scowling and making me feel about three apples high.

Great. Now I couldn't even *think* about football without getting embarrassed? Was this pesky, ridiculous memory going to bug me for the rest of my life?

Skip ahead a month and a half to today. A flight to New York this time, connecting once again through Dulles (gotta love Independence Air).

Enter George.

George walked onto the plane wearing a plush birthday cake hat on his head. He was so tall, the candles crushed against the ceiling as he made his way down the aisle to find his seat.

"I like your hat," the flight attendant said.

"It took me forty years to earn this hat," George announced to the whole plane. "I like it too."

George's companions, who were spread from the first row to the last, teased him about breaking open the bubbly. "The champagne's on me!" George cried out, and he cracked a good joke in reference to the scattered group about "spreading his girls around." We all laughed. Before the flight attendant played the safety instruction recording, she wished George a happy fortieth over the intercom. Everyone on the plane cheered and applauded.

The celebrity guest who read the safety instructions was Mia Hamm.

George's pals made good on the champagne threat. About fifteen minutes into the flight, a cork hit the ceiling like a gunshot. There were cries of excitement and dismay as the champagne sprayed the flight attendant, George's friend, and most of George's friend's neighbors. The rest of us smiled and laughed. The flight attendant went back up to the front of the plane to get napkins and make an announcement about what had happened, for those folks who might have missed the violent popping or the rich smell of champagne that filled the cabin.

Those were probably the same folks who didn't know how to fasten their seat belts.

At the end of the flight, as we taxied into the gate, George turned on his cell phone and called his friend Alan, who had also just landed in Dulles. We all found out at what carousel George planned on picking up his baggage, where he was getting his car, and approximately how long it would take him to drive to where he was going.

I thought about wiping the silly grin off my face, but I didn't really want to.

The seatbelt sign dinged off, and we all jumped into the aisle. While we were waiting to disembark, I turned around and wholeheartedly wished George a very happy fortieth birthday. And I meant every word.

Because now in the back of my head, when that scowley whack-a-mole guy pops up and motions for me to pipe down, George yells, "Put a sock in it, buddy!" and squashes him beneath his cowboy boot like the cockroach of a memory he is.

He leans across the aisle—elbows on knees, chin in his hands, and cake-hat candles wobbling. Enraptured, he says to me, "So *then* what happened?"

The Year of the Rooster

June 12, 2005

"It is easier to lie with familiar demons than to walk with strange angels."
- Unknown

Growing up with Greek customs, a child learns to watch what she says, and to spit. A lot. It's not an expression of disgust; it's more like knocking on wood. If you say something good, you spit so as not to tempt fate. If you say something bad, you spit…and cross yourself a few times for good measure. Two of the most important things I learned growing up were: 1.) think before you speak and 2.) stay hydrated.

Words have power. If you don't spit or cross or knock or scratch your butt or follow through with whatever your own personal appeasement to the gods is, then the words that have just left your mouth have the potential to curse. You don't have to intend malice—

it just happens. A beautiful child will turn ugly; a well-oiled machine will break down; the best-laid plans of mice and men…well, you get the point.

Everyone has this ability, this unrealized power. *Everyone.* You have to wield it with care.

Last August marked the inception of the first (and hopefully annual) Codex Writers Group's Halloween Writing Competition. Jason D. Wittman was the one who suggested the idea, and who ended up being a sort of Master of Ceremonies when things all fell into place. The rules of the contest were as follows: all the participants' names were randomly selected out of a hat and put into a list. Each of us then thought up an idea—not the whole plot, but the seed of a story—and passed it to the next person on the list (my victim was Cathy Bollinger). The stories had to be downloaded onto the server anonymously by October first, at which point Quinn Reid, our administrator, sent them all out in a zip file for us to read, pick the top three, and vote on. First Place got three points, Second two, and Third one. The story with the most points won. Easy peasy.

I had never done such an exercise in all my life.

Possibly the most difficult aspect was coming up with a story idea that I was willing to part with. I think I came up with three—all of which I fully intended to keep (that I should have written down because now I can't remember not one of them). But I had to give Cathy *something*. My parents were in town, and they tried to help me, but nothing was clicking. I had to pick something, something totally out of the air, something I had no connection to and had no intention of thinking about beyond typing it in an email and sending it off.

Finally, I figured out how I was going to do it. I was going to give Cathy a list of three things her story must include. She could do with them whatever she wished. I wrote the three things down…and then spent the next paragraph apologizing to Cathy because it was such a horrible idea, and should she need me to give her another one I gladly would.

Brave soul that she is, she kept them.

The three things I had given her were: a boy, a haunted bicycle, and a fairly intelligent chicken.

I felt like a monster.

I had actually received a decent story seed about a painter (courtesy of Eric James Stone) and had the brilliant idea of not only incorporating the legend of Jack O'Lantern, but also subtly sneaking various members of our writing group into the story. I had images of the members of Codex chuckling to themselves as they recognized each character and looked for others. I wrote the story in two days and turned it in before the deadline. It was called "Violent Crimson," after a misunderstanding I had on the phone with Sami when she was trying to list all the different shades of red paint.

"Vermilion…violet crimson—"

"What?!?" I asked, and the rest is history.

The stories were amazing. Every single one. It really was hard picking three best, because there weren't three best. They were *all* the best. (And I still maintain that one day someone's going to pay us scads of money to recreate it into an anthology.) Cathy's was an amazing tale about a ghost who haunted a bicycle and a shack in the deep woods where witches turned little boys into chickens and kept them as pets. They named them after their favorite desserts. It was marvelous.

The very close race was won by Quinn Reid, James Maxey, and Tom Pendergrass. (Turns out, believe it or not, that I was a little too subtle for my own good.) We joked that Quinn rigged the contest so that she would win. We patted each other on the backs and thanked Jason for a wonderful time. But the best bit was the email I got from Cathy shortly after the contest.

She told me I had cursed her with a chicken.

A man down the road from her had apparently purchased a bunch of chickens to have at his house, and this particular little gal wandered off. She hung around Cathy's yard…and decided she liked it there. So Cathy and her husband left out food for the chicken, and in return it kept their garden clean of pesky snails and such. It even made friends with Zeke, their cat. And in honor of her beautiful red and gold plumage, Cathy named her Mustard.

Cathy mentioned Mustard to me in her emails from time to time. I even got a picture—quite a pretty little hen, really.

In February, Jason suggested another contest to get our creative juices flowing (which was very originally entitled: The Get-Your-Creative-Juices-Flowing Contest). I felt bad, because due to my workload, I wouldn't be able to have something by April first. In fact, when I did come up for air and think about entering, I realized that the deadline for the contest was *that* night. It was never going to happen. But then the deadline was extended…and then it was extended again…and I figured it was meant to be, so I opened up a notebook and scribbled something down.

The story was called "Crocodile Baby" (which later became "Alligator Baby" when it was pointed out to me that I was in the wrong hemisphere for crocodiles), and I wrote it in about five hours. To add to the challenge, I decided that it was only fair to curse myself with the chicken this time. So to the core list of seeds we were forced to pick from and include, I mentally added, "fairly intelligent chicken." But it wasn't just any chicken; it was Mustard.

She was my muse. She was a star. In fact, she was an angel—an angel cleverly disguised as a chicken. Cathy (who I also inspired to scribble down a last-minute entry) recognized the story as mine right away. She praised it and thought it grand indeed that Mustard played a pivotal role.

The story tied for second place.

Last month, I was in New York. I missed seeing Cathy's email until I got back to work. It was entitled "A Farewell to Mustard":

Last Thursday, I was wakened from a sound sleep at 1:30 in the morning. Outside my bedroom window, I heard the eeriest, most frightening sound I've ever heard. This was no domestic cat argument between my beloved 15-year-old neutered male, Zeke—who insists on sleeping outside under the bedroom window on warm nights—and a neighborhood troublemaker feline. This was different.

I run outside in my nightshirt, after slipping on the garden clogs handily stationed by the door. I hit the outside lights and go charging outside, as my spouse slumbers on in bed. I call Zeke's name and head toward the edge of the front deck into the darkness lurking beyond the reach of the floodlights. As I do so, a little voice in my head is starting to wonder aloud if this is such a good idea. I find Zeke cowering against a step, looking more terrified than I have ever seen him. But he seems untouched. I point my flashlight into the darkness toward the sound that has receded just beyond the reach of the light. It is a high-pitched muttering that rises and falls in pitch, and it sounds very angry. It made me seriously wonder in my sleep-fogged condition whether demons had invaded my woods. I did the only thing I could think of. I said in my loudest, most dramatic voice (and I have a BIG voice), "Begone! You are not welcome here."

Much to my relief, this seemed to do the trick. The creature continued to mutter and curse loudly, but as it did so, I could hear it crashing through the underbrush as it headed down the hill toward the creek that borders our land. I stood there, trying to follow the sound with my flashlight, as the demon cursed and muttered its way down the creek.

About that time, Tom, my sleepy spouse, came stumbling out to look for me. Zeke, who usually refuses to sleep in the house at night, voluntarily charged through the door and, after we calmed him down and checked him over, crashed on the living room floor with obvious relief.

Since that time, no Mustard. Anywhere. Not even a feather. We think she gave her life for Zeke. You see, they'd taken to sleeping beside each other—my still-active hunter, Zeke, and this feisty hen. After talking to my vet and a wildlife vet, we concur that the demon was most likely a bobcat, who followed Mustard's scent up the hill (she wandered everywhere) to the spot where they often slept. Mustard wasn't there—I would have heard her squawk. But Zeke was, and the demon, I suppose, after polishing off Mustard earlier, was hoping for a second helping. Instead, the bobcat found Zeke, cornered him, and was enthusiastically telling Zeke how he was going to die when I intervened.

We kept Zeke inside several nights, until we no longer found strange scat in the driveway. All is <knock wood> quiet now. Too quiet, really, now that our uninvited feathered friend has departed. We'll miss her, and it's nice to know she has her very own story as a memorial, thanks to you.

Farewell, Mustard, and thanks, Lee.

I opened my desk drawer for my toilet paper stash to soak up the tears that were streaming down my face. I hiccuped a laugh—how silly I was to be crying over a chicken. But she was *my* chicken. My angel. And a demon destroyed her.

We writers live in a strange world. We walk so fine a line between reality and fantasy, sometimes it's hard to remember which is which. There are the things that life gives you, and the things you make of them. And one can be just as fantastic as the other.

Was Mustard just a coincidence? A ship passing in the night? Was she just a funny story that a couple of authors made up between each other? Or did we, by somehow tapping into that vast power that we careless wordsmiths have, actually *create* her?

Are curses real?

Well if they are real, at least we can say for sure that they aren't all bad. And even if she was just a strange coincidence, Mustard brought joy to the lives of a couple of women in her brief time on this planet.

Two women who, in gratitude, made her immortal.

These Boots Were Made for Moderatin'

June 2005

I grew up in a two-story brick house on a lake in South Carolina. In the fall we raked pine straw instead of leaves. In the winters we played rainy-day games and sent childish wishes to the stars for even a glimpse of snow. In the spring we watched the azaleas bloom and tested the water with impatient toes. In the summers, we were fish.

Rain or shine, with clothes and without and every form of dress in between, we ate, bathed, and slept in the water. There were rules, of course. Common sense stuff. Universal truths. You can swim if there's thunder, but everybody out if there's lightning. No calling for help unless you really mean it. If you swim to Ian Chillag's house across the lake and decide to stay, call home so someone knows where you are. Whoever holds their breath longest wins. And the best way to get in the water is a cannonball off the end of the dock. The cold only shocks you for a second.

Total immersion is the best way to do most things. Baby steps are for babies.

Hypericon in Nashville was last Friday. On Monday, I got the invitation from Fred Grimm to be a guest. An official guest. And I could be on some panels too. This was it. I'd been a "Guest of a Guest" before at a couple of cons and workshops, but never an actual "Hi, we'd like to have you on a panel."

Fred asked me for a short bio. I gave him one. He asked me if I wanted to be on a fantasy panel. I told him I probably wouldn't have much to add, but if Sherrilyn Kenyon was going to be there I would be there anyway. "Good," he said. "Then you can be the moderator."

Gulp.

Max said the worst job in the world was that of moderator. I didn't really know *why* he said it, but I guessed I was going to find out. From glorified guest to the worst job in the world, right in front of Sherri, Glen Cook, J. Ardian Lee, and a nice big audience.

A cannonball right into the chilly deep end.

I had a mental list of questions ready and borrowed half of Sherri's wardrobe for moral support. I kept my hands on the table so no one could see them shaking. At one point I was so caught up in what the authors were saying, Julianne Lee had to remind me to take a question from the audience. Sherri had to pass her watch down the table to me so I could keep track of the time. But everything went fine, the audience asked questions and the authors talked and we filled up the whole hour and then some.

Sherri and I hung out after the panel and then went to Hard Rock for a ridiculously late dinner with two of my new best friends, Derek and Eddie. That night I even slept okay because the hard part was over. I had done the worst job in the world and come out alive. The two panels Saturday would be cake, right?

Right?

The two panels were back to back. One at 12:00 pm and one at 1:00 pm. The first one was a short story panel with Randy Fox and Geoffrey Girard…whom I squealed about when I realized that not only was Geoff *there* but I was going to be on a panel with him. We met through the Codex Writer's Group, and Geoff had edited a couple of my stories for me. A genuinely great guy. It was fun to see how long it took him to realize that he knew me. It wasn't too long. And when he did, he shook my hand and introduced himself to me again.

That panel magically lasted almost the whole hour, and afterward I got sidetracked hearing the amazing story about a man's novel series…I checked in with Sherri quickly and then grabbed Eddie out of the dealer's room and pretty much ordered him to walk up to the big Genre panel with me. I knew I was late and, four-inch-heeled boots or not, I was too chicken to go by myself.

Sure enough they were all there: Brian Keene, Mary Buckner, Glen Cook, and David Harris. And they were all waiting on me. There was an empty seat right beside Brian. And as I went for it, Brian said, "We made you moderator."

"What?!?" (I'm pretty sure that was out loud.)

"Last one to the panel gets to be moderator," said Glen Cook.

Who the hell made up that rule? The Rotten Egg Police? "Oh, shit!" (And I'm really afraid that one might have been out loud as well.)

Did I mention that the entire convention was in the audience? Well, if they weren't, it certainly felt like it. I quickly found a couple of familiar faces in the crowd: Lillie, who was sitting somewhere in the middle, and Jason Sizemore, who was right up front. I sat up straight and introduced myself to the room. And when the introductions were over, I pulled a question out of my butt and the games began. Jason yanked me out of the fire once when there was a lull in the Q&A, and later even Brian chimed in to ask a question of the panel. You know, I think I might have even contributed a sentence or two that didn't sound too terribly inane.

The rest of the day was kind of a blur. Sherri got a terrible migraine so I played mama hen for a while...the air conditioner in our room broke and we had to repack all our stuff and move to the end of the hallway (you know you talk to the front desk too much when you dial "0" and say, "Charles! It's your favorite person!" and Charles knows exactly who is on the line)...and finally Sherri told me to leave her and go up to the party floor and have a good time.

Right. Party. Me.

By myself.

Right.

I could do this.

Hey, I could moderate a panel. I could do anything.

I made up a strategy in the elevator. I would not wander around the party rooms looking lost. I would be looking for a friend. Right. What friend? Okay...Derek. I would just peek my head in the doors and scan the rooms and tell people I was looking for Derek. Right. It's a plan. Stuck my head in the first room. Lots of people...girl in a bra...no Derek. Second room: streamers hanging from the ceiling, video camera pointed into the room, and the picture projected on what seemed like hundreds of monitors. No Derek. On any screen.

Back into the hallway again. Someone parts the sea of people for me to get by. Breathe. Remember Douglas Adams. Don't Panic.

I did find Derek soon after and ended up in the *House of Blood* room, where within three seconds I was asked by the lovely and bubbly Rachael Wise—Hostess Extraordinaire and Cutest Woman in the World—if she could get me anything. There were no naked people or scary cameras—just chocolate cake, beer, and a bunch of people sitting around and talking. *This* I could handle.

The venues and the people changed a little as the night went on...I lost Fred and Darryl to some convention business and picked up Eddie, Brian Keene, and Tom Piccirilli (whom I've officially dubbed the Nicest Man in the Universe). I had the absolute time of my life sitting around and chatting to these guys into the wee hours of the morning about comics and TV shows, books and other authors, dreams and bitterness, everything and nothing. (Pretty much in that order.)

And the boots witnessed it all, their patent leather and laces even threatening to kick Brian Keene's ass at one point (and wasn't *that* an amusing conversation to remember on the way home the next day). I took those boots off before I snuck back in the room and crawled into bed sometime really close to 5:00 am (I only know what time it was because Sherri pointed it out to me the next morning. Once a mother, always a mother...).

The Sunday after a Con, most guests check out and go home. Sherri and I checked out with all the intent of finding something to eat and doing just that...and ended up hanging out in the Consuite until 6:00 pm with the fabulous convention staff and the rest of the peanut gallery.

Sunday begs to be mentioned because it was the day I fell in love. He was a genius with long blond hair, the most incredible blue eyes, and the perfect pickup line for a picture book writer. He walked over to me and recited the alphabet. I fell for him instantly. He hung out with us at the table for most of Sunday, and we laughed and sang...he made me feel like I was the center of the universe. He drooled all over me.

Literally.

And when Melissa Gay came back from tearing down the art show to pick up her two-year-old son, she gushed about how astonished she was that we had bonded because Brendan just doesn't warm up to people (which I seriously can't believe for a second), and how grateful she was that he had found a friend to keep him company (which I do believe). Of course, I didn't realize how grateful until she gifted me with the most beautiful matted print and I almost cried. See, like a moron I hadn't bought anything for myself at this convention—the best convention I had ever attended—and now I not only had something to remember it by, but I also had something precious, something that would tell me the story of the weekend every time I looked at it.

That night I took home with me a print, a boatload of new friends, and a new set of universal truths: Brunettes are cool. Yankees put brown gravy on everything. There is a lot to be said for a well-stocked Consuite. All friends are worth making (well okay, that's an old one, but I was reminded of it once again). What happens at Frolicon...well, I really would prefer that it stay at Frolicon, 'cause I don't want to hear about it. Beware the breakfast buffet because the zombies like brains in the sausage. Every Con has a list like this that six people will laugh at and the rest will go, "Huh?" Hypericon was really awful and you don't want to go next year, you really should leave all the fun to me. Last one to the panel gets to be the moderator. Let it slide. And most important of all: Don't Be Stoopid.

Well, I've gone on too long again and it's past my bedtime...I'm staring at the blue Archangel of the West and thinking about a little boy in my lap who knew that W-A-T-E-R spelled water.

You jump in the deep end and sink or swim. Sometimes you hold your breath for so long that you feel like you could stay down there forever. Part of you is convinced that your body could adapt...you could get the oxygen out of the water from osmosis through your skin. But the rest of you knows that it's just a dream and eventually, reluctantly, you have to come up for air.

I came back to the Real World with a watery print to remind me of my foray into that deep end...a signed, limited print numbered 13 out of 100.

Lucky number 13.

Which reminds me—-I need to return some emails from my new best friends in horror. Horror…the redheaded stepchild of the speculative fiction genre.

See? Everybody loves redheads. Even me.

Murphy Is My Copilot

July 2, 2005

I told my new friend Tom Piccirilli that I was looking forward to the nine-hour drive to Charleston, SC this weekend to visit my sister. I just really love being alone in the car, windows down, music blaring, singing at the top of my lungs for so long that I'm hoarse by the time I arrive. I always bring a few books on tape, but I lose patience with them quickly. I crave the meditative nothing time, the selective sensory deprivation. My brain needs time to defrag its hard drive.

Surrounded by music and fresh air I am free to plan my life, organize manic thoughts into boxes, and tell myself stories. I have discovered that I get some of my best ideas in the bathroom, and in the car. I'm sure there's some sort of complicated psychological explanation that involves ordered brain wave activity in a relaxed state, but mine is not to wonder why. Mine is to laugh and gasp as brilliant thoughts come pouring in to entertain me…and to try not to wreck while writing them down.

(And yes, because everyone inevitably suggests it at this point. I *have* a mini tape recorder. My parents bought me one every year for a while until I finally convinced them that it just doesn't work like that . Believe me.)

I've made quite a bit of headway on my fairy tale story for the latest Codex competition…so much, in fact, that I've decided it will just have to be my next novel, and the Codex entry a boiled down synopsis.

So if you think about it, I'm not entirely alone at all. I won't name any names, but I know for a fact that I'm not the only writer whose characters keep her company in the dark and quiet hours of the night.

And then there's Murphy.

My mother was raised Catholic. She believes in guardian angels. She says that everyone has a guardian angel, sometimes more than one, and they are eager to be of use. You ask them for favors, like a good parking space or a great deal on a sofa. Mom also says that if you ask them what their names are, they will tell you.

Me, I'm not very religious at all—at least, in an organized way. It's not that I don't believe in Things Greater Than Myself, there just doesn't seem to be an established label for what I do believe, and I'm okay with that. Mom's angel theory sounded nice, had the potential for some really great stories, and was the best excuse for a glorified invisible friend that I'd ever heard. I envisioned my own guardian angel, beautiful and timid, waiting in the wings to be recognized. I thought of maybe calling her Mary or Marie. And then I promptly forgot about her.

Murphy started out as a joke. It's what I used to tell people I'd name the kid I'd never have. Murphy's Law was more than a saying; I had come to accept it as my way of life. It would only be fitting to name the non-existent fruit of my womb after my patron saint.

I haven't been writing in this blog for a year yet, but if you've kept up at all you have a sense of how my life goes, the good and the bad, one adventure after another. After more and more ridiculous and amazing things started happening to me, I did what every human does—I blamed it on something. I put a name to it, whatever it was, completely arbitrarily and without thought. It was an entry here, as a matter of fact. I named my imp, and I called him Murphy.

Anyone who has ever read fantasy is familiar with the recurring Magical Tenet that names have power. If you know someone's true name you have power over them—power to manipulate or destroy them. Conversely, by giving something a name you give it power. Make it real. Sure, most of fantasy's tenets derive from folklore and legend and once upon a time truths, but they aren't normally worries that stay in the back of your mind on a day-to-day basis. It's just fantasy. Only…the more things happen to me, the more this whole invisible friend thing makes sense.

It began, as Murphy's Law does, with the bad things. Coming home from London the day *before* my birthday. Getting a rejection from Writers of the Future once again. Getting sick right before a convention. Sending an email to someone you *totally* didn't intend to send it to. If you're the kind of person who believes that everything happens for a reason, and that the bad must come with the good, then you take it all in stride.

The coincidences that make the hairs on my neck stand on end are the ones that feel like communication. The ones that remind me of being tortured by my older brother as a kid. I'd think and complain about how I never got out of the house, away from the computer, and that I needed to spend some time outside for my own good. That weekend, Sherrilyn Kenyon and I got locked out of the house. Away from our computers. I found myself sitting on the steps in the blistering Tennessee summer heat. I listened to Sherri rant about her cleaning lady as the sweat dripped down our faces and I smiled to myself. It was twisted, but I was outside wasn't I?

I have almost 900 songs on my iTunes at home. In the mornings and after work I stick the entire library on shuffle and go about my business. The week Max was in Dublin, I heard "Ireland," a song off Tori Amos's new Beekeeper album, no less than five times before I screamed, "All right! *I get it* already!" The last day he was there, I made myself lunch from whatever was left in the fridge. Spinach, some grilled salmon, and sweet potatoes. I threw it all in a bowl and I was walking out of the kitchen when I looked down and realized what I was really having for lunch: the Irish flag.

I shook my head and sighed. "You think you're funny, don't you?"

It's not malicious, though. The bad things that happen to me seem to happen…in the best way possible, if that makes sense. I get stuck in traffic or in a long line when I'm so incredibly frantic that I *need* to be made to stop and smell the roses. I remember something I've forgotten when I'm turning the key to lock the door, and not twenty miles down the road. My car breaks down in the parking lot at work and not on the highway somewhere away from everything.

I don't waste my time asking for things like decent parking spaces or winning lottery tickets—my wishes are better spent on eradicating poverty or achieving world peace. If there really is a Murphy, I think he knows that. He's not specifically good or specifically bad. He's just a friend of mine who hangs out from time to time…and just happens to be incorporeal.

My mother's Cadillac (which I've been driving ever since the Saturn broke down in said parking lot) doesn't have a CD player, so I was forced to dig out tapes from back in the high school days when mixing tapes was a favorite pastime. For hours I was reminded of what fun my friends and I had making these for each other, and what incredibly good DJs we were. The third tape ended right before I got stuck in Atlanta rush-hour traffic; I popped it out and turned on the radio. What should have been a twenty-minute drive around the perimeter took me the better part of an hour, but 99X—one of the best alternative radio stations ever—was in the middle of a weekend marathon of the top 1000 songs of all time. I had reception from about number 802 to about 764 (if you'd like to see the playlist of most of my drive, 99X will have it up on their website Monday).

The weather was awful, summer storms pouring down rain in blinding sheets, and the traffic was worse…but the ride was actually kind of fun. I called Kit and told him I wouldn't make it to Columbia in time for dinner, but I still planned to stop and see him. Luckily he didn't have any previous engagements, so I was still (and always) welcome. I finally showed up at his house two and a half hours after I had meant to be there.

Sami was mad that I was stopping at all—she wanted me to hurry up and get my butt to Charleston and knew that I would spend more than my designated hour catching up with Kit. She was a little bit right. Kit and I parted reluctantly at 11:30...wishing as always that we had had more time, but knowing I should get back on the road. The night was cool, and the weather had cleared up. I was still wired, but I'd had a nice break out of the car. I looked forward to it. A couple hours and I'd be at the beach.

Two minutes down the road, I was in the parking lot of the senior center checking my oil under a street lamp.

The car felt like it had a plugged fuel line, revving and jerking as I drove down the streets of Kit's neighborhood. It idled worse…sounding at times like it was just going to flat-out stall. I knew I had pushed it a lot, between the rain and the overheated stop-and-go driving, but Mom had driven it down from Virginia under similar conditions and it had been fine.

Super-anxious all over again, I called Kit and asked him what he knew about cars. I drove back to his house. He told me to just spend the night. We'd take the car to get it checked out in the morning, and I could be on my way. He tried to calm my nerves with Oreo ice cream. He did a good job.

Sami was mad, but I couldn't be too upset. I *had* wanted to spend more time with Kit. And now I was. I just hoped it wouldn't be to the tune of several hundred dollars…several hundred dollars that I didn't have to spare.

I lay down at 1:00 am, my nerves humming like a tuning fork, and slept fitfully. In the morning we dropped the car off at the closest Precision Tune and explained what was going on. Kit took me to a Barnes and Noble and bought me some Starbucks. Books and coffee and a discussion about my favorite cover artists calmed my nerves. My friends know me all too well.

Forty-five minutes later, we went back to Precision Tune. The extremely friendly mechanic took me to where the Caddy sat with its hood up and pointed to a small black box on the side of the engine that he described as the idlesensor-control-module-regulator-thing. It was all very technical. Kit and I hmmmed and nodded like doctors.

"It's what keeps your motor from stalling during idle when you've got your air conditioner or radio on," the mechanic said. "When it starts to go bad, sometimes it sticks. And then it'll act up like it does when you're idling, but it's fine when you press the gas and start going."

Which explained perfectly what was happening to the car. A rarity to find not only a competent mechanic, but one whom can explain what's going on in non-condescending terms you can understand. I appreciated that. I waited to find out what the rest of the damage was, and how much it was going to cost me above and beyond the $47 diagnostic.

"…so Joe there hit it with a stick," he said as he shut the hood. "You should be fine for the rest of your trip, but you should get it replaced when you get home."

I blinked twice and resisted the urge to shake what he had said off like a wet dog.

Hit it.

With a stick.

I couldn't complain. I once made almost $1000 an hour writing a picture book. Who was I to begrudge Joe $47 for a deft flick of the wrist? That $47 also bought me peace of mind for the rest of my journey and a few more precious hours with an old friend I didn't talk to half as much as I wished and saw even less.

I called Sami and told her the ridiculous news. I called my parents, whom I had contacted to find out about the Cadillac's history, and told them not to worry. I hugged Kit for the tenth time and hit the road once more, still looking forward to blue skies and music, with my family and the ocean at the end of my journey.

I'm currently writing this from a beach towel in a field next to the BP station at Exit 136.

There's an accident six miles down the road—I know because the digital signs that the brilliant S.C. Department of Transportation placed along the highway this weekend told me so. I'm listening to my iPod and feasting on my second gas station meal of the trip (diet soda and Pringles; yesterday it was Combos). I've received funny looks from the people walking their dogs and filling up, people who have stopped for a potty break or to change drivers. I am reminded what "normal" people on vacation act like, in their Salty Dog Café T-shirts, flip-flops and jeans rolled up to the knee. They stretch; they call their loved ones on cell phones; they get a CD player or a hat out of the back seat; they yell at their kids to hurry up and finish choosing what candy they want before Daddy comes in to pay so they can get back in line on the interstate.

I just smiled at a girl who had gone into her trunk to change her shoes. Who knows what she and her boyfriend think of my makeshift picnic out here in the sun? Well, they wouldn't be the first ones to decide a writer was crazy. Little do they know that it's mostly self-preservation—what I must do to appease my parents, to prove that I'm not risking life and limb getting this all down in transit. I'm betting that in ten minutes, when they've made it a mile and a half down the road, they'll envy this crazy woman all alone in the field, with no one but her imaginary friends to keep her company.

"You want to be alone?" Pic said to me. "Come to Colorado. I'll take you up to Pike's Peak and leave you there."

Sounds like a plan.

Sign me up.

But first...eventually...I have a date with the beach.

"At least we know, if all else fails, we have lobsters in our future."

-Soteria "Sami" Kontis

PART THREE

The Life of Hymie

Tom Piccirilli says...

I was just starting in on the second half of a bottle of rye, my gun digging painfully into my hip, when she walked into my office. I swung my feet off my desk, thumbed my hat back, and took a long gander. She looked like a girl next door type, who appeared sweet and delicate and normal as the cherry on a sundae, but I knew from experience they were sometimes the oddest dames of all. She had a smile that brimmed into her eyes, and straight hair halfway down her back that swirled wildly when she stepped in front of the fan.

I tipped the bottle in her direction and she shook her head.

"You've got nice wheels, lady," I told her.

"Wheels?" she asked.

"Gams."

She blinked at me. "Gams?"

It was times like these that I remembered how old I was, while the rest of the world often seemed so young. "Legs."

"Oh, thank you." She sat down opposite me and stared at the wall where my first secretary had tacked some of the news clippings. They were yellowed and cracked now, but the headlines still told about the cases I'd cracked. I tried to remember the secretary's name. She'd taken a stiletto in the back during THE CASE OF THE GOLDEN FRAMMIS.

"Your name, miss?" I asked.

"Alethea Kontis."

It was the kind of name that had reams of backstory to it. Her deep black eyes seemed to bear that out. I lit a Lucky Strike and offered her one from the pack.

She said, "Lucky Strikes? I didn't know they still made those. And no, thank you, I don't smoke."

Curious, I thought, a well-bred dame like her not drinking or smoking. I knew she was going to be a femme fatale who'd try to ice me before the end of the day. "And what can I do for you, Ms. Kontis?"

"I need you to find my boyfriend," she said, and those emotive dark eyes were already getting teary.

"I see. When and where was the last time you saw him?"

"In Tennessee. Last month at Dragon Con."

"He's a con?"

"No, no. Dragon Con. It's a convention for writers."

"And he met with foul play there? Did he get on the wrong side of a grift and japped for his moo?"

"What?" She shook her head and shrugged it all off. "No, no foul play. He just left."

"And where do you suspect him of being now?"

"Sweden."

"I'm afraid that I don't work outside of L.A., miss. Maybe you should—"

"And you need to find out why the alphabet is running backwards."

"The alphabet is—?"

"Yes, the *AlphaOops*. It should've corrected itself by now."

I had been right. I was dealing with a very disturbed individual. My gut had never been wrong. "But Ms. Kontis, I—"

"It's available at all the finest booksellers."

"It is?"

"Yes."

"Look, about this guy in Sweden, I really think you should—" At that moment, the delivery kid from Burger Emporium came in with my lunch. I gave him a buck and tipped him a dime.

"What the hell is this?" he asked.

"Keep the change, buddy."

"The bill is $9.75, and don't try to lay off a quarter tip on me. I want at least three dollars gratuity."

I paid up. These vacqueros and zoot suiters were becoming a big problem since the end of the war. I hoped Eisenhower closed the border soon.

I opened up the bag and got out my burger, hoping I could take at least a couple of bites before having to call the men in the white wagon to come pick her up. L.A. was already crowded with the demented, maybe the soldiers had brought some kind of disorder back with them from Germany, and it was spreading.

Alethea screamed, "Ketchup!" She flung herself out of her seat and backed up against the wall, stricken with terror.

"You're afraid of ketchup, lady?"

"It's horrifying! You see, when I was a child, I was frightened by a wild man wielding ketchup packets!" She returned to her seat, broke down, and began to cry into her hands. "Oh God, the ketchup! It was everywhere! I'm sorry, I thought I was over it, but the therapy hasn't taken yet."

"Did he do this to you in Sweden?"

"No no! My boyfriend is in Sweden! You must find him and bring him back!"

"What's he doing there?"

"Writing books!"

"In Sweden?"

"No, he's English."

"If he's in Sweden doesn't that make him Swedish?"

"No, you dolt, he's English."

"The jerries gave them a rough time during the blitz. You sure he's not in some bombed out building in London?"

She stormed out of my office then, and I finished the second half of the rye, thinking about how strange the world sometimes got. The phone rang then. It was Bogie. He wanted to know if I wanted a free pass to his new film. It was about a bird.

Toothpick Princess

June 24, 2005

For several years when she was younger, it seemed like every time I saw my niece Alana, she had a cast of some sort on. And, since she had a tendency toward Prima Donnaism, I dubbed her the Toothpick Princess.

I am constantly reminded that not all pain is physical. I've been learning it since I was a little girl myself—you'd think I would have caught on by now.

Sometimes words hurt. Sometimes not hearing words hurts more. Stress kills. Sleeping sucks. It's not just Alana. All women are fragile. And they are all princesses.

The other lesson I've been trying to learn over the years is to not be a doormat. To stand up for myself and demand that everyone recognize me for the princess I am. That's easier to do some days than others. On the days when you just need the world to keep turning, you would sell your soul to make someone you love smile…and sometimes you do. And you try not to hate yourself for it.

I went to the doctor yesterday—a feat almost as remarkable as me picking up the phone. I've felt crummy for the last week. My throat is tight, my chest hurts, my back aches, and I'm constantly tired but I can't sleep. I have so much energy that I don't feel like I'm accomplishing anything unless I've got ten things going on at once…but I'm so scatterbrained that I can't even concentrate long enough to read a book or watch a movie. I've had patience for nothing but poetry and the raw essence of emotion it invokes.

I spent six years of my life depressed as a result of a birth control shot—the origin of my huge fear of medicine of any type. So when I have all this energy, I don't know what to do with it except find outlets for its use. It's just a little frustrating to see it wasted down black holes. I call and talk to people who don't seem to care. I write incredibly long emails that friends and family respond to with a few sentences…if they respond at all. I write stories that no one talks to me about…if they read them at all. I know people need love—there's certainly not enough of it in the world—and I shine it out like a beacon. I know it's selfish for me to expect any of it back. But I miss it.

And the doctor can't find anything wrong with me.

I'm tired because I'm tired.

I'm being a Toothpick Princess.

So I lie in bed at night on my back that's not supposed to hurt, with a pillow under my neck to support my imaginary sore throat, and I try to relax. I try to think up stories and tell them to myself in a futile effort to jumpstart a dream. What I end up wondering instead is whether or not it was a good thing to tell my boyfriend how I felt because if maybe I've said the wrong thing then maybe this time will be the time he goes away forever and exactly how scared am I about being alone? I really should put my gardenias in pots because they're dying in my utility room. And if my birthday was on a Tuesday this year can I figure out what day of the week it was when I was born? Taking into account leap years at some point I have to divide by four…and subtract…

And in between the manic musings come snippets from the day—the week—and they cover me like fire ants and take little venomous bites of my soul.

"Well, darlin', looks like you're stuck with this idea…"

"Gotta go…write back and stuff."

"I can hold places for them for a week or so, but not much longer."

"My deadline is next Wednesday…"

"I was just thinking about you today."

"Lord, writers are a sensitive bunch—and you thought YOU were insecure!"

"My mother says it's probably exhaustion."

"Your mother is probably right."

"You just wished pneumonia on yourself? Are you nuts?"

"I doubt you'll hear from me again today. I am going away."

"It hurts me when you don't say anything. Please don't do this. Please."

"Look, what's with the ketchup? You really scared me with the ketchup story. I'm still obsessing on it."

I bought some over-the-counter sleeping pills today, and I hate that I have to take them. I'm sitting here with a glass of water in one hand and this blue-and-white capsule in the other. It's only one pill. Mom told me to take it. It's not going to kill me.

One stupid blue pill.

Kitti walked into my office today and told me that men don't really exist. They're just figments of our imagination.

Gulp.

Boy, I hope she's wrong.

This depressing little essay was far too personal at the time to actually publish on the Internet. (Mom would have flown down and booked me into an asylum or rehab or something, I'm sure.) But in light of the events that came soon after, it seemed important. I sent the essay out to only a few of my friends, including Tom Piccirilli. That night, Pic hunted down my number and called me at home.

I still have the beginning of that conversation on my answering machine. "Are you off being stoopid? You don't return the emails; who the hell knows what kind of crisis of faith…" I play it again whenever I'm feeling particularly stoopid.

Ironically, this was not the Birth of the Princess. But you can see how the seeds were always there, dancing in the background.

The pill referenced at the end of this essay was a Tylenol PM. The doctor, who couldn't find anything wrong with me beyond exhaustion, elected to take an x-ray of my chest, for lack of anything else to do…

Dr. Cookie's Rx

August 11, 2005

I apologize in advance to everyone who hasn't heard this from the horse's mouth already (that horse being me)—but seeing as it took me almost two months to personally make sure that everyone knew about *The Telaphab*, I just don't have that much time to spread the word about my tumor.

Yes…I said the "t" word. They found it by accident in a chest x-ray I got when I apparently wasn't sick, and they want it out of there (it's between my spine and my lower left lung).

Eddie's started calling it "Hymie."

The surgery to have it out is no big deal…like having a gall bladder removed. And I was going to wait until the end of September to do it—after Max comes to visit and Mom and Dad go to Turkey and Bookville's Fall Publisher's Showcase have all come to pass. But I wimped out after a week of knowing that this little (3cm) grub of a monster was inside me, so I'm having the surgery on Monday. Yes, this Monday the fifteenth, and I'll make Mom come on and update while I'm laid up so that everyone knows I'm going to be okay.

But that's not the point of this post, that's just the backstory.

The point of this post is to tell you the reason that I'm staring at three bite-sized carrots.

For those of you who don't know my dad, he's a little bit psychic. Not psychic enough to have won the lottery or anything (dagnabbit), but enough to tell stories out of the pictures he sees in coffee grounds… stories that sometimes come true.

Like all wives, Mom only listens to half of what Dad says. The sensitive comments from the genius engineer get taken to heart. The ramblings from the over-opinionated crotchety old man go in one ear and out the other. And when Dad says something totally out of the blue, she pays attention.

In my family, you just learn to pay attention to seemingly random events which could be crucial to the order of the Chaos of the Universe.

Like fortune cookies.

Last week, Mom and Dad went out for Chinese. The fortune cookies were delivered with the bill. Dad held them in his hand and told my mother to pick one. She felt them both, and chose the one that "called" to her. Dad went to open his. And before he did, he was struck by the thought: *This fortune is for Alethea.*

He opened it up, read the slip of paper, and stared at my mother wide-eyed before reading the fortune:

"A carrot a day keeps cancer away."

My mother felt compelled to tell me this story—its importance was right up there with the report that my Nana had gone to church and lit a candle for me. She also felt compelled to *mail* me the fortune, in a card that I haven't received yet. (Guess I better check the mail.) But most importantly, I had to promise her on the grave of every ancestor we've ever had that I would go to the grocery store *immediately*, buy some carrots, and eat one every day.

And did I? Did the woman who can't seem to remember to get her oil changed go out and buy a bag of mini carrots? You bet your sweet bippy I did. Right that minute. And I've had at least three (always odd numbers) every day since.

Coincidence?

Probably.

Silly?

Absolutely.

Will it make a difference?

Who knows.

I'm just trying not to think about the fact that the expiration date on the bag is Monday the fifteenth. The day of my surgery.

Wish me luck!

I'll keep you posted.

Like Martyr, Like Daughter

August 31, 2005

So the deal was, Hymie was either a really dangerous nerve sheath tumor—in which case I had about a year to live—or it was a congenital birth defect called a "bronchogenic cyst." Since I'd never had bronchial problems in my life (and therefore no baseline chest x-rays), I feared the worst. Suffice it to say, I've never been so happy to have a deformity in my life.

The down side? Hymie had absolutely nothing to do with why I'd been sick. That was 100% exhaustion, plain and simple.

If you were ever a dedicated reader of the classic comic strip *Calvin & Hobbes*, you know that Calvin comes by his imagination honestly. His mother can make up reasons for him to eat his dinner at the bat of an eyelash, and his father tells him equally gigantic lies.

It's all in the family.

Having Mom visit me during post-tumor-extraction recovery was an absolute blessing. She's such a trooper, putting up with me when I am whiny and fussy and uncomfortable and frustrated (me at my best, I assure you).

But there were moments when the tables would turn, like the morning Mom kept saying she had a really bad headache. So I tried to downplay the Poor Baby Princess and take some pity on my mother. Did she need some Excedrin? Some breakfast?

Her answer: "I've had three cups of coffee and a bit of that chocolate cake. I'll be fine."

It still makes me laugh. (Three cups of the kind of coffee my mother makes is enough to make an elephant climb the walls.)

Meanwhile, my father was in between Virginia and Florida, moving house without my mother's assistance. He called every day to update us on the yard sale, the movers that didn't show up, and when he was on the road. He promised to stop when he got tired and to not drive into the wee hours of the morning.

"Don't worry about me," he said. "I'll be fine."

Only he lied. When he finally *did* get back to Florida, he confessed to my mother that he had driven far too long into the night and gotten up far too early in the morning to go the distance. My father is no longer the Spring Chicken Distance Driver he used to be when we made the Burlington-to-Ft. Lauderdale all-nighters I remember as a kid, but apparently he still thinks he is.

Mom's worry alternated between her broken daughter and her dear husband, both of whom were constantly trying to accomplish way too much in their current conditions. Max empathized with her—he said that taking care of one of us was enough, he couldn't imagine having to juggle two. (Still not sure how to take that one.)

Mom left just as I was feeling better, and Dad got everything moved like a champ—they can now take their upcoming vacation with no worries. Good for them.

As for me, well, I'm back at work doing half days until the ninth. And I am still driving to Atlanta tomorrow and attending Dragon Con this weekend. Look for me—Max and I will be doing a number of panels on the Goth track (mostly on Sunday), and we'll definitely be at the Dune 40th Anniversary Celebration on Friday at 1:00 pm

The hotel where we're staying is a mile away from the con. I've promised not to carry anything and to take naps (hah!). I've packed both my sensible and insensible shoes and plan on running on caffeine and adrenaline all weekend. It's gonna be *great*!

Don't worry about me. I'll be just fine.

Geek Chick Summer: A Life in Conventions

Apex Digest
Winter 2005

Tell me what your calendar is, and I'll tell you who you are.

Each of us has our own way of cataloguing memories. If I pick a year, chances are you could tell me what television shows were popular, who won the Superbowl or the World Cup, what book won the Pulitzer, where you were living at the time, or what films were in wide release. I will instantly know if you are a couch potato, football fanatic, bibliophile, Army brat, or movie theatre projectionist.

If the major events in your life can be broken into SF conventions, it's safe to say you are a geek.

Hi. My name is Alethea Kontis, and I am a Geek Chick. (Yes, we do really exist.)

It's certainly no wonder why speculative fiction conventions are the opiates of the genre-genius masses. Computers definitely play a large role in the convention's resurgence: in a world where agoraphobic, superbusy, hyper-intelligent folk spend all day online working, chatting, playing *Everquest* and downloading episodes of *Doctor Who*, the convention is a Mecca. It's the place where these people can exercise their social muscles, spread their creative wings and preen their feathers among their peers. It is a haven where the rocket scientist, the rock star, the *New York Times* bestseller, the elven princess, and the closet Goth girl can share a table and discuss their guilty pleasures free from the prejudices of society. Or where you would find all these traits in one person.

Welcome to my way of life.

Since I've been getting out more in the literary world, I decided I needed to brush up on doing it in person. So, I made it one of my 2005 New Year's resolutions to attend more conventions. As many as I could. Sure, I had been to Dragon Con and one or two very small, fairly local conventions, but this year I would seek them out. If I had a free weekend and it was within driving distance, I was there. I would make friends and reawaken the dormant social butterfly that I knew lay deep in the cocoon of my soul, craving interaction.

I started out with a day trip to Chattacon at the end of January. It was fun and low key, and a much-needed distraction. I had just met the love of my life in London and lived a fairy tale for twelve glorious days, but other than some nebulous summer plans, I had no idea when I was going to see him again. My house was cold and dark and quiet. My writing life was on hiatus. Despite being full of dreams, my heart was numb. It was nice to see friends again. To be yelled at from across the room and embraced. To be wined and dined by publishers. To be called pretty. To remember that I was special. To drive home in the snow.

Life picked up slowly after that, but the markers were few and far between. I got the ball rolling on an anthology we never thought we'd be able to pull off. I polished up the novel I was working on. I wrote a story in five hours and won second place in a Codex writing contest. I saw my family for Easter. We got the contract for the anthology. I edited at least two more passes on the picture book.

One by one, days would pass and then months. Summer got farther and farther away…and I was still alone. Friends forced me to get out every few weeks, and I was glad they did. But late at night, in the dark, it was difficult.

June twenty-first was fast approaching. The first day of summer. Max had said he would come, and he had promised to never disappoint me. I believed those two things like I'd never believed anything before—clenched them in my fists and never let them go.

It was still difficult.

Little did I know it was going to be the most difficult summer of my life.

HYPERICON I
JUNE 17-19

I was sick.

Okay, I hadn't officially succumbed to anything yet, but a sinus infection was imminent, I felt sure. I'd had enough of them to know. I was tired all the time, my head ached, and I kept waking up with a sore throat.

It was just a small local convention. Did I really want to go? Yes, I had finagled my way onto the guest list—a real guest who would even be on panels and stuff—but the daily 40 minute each way commute was going to kill me, I was sure. It was going to be hell. Especially when I didn't even feel like getting out of bed.

My phone rang on Wednesday. It was Sherrilyn Kenyon. "Come

on," she said. "I'll get us a room, so we don't have to drive home. We'll go Friday after you get off work and come back early Sunday morning. We won't stay any later than we have to, okay?"

Fine.

I called in sick that day, and told her we could leave whenever. I packed two sets of clothes in a small bag (both a girl thing and a geek thing)—one set for if I felt particularly cute and enthusiastic, and a standby set of comfy jeans and horror movie T-shirts. I drove to Spring Hill, tossed the bag into the back seat of Sherri's Mustang (mainly because the trunk was already stuffed full of her convention trousseau), and we were off.

I had to moderate a panel Friday night with Sherri, Glen Cook, and J. Ardian Lee. It was the first panel I had ever been on, never mind moderated. At the very least, I hoped the adrenaline would chase away my malaise. I decided to try to look the part while Sherri decked herself out in vampire gear. My lame attempt consisted of borrowing heavily from Sherri, a woman who had packed more for a 48-hour trip than I had for my entire stay in London. I donned the clothes as if they were light-Goth battle dress, telling myself it would make me feel better. If I *looked* like the hot author chick, I would *be* the hot author chick.

Besides, it wasn't just for me. Letting me raid her portable closet would appease Sherri's big sister instinct. (She secretly hates me because her jewelry looks better on me, I know it.) She had gotten me there, dressed me up, and I was going to be a star. A princess.

And I was.

The moderating was tenuous, but a good start. I handed out cards and got stopped in the hall by someone who talked to me for so long I was late for my next panel. I didn't spend a penny or lift a finger. I met Brian Keene on a good day, and fell in love with Tom Piccirilli. I made friends with Jason and Derek and Eddie and Fred…and pretty much everyone else from the convention staff to the hotel desk clerk. Better than friends. Family. It was magic. I was Cinderella in four-inch-heeled black boots, and the rest of the world disappeared.

That Monday everything came crashing back.

I hated my job. I hated my life. I hated the fact that my boyfriend was still in another country and we couldn't even have a decent fight in person. I hated the fact that I was still waking up with a tight throat and a sore chest. I gave up on Wednesday, left work and went to the doctor.

They couldn't find anything wrong with me.

It was a really bad cold. It was exhaustion. It definitely wasn't a sinus infection, or walking pneumonia, or anything else that would have garnered me an orange plastic bottle of capsules that I could carry around to brand myself a victim. Since I only got sick enough to go to the doctor once a year, they took some blood and a chest x-ray "just in case," but they knew it was nothing. You could hear it in their voices.

It was psychosomatic.

It was depression.

Tom hunted me down and talked me out of the pit of despair. My boyfriend and I made up, and I felt whole again. I laughed again. The anthology was well underway, and I switched gears from newbie picture-book author to hard-nosed adult SF editor. Jason signed me up here at Apex and had assignments in hand when he did so. It was good to feel important again. To feel needed. That blood test came back, and it was fine…but I could have told them that. The chest x-ray came back equally virus-free, but they called me in anyway.

They called me in to show me the 3cm mass they had found on my lung.

LIBERTYCON 18
JULY 30-31

As I walked up to the hotel, the first person I saw was John Ringo. He was standing outside with a group of the Baen boys, smoking a cigar. He opened his arms, and I gave him a hug. I needed it much more than he did.

"How's it going?" he asked.

I smiled. Other than a couple of brief phone conversations with Derek and Eddie while I was stuck in traffic, I had cried most of the way there. "My life has gone to hell."

John rolled his eyes. "Tell me about it."

I held out my hand. "Bet me. Oh, just bet me. 'Cause I'll win."

We shook on it.

I went inside to register.

I wandered around until John had another panel, and I hid myself in the audience. David Drake and Julie Cochran were both speaking as well. I think it was about world building. I can't remember one word of it. John went outside to the lobby to sign books afterward and I didn't want to bug him, so I sat with my dear Chuck and Lillie, who were one table over.

"I didn't get to see you before you left work for the doctor's yesterday," Lillie said. "How did it go?"

Do not cry. *Do not cry.* Smile. Smile because it's ridiculous. The whole world is fucking ridiculous. "I have a tumor."

They weren't the first people I had told. I had called my mother from the parking garage at the hospital. My little sister had bought her very first house that day. Mom spent twenty minutes telling me all about it. She was so happy and excited… and then I made her cry. I hated myself for that. I had called Robin and Kristi at work and told them I didn't want to be alone. I had called my friend David and told him that I was going home to get a change of clothes that I would be staying with Kristi and leaving for the convention from her house the next day.

But Chuck and Lillie were the first people I told in person. The words came out as if I had already written them down in my head, as if I were talking about somebody else.

It's a tumor. I saw it on the CAT scan. There is a very small chance that it could be a cyst, but since it's nestled between my lower lung and my spine, it's not in a good place. The doc wants to take it out. He's a friend of the family, and I trust him completely. He thinks I should have it done right away, but my parents are in the process of moving from Virginia to Florida and I just can't pull my mom away from that. Plus, we finally made plans for my boyfriend to come in September for Dragon Con. He is going to come and I am going to go to Dragon Con, no matter what. It's just a really inconvenient time to have this. But the doc says that even if it's malignant, tumors like these grow like snails. So I'm going to wait and have it out at the end of September after everything is done and everyone has a little more free time.

The part I didn't say was: *I'm going to wait and have it out at the end of September, in case I die on the operating table and don't at least get to do the two things I really want to do this year.*

I felt a strong arm snake around my neck and clasp me around the shoulders. "You win," John whispered in my ear.

I floated through the rest of the weekend. Chuck and Lillie kept me company. Panels kept me distracted, as did my new best friends from Hypericon. Derek showed up and kept me occupied with shopping the dealers' hall and discussing plans for the Goth track at Dragon Con.

I took my life in my hands and rode with John and Miriam to the Baen dinner. Eddie sat beside me and kept me entertained with viciously dirty tales of his youthful exploits. We rode back to the hotel in a limousine with Fredrick Pohl and David Drake, and I finally had the chance to thank Dave for both contributing to our anthology and suggesting, when we had met three years ago, that I go introduce myself to Andre Norton since she only lived two miles from my house. A suggestion that started an amazing friendship I will never, ever, forget.

Fred from Hypericon was there too—he hung out with us in the lobby until the wee hours of the morning and kept me laughing. Eddie let me go to his room and check my email. Derek walked me back to my hotel.

I cried myself to sleep.

The next morning I woke up early enough to have breakfast at the hotel. I attended a panel about hosting conventions, and then sat, fascinated, through the one-on-one with Fred Pohl. I skipped lunch and trekked outside to one of the very last panels: an informal "Women in Science Fiction" that was held in folding chairs under a tent on the lawn behind the pool. By that time, almost everyone had gone home, so the attendees essentially consisted of me, Toni Weisskopf, Sara Hoyt, Rebecca Lickiss, Eric Flint and his wife, and Fred Pohl's wife, Ann.

I was surrounded by all these amazing people, and yet my brain was full of how it was getting hot and late and I should probably be heading home.

We assumed it was time for the panel to be over when other folks started wandering outside to join us. Miriam came and sat down beside me. "I guess I should be going home," I mumbled.

"No way!" she said. "You've got to stay for Hank. That's why we're all here."

I vaguely remembered the last slot on the program. "Shovels and Rakes and Instruments of Destruction: Weapons Demonstration by Weapons Master Hank Reinhardt."

Hank was a great guy. Miriam was all excited. So I stayed. We helped Hank and Toni carry swords and clubs and maces and cardboard tubes from the car to the table set up outside the pool.

It was fascinating. Hank explained the history behind each weapon and then, brave man that he is, passed them around so that we could all look at them more closely. Feel their weight. Touch the designs. See where they wore when used. Unbelievably, we all trusted Hank when he told us they were sharp, and there was no blood shed. Even more unbelievably, he set up the cardboard tubes one by one and let folks try their hands at a little sword slashing.

Miriam went first. She looked like something straight off the cover of one of their books–a tiny little thing in fashionable heels wielding a sword that was almost as big as she was. After Miriam, John had to be macho and take a turn. Doc Travis (Taylor) volunteered, and then Patrick, Toni's faithful assistant.

I should have raised my hand, but I didn't. These were the authors. These were the folks who deserved the spotlight. Not me.

One by one they exhausted the supply of tubes, and Hank resumed his talk. As he came to a close, Eric Flint called out, "Hey, there's one more there on the ground!" He was correct; one rogue tube had indeed rolled off the table and was hiding in the grass. Hank set it up on the table.

"All right, who wants it?"

I couldn't have asked for a better sign.

I raised my hand.

I walked up to the table, and Hank handed me the sword. It was warm from sitting in the sunshine and a little bit heavy, but not overly much. I stared at the tube and concentrated, thinking back to my year of kickboxing and all my yoga training. I had held a sword before, but never with the express purpose of actually cutting something. I grasped the hilt in both hands and swung. The blade got stuck halfway in.

There were cheers from behind me as Hank took the tube off the blade and set it back on the table. "Try again," he urged. I focused on the tube once more. And then I heard them:

"Go, Alethea!"

"Come on, girl!"

"Find the sweet spot!"

"You can do it!"

I looked over my shoulder. The seats were filled with almost every honored guest that had been invited to the convention. I was up there holding a sword and being cheered on by some of the most talented minds in science fiction. They were cheering for me. This was my life, this fabulously surreal thing that it was, and I was at the very beginning. There was no way in hell it was going to end anytime soon.

I took a swing, and the tube went flying across the lawn in pieces.

DRAGON CON 19
SEPTEMBER 2-5

I lasted a week.

I joked about it, told people I was going to play the tumor card to the hilt and see how much free stuff I could get out of it. I urged them to do the same, but only if they came back and told me the stories of what they got away with. I was going to make a bumper sticker that said: "My Tumor is smarter than your Honor Roll Student" and put it on my car. I was going to ask the hospital to put it in a jar so I could take it home with me.

I had a long talk with Tom Piccirilli. "I don't get you, *Mimou.* You're a mess when you're a hypochondriac, but when you have a tumor you're just fine."

It made perfect sense to me. When you're a hypochondriac, you *know* there is something wrong but you don't know what, so you can't do anything about it. When you have a tumor, you have a plan. And when you have a plan, there's really nothing else you have to worry about.

I smiled and laughed. I talked things through with my coworkers and Human Resources. I worked like a dog to get everything done before I left. People told me I was handling it very well. They told me I was brave. Friends would find any excuse to stop by my office. They all told me if I needed anything to just ask them. Did I need anything? It got to the point where I was just making up stuff for people to do. Yes, I would love a Coke from the cafeteria. As a matter of fact, if you're headed that way, you can pick up that spreadsheet I've just printed out. Why thank you, I guess I had forgotten to check my mailbox this morning.

Inside, I was going quietly insane.

My first assignment for Apex was to interview Brian Keene. In preparation, I read his latest book: *Terminal.* Of all the books of Brian's I could have chosen from *that* was the one I had on my shelf. I had to put it down several times to cry like my heart was breaking.

By that weekend, I was tired. I was tired of wondering about what-ifs and dwelling on forethoughts of doom. I was tired of people being nice. I was tired of being introspective. I was tired of, after a few minutes of said introspection, being asked if everything was okay.

I called Mom on Saturday. If I could get the doctor to agree, would she drop everything and come right now?

She did.

When I announced my intentions to the world the next day, everyone was thrilled that I was getting it taken care of right away. Everyone except me.

There are a lot of things they don't tell you about the hospital. They don't tell you that they're going to have to take blood continuously and that by the time you leave you will feel like a gigantic pincushion. They don't tell you that if the surgeries before yours have complications, you might lie in pre-op for five hours while they freak your mother out in the waiting room regaling her with worst-case scenarios. They don't tell you that the narcotics in the epidural will make you itch so badly you can't sleep and there is nothing they can do about it. They don't tell you to drink several gallons of water the day before you go into surgery because you won't be able to drink anything again until the doctor sees you almost 48 hours later. They don't tell you that when you come in for pre-surgery you will sit down in front of a computer that goes over what will happen in your surgery while giving you a quick lesson on the lung cancer that you don't have and all of its possible horrific side effects. And there *is* a pop quiz at the end to see if you were paying attention.

I was crying so hard by that time, I got one wrong.

All in all, though, I had quite a good time at the hospital. My doctor was brilliant. The nurses were as sweet as could be and treated my mother like a queen. The hospital itself was beautiful. Every one of the anesthesiologists was exceptionally good looking. Friends came to visit me every day, and I got flowers and candy and cards and goodie bags.

The best part: the tumor was a benign cyst. I had survived surgery, and I had the rest of that fabulously surreal life to look forward to.

Max called the room the morning of the day I left. I had made sure that Robin and Kristi emailed him to give him my information, tell him everything was okay, and update him on my progress. I figured Robin would have also told him to call, but I never thought he would actually find a way to do it. The second the phone rang, I looked over at it and said, "No *way*." I was smiling before I even picked it up.

A nurse came in about five minutes into our conversation to take my blood pressure. My mother waved her politely aside. "She's talking to her boyfriend in Sweden," she whispered. The nurse smiled, nodded knowingly, and never came back.

Max flew into Nashville the day before we drove down to Atlanta for Dragon Con.

They all told me I was nuts for going. But Dragon Con was my first convention, my favorite convention, and Max and I were both on the guest list as well as being on panels. I had friends to see and schmoozing to do. Of all the conventions this year, Dragon Con was the most important of all. There was just no question of not going. No question at all.

People ask me if this was the best Dragon Con I've ever been to. Honestly, I have to tell them, I have no idea. I'm pretty sure I had a great time and did some wonderful things. But each memory is seen through a purple haze of absolute pain.

I was stubborn and horrible and brilliant and charming. Max was a Golden God and my arm to hold. I remember some amazing moments. I remember how irate Peter S. Beagle was that he didn't get a chance to be in the anthology, and he wanted to make sure we invited him to the next one. I remember leaving a party just as Jewel Staite was arriving. I remember being smacked by Kevin J. Anderson for saying bad things about my own writing. I remember transforming into the smart-assed host of "An Hour With Sherrilyn Kenyon" and not being one single bit afraid of cracking jokes in front of an audience of two hundred people.

I remember it all, but I can't wait for next year when the Incredible Whirlwind of Beauty and Dynamite is back in top form.

Next year is going to be amazing.

Having Max there was bliss. It was fabulous. It was wonderful. But it wasn't surreal. It was absolutely, perfectly, and in all other ways completely…

…normal.

I loved every second.

This time we planned his exact return before he left so that things were not so nebulous. So I would not shrivel into nothingness after eight months of solitude.

I looked at the calendar the day before he left. "I can't believe that Thursday is the equinox," I said. "Summer's almost over."

Max shivered. "Don't remind me."

I'm sure he was thinking of the very, very long Swedish nights that lay ahead of him. I had some of those nights ahead too—maybe not so long, but just as dark.

But I would see him again in January, for my birthday. Three months. That wasn't a long time; it was a vacation. I had a lot to do, so the days would pass quickly. A hundred days. A hundred days until the love of my life came back home to me. A hundred days until I turned thirty, and I *would* turn thirty.

And only a hundred and nine days until Chattacon.

I'll see you there.

A Quartet of Alethea Experiences

by the Gamber Family

DAN

Once a year, the largest science fiction and fantasy convention in the Southeast takes over downtown Atlanta. With numbers hovering around 30,000 strong, fans of the fantastical descend on the Marriot, Hyatt, and Hilton hotels near Peachtree Center. To truly appreciate all the flavors of the convention, known simply as Dragon Con, I descended through the different layers of this colorful celebration of all things fantasy and science fiction.

I was innocently making my way to registration when I spotted the unthinkable. A double-take confirmed Darth Maul and Sailor Moon riding the escalator together. In the lobby, all sorts of beautifully horrific creatures were holding court and feigning affection for the cameras—including a tired, dejected Jack Skellington. A blue sprite of a fairy beckoned me closer.

I continued on my journey.

I passed shopkeepers and merchants of all sundries fantastic. The next surprise was nestled in between the rows of books and action figures. Was that Colonel Wilma Dearing? This time it was no costume, but really Erin Gray! I was transported in time back to acne and puberty-induced clumsiness, overtaken by the impulse to tell her, "You Rock!"

Finally, my relatively safe wanderings took me to the scariest depths of Con. I descended to the deepest, darkest level. There, I came face to face with the thing that made the hair on the back of my neck stand up, made my mind shudder a vacant 'noooo…'—the literary track, where authors and those who could read hung out.

I poked my head into a panel, timid and afraid, not sure if I'd be accepted or torn to bits as an outsider. Eventually, I slinked to the back of the room where the least scary person was standing, her attention on the verbal tennis match at the front. When I stole a glance at her name badge, I found myself stunned. The fates had smiled upon me. Had they even offered me safe passage through this dungeon?

I reached out my hand, unsure if my gesture would give offense. My impertinence made me falter. "Hi, I'm Dan," I stammered.

She smiled, and I sighed in relief.

"Alethea," she offered. "Alethea Kontis, buyer for Bookville Books."

And suddenly, I knew all would be okay.

BEN

The splashing of my hurried feet in puddles echoed down the empty street. Rain soaked my hair. I did my best to huddle beneath my overcoat, but the parcel I concealed took an uncomfortable amount of space. A quick glance behind showed nothing in the street, so I paused momentarily to catch my breath.

It had all begun with an idea. A sudden inspiration, an unbidden thought. Though imagination had been outlawed here on planet Ringam, mine had roamed free. A story had developed. It was so stunning, so real, that I simply had to write it down.

It was one thing for a person to imagine a story. But when I wrote the story for other people to see, I became marked as a criminal. Now I found myself running down a wet, empty street, trying to find the meeting place for others like me.

When my breath recovered, I continued. I looked for signs people had told me about, pointing the way. I found the first of them, wet and stuck to a post. As I looked down the street, I saw more. At the end was an arrow. It was subtle, but from my point of view, I saw it. I knew I was close.

There was a sudden bright light.

Police surrounded me. My hands were cuffed—my parcel taken from me.

Next thing I knew, I was placed in a conveyer and taken to Ringam's Spaceport A-3.14, the boarding platform designated for space prison. There was no jury, no judge, I was caught with my story—the evidence—in my hands. All that was left was my execution at the prison for the Criminally Imaginative.

I suddenly felt alienated. There were very few people here, most were extremely muscular and had many tattoos. I seemed to be the only human.

Then I saw a small slip of paper near my foot. I picked it up, looking around for who could have dropped it. No one seemed to be searching for it, so I read the message. *I know what you've done. I can help. Watch for diversion, then slip to terminal G5. Happily Ever After.*

I looked around at the signs directing people to their terminals.

Terminal E… F… G. But the sign stopped at G 4, so I crept closer, and saw a small sign that had been scribbled at the bottom, G5. It indicated a small path that navigated through a section under construction. I memorized the path, then went back to take a seat.

Suddenly, two other prisoners began to fight. An officer dashed over to break it up. I saw the opportunity, and without hesitation took it, running past the *Under Construction* signs. I wound my way through the halls and began to hear voices. I peeked around a corner and saw a large creature standing outside a door. He spotted me and beckoned me to him.

The large alien showed me to a docked transport called *Happily Ever After*. There were several people inside, both human and not. One person sat just a little off to the side wearing a uniform. I walked slowly over, noticing it was a woman, a human. She turned and smiled. She stuck out her hand, and I accepted the greeting.

"Alethea Kontis, flyer for Ringam crooks," she said with a wink.

I finally let out my breath.

ELLEN

I heaved a sigh as I stared toward the sky full of pink-rimmed clouds. The sun peeked out from its hiding place behind a blanket of hills and forests. I sat up from the flower on which I had slept, shaking my wings to loosen dusty orange pollen. Stretching my arms, I rose, examining the forest around me.

A night's rest hadn't given me any more energy, and my hope was still gone. I perked my ears and tried to listen for the gentle music of a running river, hoping it would guide me. All I heard was the song of birds and crickets who insisted on performing. I sighed again and waved my wings, getting ready to fly toward the trees.

As I leapt into the air, I got a better view of the forest. I hovered toward the trunk of an oak, grasping the bark and holding on as my wings continued to flutter. Craning my neck and squinting my eyes, I saw an iridescent shimmer below, near a clump of friendly-looking mushrooms. I realized what I must be seeing and let go of the bark, eagerly whirling myself toward another fairy.

"Hello!" I called. The fairy looked from behind a mushroom. She had long hair and sparkling emerald-colored wings.

"Hi."

I landed delicately in front of her and lowered my wings. "I haven't seen a friendly face in a long time," I said. "Are you headed somewhere?"

"Yes," she replied.

"Would you mind if I traveled with you for a while?"

"Of course you can." Her friendly smile glowed in the early morning light. She walked toward the edge of a mossy drop-off and readied her wings. "Do you want to fly?"

"Sure," I answered. She flew upward and turned before she neared a tree, and I followed. "Are you going to the gathering?"

She smiled again. "Yes."

"Me too, but I lost my way. I can't find the river."

"Then it's a good thing you found me," she said. "Listen."

She turned around a group of trees, so I took her lead. Then I stopped, hovering. I was startled to find she had led me straight to the river. "How did you know how to find it?"

"Why, I'm Alethea Kontis," the fairy said. "Finder of singing brooks."

I listened, and the clear water really did seem to sing as it flowed past rocks and fallen trees. And more than that, I heard the laughter of the gathering fairies downstream.

"Thank you," I said, and I raced her to the celebration.

JACKIE

I should have felt at ease among the walking dead. Amid muslin-pale faces and colorless eyes. The gothic horde, wedged shoulder-to-gaunt-shoulder and muttering fashionable discontent from kohl-lined lips, should have made me feel at home. But I felt as alien as ever.

I alone was real.

Curiosity had at first drawn me to the Gathering. There had been talk among my people of great, unfolding crowds of like minds—among them, story benders. I had heard of many story benders, had partaken in reading their written gold from the shelves of my city's Treasure Library. It was a venerated class, a specialized field reserved for the worthy, the select and blessed few. The Gathering was to be my chance to meet story benders for myself, to kneel and touch my forehead to their hallowed, hooded cloak. To hope a passing of their shadow might somehow bestow a faint shudder of blessing upon my own.

And, deep in the labyrinthine innards of the Gathering Temple, passing through the stone archway to the Forum of Partaking of Knowledge, I did feel the thrill my silent heart had been hoping to experience. I sat at the feet of story benders, absorbing their wisdom like a desert drinks rain. And my desire—my secret, forbidden yearning—to be one of them flourished.

But in the hallways, in the hazy corridors filled with gauzy figures, I grew disgruntled. All around were painted faces and hollowed-out smiles. Pierced mouths and drawn scars. To the inexpert eye, their gloomy visages appeared genuine. But to me, a true citizen of the city of haunted dreams, these wingless impostors were an affront. Black-dyed hair and spiked collars were only costumes; when I looked into their eyes for kindred, no reflection came back to me. They failed to recognize the true pain of an unmined soul.

Then I sensed someone. Across a room, beyond a sea of black leather and Mohawk haircuts, I spotted her. She was quiet. Smiling.

But within her eyes teemed understanding. I made my way toward her.

Then, without warning, her hand shot out for the nearest cloaked figure. She bent him backward, exposing his creamy, wanna-be throat, and sank impossible fangs into his flesh. Then she dropped him, dazed and dreamily-smiling, to the floor.

She stepped over his body as he sighed and curled up to sleep. "Hi," she said, extending her hand. "I'm Alethea Kontis, biter of wingless kooks."

"Brethren," I said. And heartily gripped her hand.

Werewolves of London

October 31, 2005

There are times in your life when you really just want to be somewhere else. Today was one of those days. Not that it was a bad day here—I got lots of compliments on my costume at work (I don't think I've had so many doors opened or chairs pulled out for me in my life. But what are you gonna do when you look like some Satanic fetish dream?) and nothing *bad* happened…but I spent most of the day staring at my little altar at work.

Yes, altar. Some people call it their hard drive. Paperweights and post its and other various nonsense find their way underneath your monitor to collect dust, but I call it what it is. On my little altar I have a miniature statue of Buddha surrounded by a chunk of rose quartz, a dried yellow rose, a feather, and various scattered bits of confetti that my friend Gretchen sprinkles on our desks like the Office Holiday Fairy. I have a paperweight of a fish that a colleague gave me for

Christmas after I had only been working at Bookville a month—I don't think he knew of my love for the ocean, but he was right on the money.

I also have what I call the "Publishing Baby"—there's a publisher who sends a King Cake to Bookville every Mardi Gras, and this year, I got the baby. Well, since the publisher furnishes the cake I'm off the hook…but other people have their superstitions about what the King Cake Baby signifies. Some say you'll have good luck. Some say you'll actually have a baby. And the latter is pretty much impossible, unless you're like some authors and consider your books your children. In which case, I wish heaps of luck on my children, and I make sure to kiss the Publishing Baby as often as I rub Buddha's tummy and wish for an ounce of his eternal, jovial patience.

The other thing I have on my altar is a miniature snow globe I bought it on our very last day in London, the day before my birthday. It's of Buckingham Palace. Shake it up and the glitter shimmers down onto the palace where the flag is flying: the Queen Mum is in residence.

Only…as the glitter falls the Palace becomes smaller and more softly lit. The sky behind it is black, and there is a mist in the air and no stars—they are hidden behind the clouds. Through the trees you can see that Big Ben is about to strike 9:00. And Max puts his arm around me as we walk along the park. It's warm for a London night in January, warm from the walk, and probably too warm to be huddled up this close to one another, but I don't want him to let me go. Max is there right now, in London, taking a much-needed break from writing and seeing one of the finest performers I've never seen—Roddy Frame. As cute as I am, in my black fishnet stockings and little red horns, I wish nothing more than to be there with him.

I should probably do as Robin says and take myself out tonight—celebrate finishing my novel rewrite…but I can't. I'll go home and wash off the brazen sexiness, change into jeans and a t-shirt and wait until Max gets back to the hotel so he can tell me all about his day. So he can tell me stories and I can pretend to live them with him.

You dress up for Halloween so that when the spirits come looking for you they won't be able to find you. Well, this morning they certainly wouldn't have recognized me. And this evening…this evening I may look like myself, but I'm not really here. I'm in a hotel room in London. My ears are still ringing and my nerves are still humming from the fabulous concert. I'm singing "The Birth of the True" under my breath and holding Max's hand as I fall asleep. The flag is flying at the Palace, and the Queen Mum says hello.

Sweet dreams…

Happy Birthday to Me
(redux)

Spring 2005

When you're twelve, you want your life to be perfect. It usually turns out a mess.

Mom let me have my first slumber party when I was twelve. I had it all planned out. I would invite eight of my closest girlfriends. We'd start out playing Pictionary to break the ice. We'd have caramel brownies—not cake, cake was for babies—and after dessert we'd have a lip synch contest. I didn't have a ton of music but that was okay; we'd just call the radio station and request the songs we wanted them to play. Then, when it got dark, we'd settle into our blankets and sleeping bags and watch *The Secret of my Success* and *Project X* and munch on leftover brownies and chips and popcorn and giggle until we passed out.

I was going to have a slumber party that blew all other slumber parties away. It was a slumber party that everyone would be talking about for years to come.

Yup, you guessed it. Things turned to crap well before they had begun.

It started with the guest list. The first horrible thing was that my mother insisted that I include my little sister Sami in all the festivities. Couldn't she have found one of her equally annoying friends to spend the night with? Or pitched a tent out in the backyard? It wasn't too late to sell her to witches, was it?

Then, there was apparently no Saturday that everyone would be available. Casey was out of town the first weekend, and the next weekend Della had band practice and Bethany had family in from out of town. Finally—*finally*—I found a day where pretty much everybody was available (well, everybody but Leslie). It was the Saturday that all us smart kids had to take the SAT.

So not only was this fête occurring almost a month after my actual birthday, but we were all completely exhausted even before the party began. We were, however, definitely ready to celebrate.

The brownies were almost a disaster, since in my frazzled state I had put the candles in when the caramel was still hot. (My long-suffering mother tossed the pan in the refrigerator, and then painstakingly dug out all twelve of the offending wax-filled holes.)

The radio DJs were complete and utter assholes. After six phone calls and several hours of listening to Top 40 junk we hadn't asked for, Sami and I dug out the few cassette tapes we had, by which time only Della and I were interested in competing. I won, of course…but probably more because it was my birthday party and less because I incorporated an entire gymnastics routine into the lip-synched song. (Della now plays keyboards for the rock band *Caligari* out of D.C.)

I wanted it to be perfect, and everything went wrong.

Fast forward from 1988 to 2006. My thirtieth birthday.

Things are different when you're thirty. By the time you're thirty, you realize that not only is your life a mess, it always has been and it always will be, and there's nothing you can do to change it. But it's life, and it's the only one you're gonna get, so you shrug and you run with it and you try to have a helluva time along the way.

This time I didn't just have a slumber party, I had a *convention*. A complete geekfest. I even called it "Leecon." And I didn't plan a damn thing.

I picked the weekend after my birthday because it was Martin Luther King Jr. weekend, so some folks had a three-day stretch. I didn't just invite eight of my closest friends; I invited the entire Codex Writer's Group.

Scattered as we are across the globe, it was safe to say that not everyone was going to make it. I was a little worried about the size of my tiny house and considerable lack of comfortable sleeping arrangements…but I shrugged and left it up to fate. (Which is to say that I warned everyone from the get-go that there was every possibility they could be drawing straws for the bathtub.) When the dust settled I had at least six confirmed guests, two of them flying in from out of town. Just for me. Wasn't I special?

And since I hadn't really planned anything, nothing could go wrong. When you have no expectations, everything as it happens is just a pleasant surprise, right?

Enter Murphy.

Everybody, meet Murphy. He's my guardian angel, or pet demon—depending what day it was. And had I actually *looked* at the calendar, it might have given me a better idea of what I was getting myself into.

How many people do *you* know that willingly start a convention on Friday the Thirteenth?

Murphy thought it was hilarious.

I got home from work just as Mary Robinette Kowal (of *Shimmer Magazine* fame) was pulling into the driveway. She had driven up from her parents' house in Chattanooga, and graciously offered to make dinner—an offer I readily accepted because I planned to pop up to Nashville to buy a car that night.

Everything was all set. My friend and fellow Bookville-ite Kitti and I just had to drive the trade-in car up to Carmax and drive the new car home. Then we'd go pick up Jenny when her plane arrived at eight. When we got home, Max (the sexy, wonderful and prolific) and Mary would have dinner ready, and we could begin geeking out immediately.

[Wait…that was me making plans just then, wasn't it?]

[*Oh yes,* said Murphy with an evil laugh.]

Max and Mary called us while we were on the road—Jenny's plane was delayed until midnight. Which actually turned out to be a really good thing, since it took me and Kitti *four hours* to buy the car. "Easy," my Aunt Sally. To their credit, it wasn't the folks at Carmax. It was every other damn little thing. (Suffice it to say I am no longer a State Farm customer, and I still want to bash in my Ex's kneecaps. I'd owe Kitti my firstborn child if she didn't have one of her own already.) We raced home, had four bites of lukewarm dinner, and got to the airport just in time to catch Jenny getting her bags at the carousel.

The kids stayed up until who knows when but I went to bed almost directly after we got home, since I had to get up at 0-dark-early to pick up Quinn Reid (Codex founder and Writers of the Future winner) at the airport at six o'clock the next morning. I was at the same time amazingly excited and amazingly exhausted.

Isn't that how conventions are supposed to be? Quinn and I drove around aimlessly and talked for a while until we decided it was a decent enough hour to rouse the house. (Decent enough for us, anyway.)

Another great thing about being thirty is that the talents of your amazing friends include a healthy dose of self-sufficiency. Mary made pancakes for breakfast with her laptop on the kitchen counter for recipe reference (wireless internet in the house brought to me by my wonderful parents—Best Birthday Present Ever.)

Tom Pendergrass (another Writers of the Future winner) showed up early in the day…but not too early to start indulging in his homemade spice liquor. Impromptu *Dune* party? Moonshine before noon? Why not. It was a convention, after all.

Max planned a literary trivia game with no prizes, not that any were needed. We're all a bunch of natural competitors. There was cooking and eating. There were naughty puppet jokes and a knife-fighting seminar. There was slush spouted and markets dissected. There were stories read and synopses critiqued. There were Writers of the Future t-shirts on display. There were new episodes of *Doctor Who* eagerly devoured and discussed.

There was even work done. Mary rewrote a story. Quinn somehow magically managed to participate in everything, while simultaneously finishing up her entries for *Talk the Talk*—a project for Writer's Digest—completely showing off her amazing superpowers. (At the end of the weekend, even she wasn't quite sure how she had managed to pull it off.)

The pièce de résistance was the FedEx package that arrived at the door Monday morning—the package containing the cover of my very first book: *AlphaOops: The Day Z Went First.* The Codex Writers had only been in existence about two months when I received the excited call from my now-editor at Candlewick Press. The two people sitting next to me on the couch—Quinn and Max—had been there since the beginning. They had virtually lived alongside me and the roller coaster that was my life since that Cinderella phone call, so it was fitting that they be there for the final unveiling. It was the icing on the cake…or, rather, the candles in the caramel brownies.

Cake is for babies.

I met some great people in person that had been my friends online for what seemed like forever, and I had a fabulous time. The end of the weekend brought echoes of reciprocated enjoyment and talk of what the next Leecon might bring.

The *next* Leecon.

Like any Greek woman who's ever made a meal before, I knew therein lay the best compliment. "Seconds" is the finest form of flattery.

When the cars were gone and the planes had flown and the house was quiet again, I wondered what exactly had made Leecon such a success. It had had its fair share of downs…but they were far out weighted by the ups. (And, quite truthfully, the downs made one hell of good story.) There were dozens of posts in threads that made other Codexians green with jealousy. Albums of pictures with hilarious captions chock full of inside jokes popped up all over the internet. All because of me. Wasn't I special?

Just for laughs I pulled out my old trunk and dusted off the green satin-covered photo album, curious about the documented remains of that ill-fated birthday party all those years ago. There we were in living color—silly little girls balancing balloons on our heads and jamming to imaginary music and sprawled out all over the living room couches and carpet, stuffed full of brownies and popcorn and giggles.

I sat there on the floor next to the trunk for about an hour, an introspective older woman being smiled at by immortally happy girls. Murphy looked over my shoulder and asked me why I thought it had gone so horribly wrong, why that party had tormented me for so long. Because if I had stopped long enough to stop dwelling on perfection, I would have seen that everyone really did have a good time, mistakes and mess-ups and all. Everyone, including me.

The next Leecon.

Why not. True, you only turn thirty once. But hey, you also only turn thirty-one once too…

Once Upon a Horror

Apex Digest
Summer 2006

"Be careful what you wish for. You just might get it."
–Common Sense

The French call it *L'esprit d'escalier*: the Spirit on the Stairs. It's when you walk away from a conversation and much later, when you're halfway up the stairs at home, the exact perfect thing you should have said pops into your head.

Sometimes—rare times—that spirit is kind enough to whisper in your ear when the moment arises, and you have to resist the urge to sit up, eyes wide, and blurt, "My god, that's brilliant! Did *I* just say that?"

About a month ago, Tim and Brooke from Dorchester Publishing were in my office, meeting about new books.

Now there are things you have to understand about my cubicle office at Bookville: one entire wall is covered with pictures and posters and news blurbs about anything and everything having to do with *Lord of the Rings* (including my Orlando Bloom READ poster). I've got an old Tower Records Coop calendar on the side of my bookcase from 2001 that is just too cool to take down. One entire shelf is dedicated to comics—featuring Alex Ross, Neil Gaiman, Terry Moore, Clive Barker, and Tim Burton. In the corner I have one of those four-foot tall rainbow light fish bubblers. And spinning directly above my head is a mobile from *X-Men 2*. It's the easiest way to find me in the rat maze. X marks the spot.

Tim paused a moment in the entranceway. "I love you already," he said reverently.

I gave him a patented Alethea smile. "Thanks. I've always been a genre girl. Romance, Fantasy, Mystery, Horror..."

"Why do you think that is?" asked Brooke. "Do you think that it's because it's geared toward a younger market? That perhaps you're drawn to the younger writers who are breaking out in these genres...?"

Tim cut Brooke off. "Objection. Leading the witness."

"Actually," I said, "I think it has to do with fairy tales." *Huh? Was this coming out of my mouth? That's quite interesting. Let's see what's next, shall we?* "Fairy tales were my first love. My dad used to read them to me every night as a kid. If you think about it, almost all genres stem from fairy tales. The magic is Fantasy, there's always a little bit of Mystery, the dark and evil give birth to Horror. And, of course, Romance is the happy ending."

Amazing. Up until that very second, I had no idea I felt that way. Once the words were out of my mouth, it made so much sense that I completely believed it. Just like almost every psychological scar, my reading habits were all my parents' fault.

Almost every psychological scar.

A couple of weeks ago, I was Maid of Honor in The Wedding from Hell.

Weddings are the ultimate fairy tale. True love, magic, a constant string of "what's going to happen next?"…and horror. Always the horror.

It wasn't Priscilla's fault, by any stretch of the imagination. In fact, the whole Dante-dipped affair couldn't be pinned on exactly one event or one person. It takes a boatload of savants and a bad roll of every dice to make something this flamingly spectacular. Poor Cill. She only wanted something beautiful and memorable that would make everybody happy.

Yeah, we paved quite a few miles with those good intentions.

Once Upon a Time, there lived a beautiful princess named Priscilla, whose family was crazy. (For reasons as-yet-undivulged, Aunt T wore black earmuffs around the house. I completely love them all… but it still didn't stop them from being this side of certifiable.) Priscilla had the fortune, or misfortune, of falling in love with the handsome Prince Bernardo, whose family wasn't crazy.

They were evil.

So in essence, everyone but the happy couple had perfected the act of the reluctant teenager—professional bitchers and moaners who are convinced that the world owes them something.

But the princess had prepared for this. In order to save her sanity, Priscilla had conscripted as her Maid of Honor her Fairy Godsister Alethea. Not yet old enough to have come into her full Godmother powers, Alethea could only shine down optimism and a sunny disposition…and pretty much just weave the handbasket while the rest of the world went to hell.

Alethea flew in Tuesday night.

The wedding was Friday morning.

She was supposed to fly out Saturday afternoon.

She never made it that far.

It all started with the evil sisters-in-law who—because I must give credit where credit is due—actually *were* reluctant teenagers. Wednesday was the day of last-minute dress fittings and the rehearsal. Only, at the dress fittings, the evil sisters-in-law were nowhere to be found.

The bridesmaids' dresses were fabulous. Fairy Godsister Alethea was instantly transformed into a sultry 1940's lounge singer, and the hem was altered up to show the sparklies on her glass (okay, so it was clear plastic) slippers.

The dresses were hemmed and pinned…and still no in-laws. They were forced to move on. There was still much to do. Every other second was filled with errands and chores—things that Princess Priscilla should never have had to do and tried in vain to delegate, but to no avail.

Sooner than later, the rehearsal was at hand. The Fairy Godsister descended from the princess's third-floor walk-up in her pretty black dress and shiny shoes…to find herself wading into a sea of sweatshirts and jeans. (The infamous Aunt T sported a smiling Mickey Mouse.) The overdressed Fairy Godsister never missed a beat. She ignored the whispers of "We were supposed to dress up for this?" and carried herself with embarrassed grace and aplomb.

The youngest evil sister-in-law finally met Princess Priscilla at the door to the church. "Are you mad?" she asked meekly.

"Of course I'm mad," spat the princess. "*You didn't show up.*"

Exasperated sigh. "Well, I'm here *now*."

The Nobel Peace Prize was later awarded to Fairy Godsister Alethea for restraining both herself and her ward, and not kicking the little punk's ass under the forgiving eyes of Our Lady of Perpetual Help. Smiling and beaming optimism and good will, Alethea simply steered

Princess Priscilla toward the rectory.

Legend has it that the Church of Our Lady of Perpetual Help was lifted by the hand of God from an affluent old town in Europe and set in the heart of Brooklyn. The patient and benevolent Father McGillicutty (who will be played this evening by Carol O'Conner), quickly led everyone through the motions. Everyone, that is, except the Best Man and the *other* evil sister-in-law, who were notably absent.

After the run-down, Father McGillicutty then asked everyone to lift their voices in song and led us in a rounding chorus of "Happy Birthday to You."

Did I forget to mention that it was Princess Priscilla's birthday? If I did, it's probably because *everyone else* that day forgot to mention it too. Aside from Fairy Godsister Alethea's present that morning and the Father's song that evening, not a gift or a kind word had been bestowed upon the fair Princess…not even by her Prince.

Poor chicken.

And the horrors had only begun.

Somehow, they made it through the next day. More errands were run, rivers of tears were shed, and cross words clashed in the air with the lethal grace of Inigo Montoya…but they had planned for that. At the end of the day, Fairy Godsister Alethea waved her magic wand and Princess Priscilla's hair was curled and styled, complete with tiara…right before Alethea dragged her to Starbucks.

Whoever heard of a bachelorette party without caffeine?

In the history of the Church of Our Lady of Perpetual Help, only one other wedding was ever held at nine o'clock on a Friday morning. Princess Priscilla and Prince Bernardo's wedding held the distinguished honor of being the second.

The ladies were up at 5am styling hair and adjusting corsets and donning gowns. At 8:00 am, Fairy Godsister Alethea looked divine: curled hair in an angel's halo around her head and dress fitting perfectly. A few warm-up exercises and she would be ready at a moment's notice to wow the crowd with her infamous rendition of "He's a Tramp."

The photographer showed up at the house five minutes later to take photos.

Fifteen minutes after that and four trips up to the second and third floors (wearing a dress with a train) to 1.) fetch the makeup bag, 2.) adjust Queen Cathy's corset, 3.) get the princess's Chihuahua for the pictures and 4.) put the Chihuahua back, Alethea's hair was flat as a pancake, she had thrown her pantyhose in the trash, and she was dripping with sweat.

At 8:45, Fairy Godsister Alethea snapped.

Makeup bag in hand, Princess Priscilla looked pleadingly up at her Godsister and said, "I need a mirror."

Conjuring a magic mirror she could have done, but in the unfamiliar house Alethea had no idea where to find such a mundane thing. Satin train in hand, the Fairy Godsister spun around to the fifteen people standing around in the living room (watching the photographer and no doubt only moments away from popping popcorn to pass the time) and yelled, "*Will someone who hasn't run a mile already today please find a mirror?!?*"

Hey, at least she said please.

The limo was on the street, waiting to take the bride and her lovely party a full block and a half away to the church. It had rained that morning (which is luck as the Irish would have it), but was clearing up to be an unseasonably warm day for March in New York. The bridesmaids followed each other in a line through the mud and the gale-force winds to pile into the safety of the humongous white Escalade.

Across the crowded limo, Princess Priscilla's eyes met Godsister Alethea's in stark terror, and she uttered four words that iced the three-tiered Red Velvet Wedding Cake of Insanity that had been in the oven for almost three full days:

"We forgot the rings."

They were already late for the wedding. It was showtime. There was nothing either one of them could do, so they could not worry about it. And they made the mistake of assuming that one of the other twenty people who were in that limousine might walk the block and a half back to the house to get them at some point during the hour-and-a-half long Catholic ceremony. That assumption led to a talented improv by the Best Man mid-ceremony, as he proudly brandished the empty tray and went walking through the audience trick-or-treating for rings. He returned with Cousin Kim's slender wedding band and a nameless Uncle's chunky class ring.

The five of us on the stage-smiled at each other in an emotional tug-of-war between complete horror and massive hysteria. Fairy Godsister Alethea swallowed the church giggles that threatened to burst out and precede a seriously unfairylike collapse at the altar. Father McGillicutty blinked over the tray and whispered, "This is one secret we're all going to keep."

What can I say…*I'm* not Catholic.

The newly-wedded Prince and Princess left the church smiling into a cacophony of bells and the wedding party piled in the white chariot once again. They were chauffeured to a reception hall, where they spent so much time having pictures taken they barely got to take part in the revelry. Not that they had much energy left—by three o'clock in the afternoon, the pre-dawn wakeup time was taking its toll.

Hair tangled by sweat and wind, dress sullied by buffet stains and mud, the sparklies on her shoes ruined beyond repair from having been stepped on in the limousine, Fairy Godsister Alethea called the airport and spent an extravagant fee to change her ticket to the first plane out of New York.

Head Godmother Mary Grey later commended Alethea for her initiative, and commented that at least the exorbitant fee was less than therapy.

She was right.

Prince Michael (Priscilla's brother and part-time New York City cab driver), braved the side streets of New York at a heart-stopping pace through rush-hour traffic, dropping nerve-wracked Fairy Godsister Alethea gently at the curbside check-in half an hour late...when finally the series of wrongs that had clicked down like dominoes the past few days finally made a right.

The plane had been delayed an hour.

She was blessedly on time.

The Fairy Godsister kissed the dark prince farewell, tipped the curbside fellow outrageously much for her oversized bag, and—silk-wrapped roses still in hand—made her way to the gate.

I think I shook the entire flight home. My palms were marked with deep crescents from where I had pressed my fingernails into them during the harrowing ninety-minute ride to LaGuardia, but it was nothing to the scars on my soul. Of the three best friends I had traveled with down the aisle in my life—of the three best friends I had comforted and patted through nerves and tears and hysteria—Priscilla had gone through horrors I couldn't have ever imagined. So many more things went wrong that I didn't squeeze into my little story...things I witnessed, and things that happened after I left that I only heard about later...but if I told you all of them, you wouldn't believe me.

See, that's the thing about telling stories. Truth really is stranger than fiction. Bad things happen to good people and worse things happen on top of them. You know I'm right, because at some point it's happened to you. But if you write it all in a story, you cross the boundaries of the reader's believability factor. Sure, it *could* have happened, the reader tells himself, but you expect me to swallow all this? Come on.

So stories are boiled down to the events that stand out most, just enough events to let the author drive the point home to the reader. It makes you wonder, doesn't it? All those fairy tales we heard growing up, all the horrible things that tortured our heroes right before the "happily ever after" they so richly deserved…it makes you wonder how incredibly more horrific they would have been if we had heard it all.

None of us would ever have gotten to sleep at night.

My true love met me on the stairs to welcome me home that night. I had called Max multiple times during my stay to provide for him my running commentary from Hell—I needed to talk to someone, and I didn't want to make Priscilla feel any worse…her family excelled at that task well enough.

Every day, Max reminded me that Priscilla was the reason I was there and that she was the only person I needed to worry about. He would also tell me that everything was going to be okay. It never was, of course, but he told those pretty little lies so well it was hard not to believe him.

But there, there on the steps, there in the warm embrace of my Knight in Shining Armor, everything *was* okay. I was safe. And the imp of the staircase whispered in my mind as I stood in his demesne: *Never. Remember, you swore. You would never put yourself or anyone else through the hell that you know people have been through. Casey, Margo, Priscilla, even your parents…never. Never. Remember, you swore.*

Wise as he may be, humans rarely listen to the Spirit on the Stairs.

Twelve days later, my Knight in Shining Armor got down on one knee and asked for my hand in marriage.

I said yes.

I have no excuse. I'm a genre chick. I want the fairy tale.

I've got my sword polished.
Bring it on.

Cooler Than Cherry Limeade

May 5, 2006

I was invited to be a guest speaker at Blackman Middle School's Career Day today.

Wait.

Like most times, I'm starting the story in the wrong place.

Let me try this again.

Three weeks ago, I got this email out of the blue from a guy named David Summar. Turns out the world just got a little smaller: David's a fan of Max's. While doing some research online, he discovered Max's relationship to me. And thanks to the Amazon bios, he also noticed that I live in the same town where he teaches English at one of the local middle schools. And Career Day was right around the corner…badda bing, badda boom. Mr. Summar had booked his guest speaker.

I was tickled pink.

I was completely honored.

I was scared as hell.

My grade school years were huge. *Huge*. I don't know how people can just forget them so easily. School was a *very* important part of my life. It was my job and my friends and my whole world. My parents told me that I would make my "real friends" in college, and that I would lose touch with all the people I called my best friends in the seventh grade. Because of that, I did my darndest to keep in touch with those people. I still am. We're still very close friends. Two of them married each other many years later and are expecting their first kid next month.

Call it twenty years of teen rebellion.

I never thought I could be a teacher, despite people always telling me I would have been great at it. The one day I substitute taught I had a really good time. And I might have kept on doing it had I not been traumatized by a certain snotty vice principal of a local high school, who turned me away because she thought I looked too young. So as not to be accused of age discrimination, she told me I did not meet the dress code, and that what I was wearing at the time (oversized sweater, black leggings and boots because it was winter) was not appropriate for a sub in Band Class. I could go home and change, or they could replace me. I told her what she wanted to hear, and left.

The thought of going back…

But this time, I was invited.

I had half a mind to don the famous four-inch heels and red devil horns. I resisted temptation.

The first thing that sprang to mind was: you know, I wish I had had a nutcase like me visit me when I was in middle school. I would have loved for someone crazy and different who thought outside the box to tell me that it was *okay* to be crazy and different. From the ages of ten to thirteen I tried so hard to be like everybody else. I shopped at the same stores, wore the same clothes, ate the same food for lunch.

Thing about different kids is, they will always be different. There's something deep down, at the core…some strong, unique soul that will come out and imprint itself on the world. No matter what you wear, you always stand out in a crowd.

That was me. I went through hell for that.

The next thing I thought was: what do I want to tell these kids? What special Universal Life Truths do I want them to take away when they leave? I made a list. Get a job when you're sixteen. Move out of the house by the time you're twenty. Go to college, because intelligence is sexy. Be nice, because you never know who you'll meet next and the world is a small place. If you ever have the chance to leave the U.S. and visit a foreign country, do it. Learn another language. Fall in love and get your heart broken, but keep your self-confidence. You are the only one who can make you happy. Figuring out what makes you happy is the toughest thing you'll ever do. Once you do it, go after that thing like there's no tomorrow, because life is incredibly, incredibly short and you don't have much time to do it all.

But David Summar wasn't asking me to come into his classroom and be the Dalai Lama. He just wanted me to talk about my job.

Right.

So which job do I start with? The Bookville Buyer? ('Cause you have to keep your day job.) The magazine editor, essayist, and interviewer? The SF anthology editor? The picture book writer? The small publisher?

Eep!

Career Day ran from 8:15 until almost 11:00. There were six homeroom classes; one Career Day speaker to each classroom. Every twenty-five minutes, the classes would switch rooms. I had to give the same speech six times to six different groups of twenty different students.

Gulp.

And then there are the things you don't realize. On some level, I think Career Day was a bit of a pissing contest among the teachers—who can have the coolest speaker?

There was chaos in the hallway around 8:00 when the students were trickling into class, and I peeked out the door of Room 809 to see a big cherry limeade waving and shaking hands with the students. No joke. Some representative from Sonic in the room across the hall from me had brought the friggin' Sonic Cherry Limeade mascot with him to school.

That was it. I was doomed. I mean, come on...I'm just some author these kids have never heard of. How on earth was I supposed to compete with a six-foot tall plush, pink beverage? Fugeddaboutit.

Well, if I was doomed from the start I suppose it didn't matter what I screwed up, right?

The first twenty-minute class seemed to last forever. Of course, it started with a moment of silence (which apparently they do in schools now), the Pledge of Allegiance (which I haven't done for thirteen years), and what seemed like an hour's worth of morning announcements. I had forgotten about morning announcements. There was a talent show and a food drive and baseball tryouts and this club doing this and that club doing that and blah blah blah...and then it was over, and all eyes were on me.

I smiled and sipped my water and tried to not throw up.

Mr. Summar (it was hard to call him "David" when I was in school) introduced me to the class and prompted me to start. So I did. Sort of. It was sketchy. I wasn't quite sure where to start and I went off on lots of tangents. I thought maybe questions might give me a direction to go in, but asking for them was like pulling teeth. The kids seemed interested in what I was saying, though, so I just kept talking to fill the time. And talking. And talking. That first twenty minutes lasted about a hundred years.

But it was all the practice I needed.

By 11:00, twenty minutes wasn't enough. I rushed to say my last few words as the buzzer rang. I picked out a few stories to focus on. They liked hearing about horror, so I told them about *Apex Magazine* and the YA novel I was working on. They liked comics. They liked hearing about how much money you made, and how you made it. They liked hearing the story of the woman I interviewed at Walmart who had met Hitler. They liked hearing the origin of *AlphaOops*. The actress in me got better and better every time I told the stories, more animated and more fun, with more voices and expressions.

I handed out the few cards I had with me, and wrote down my website on post-it notes. I talked to a girl whose father was also an author. I answered more questions, doled out hugs, and let them play with my hair. I even signed an autograph, for Jacob, reminding him how much cooler I was then the cherry limeade.

When Mr. Summar returned to his room, I almost wished I could give the talk again—his class had gotten the rough draft, and now the performance was something solid. But my throat was dry and hoarse from the yammering and I was shaking from hunger and all the energy I had spent. I packed up my things and had that immediate crash back into the introvert—I couldn't believe I had talked about *myself* for three hours straight. I felt like I had a shirt on that said "me me me me me me me me me" all over it.

The Sonic guy knew it. It only dawned on me at 11:00. In those three hours, I had been selling myself. But I was done. It was time to go. And I think I did okay.

I followed the firefighter and the cop with the riot screen back down the hallway to the office, where I signed out. The man running for office and his entourage held the door open for me as I walked out to the parking lot, smiling.

I had just gone back to middle school.

When I worked in the bookstore, right after college, I looked up once and realized that the woman I was helping had been the principal of my middle school. I asked how she was and what she was doing—she had left the school and was pursuing some other interest which escapes me now.

"You know," I told her. "I really, really hated middle school. I mean, I met some of my best friends there, but that didn't stop me from going home and crying every single night. It was so hard...you couldn't pay me enough money to go back there."

She looked me dead in the eye and said with perfect honesty, "It was hard for all of us."

Thing is, she's right. Some people hate high school and love college. Some weirdos like me hate college and love high school. Some hate school altogether and leave to go do the jobs they love. Some go to school to find the jobs they love. Some decide they don't want to leave school at all. Ever. But all of us, *all* of us, lived through the ages of ten to thirteen. We survived it. But none of us liked it. Not the cool kids or the not-so-cool. None of us.

Maybe that's why I want to write young adult fiction. Maybe it's because somewhere, deep down inside me, there's still a twelve-year-old misfit screaming for someone to understand her. A twelve-year-old who finally knows enough about the world now that she can do what she wants to do and say what she wants to say.

Maybe not.

But one thing's for sure, paid or not, I'll be back.

And I'll be cooler than cherry limeade.

A Match Made in Cyberspace

May 9, 2006

I realized it was my destiny to be a writer when I was eight years old.

I tell people that it was the poetry assignment we had to do for ALERT. Eight lines. Forty-three words. The world clicked. I was a goner.

Of course, that was 1984. It could have just as easily been Joan Wilder.

Regardless, the desire was imprinted on my mind enough that by 1985, at the ripe-old age of nine, I sat in a movie theatre watching George McFly getting what I wanted most in the whole wide world: a box from his publisher, full of the book he had written. The movie was *Back to the Future.* George's book was called *A Match Made in Space.*

Every wanna-be writer in the world watched that scene with unabashed longing. Ask any SF author…they might not recall the title of the book (I had to look it up), but they will remember that scene with perfect clarity.

I've been waiting on that box for twenty-one years. Last night, there were two of them on my doorstep.

I work at Bookville Book Company. I am a buyer for 14 publishers and a distributor. I get boxes of books every single day.

This was so different.

I made myself check the mail and bring in everything from the car before tossing the boxes over the threshold. I leaned over them with the box cutter, wondering why I was slightly out of breath. At which point it occurred to me that the high-pitched squealing noise that was aggravating the neighborhood dogs was coming from me.

I can't remember the exact order of events after that, but they definitely involved tossing packing material, hugging and stroking and flipping through the pages of *Elemental.* I ran my finger over the dedication to Jack Chalker and Robert Sheckley and Andre Norton, and I cried. And then I threw my head back and screamed again, that one special scream full of joy and hope and everything else all rolled into one. That special scream that's set off like an Emotional Overflow Warning.

I screamed that scream in the car the day I told Quinn about the man I'm going to marry. I screamed that scream not two weeks ago, when I sold the novelette "Sunday" to *Realms of Fantasy*. And just like I did on that day, I immediately called my mother, and got excited all over again.

Okay, so *Elemental* is not the first book I wrote. In fact, the only evidence of my written contributions are the author bios that introduce every story. But I put that book together. I sold it to the publisher. I communicated with every author and edited every essay. I got every contract signed. My name is on the title page, and on the copyright page. It's on the cover, right above Arthur C. Clarke. On Michael

Whelan's immortal artwork. If you take off the dust jacket, it's embossed on the blue in silver letters.

I skipped to the end and skimmed the afterword, looking for one tiny, but very important-sentence.

"*She said yes.*"

That *she* is me.

The book I held in my hands wouldn't have happened without a lot of caring and selfless people, without the internet, without an exceptional amount of luck and several celestial bodies aligning. But there, at the very beginning, it wouldn't have happened without me.

I've never been so proud of anything in my whole life.

Elemental is a beautiful book, with a heart and a soul and more stories than the ones on the pages inside it. It's going to look great on your bookshelf.

It's going to look great on mine—just as soon as I let go of it.

MR. UNIVERSE

June 29, 2006

In fond memory
Jim Baen
October 22, 1943 - June 28, 2006

In the fall of 2002, the Southern Festival of Books was invaded by a horde the likes of which literary pretentious Nashvillians had never seen: namely, David Drake, David Weber, and John Ringo.

Simon and Schuster, the distributing publisher of these SF stepchildren, contacted Bookville to invite the buyer to dinner on behalf of Baen Books. My dear friend Kristi, who was the buyer for Baen at the time, freaked out. And not in a good way.

See, Kristi's favorite authors are Jane Austen, Flannery O'Conner, and Pat Conroy. She majored in English, with a concentration in 19th Century British Literature. Not only had she been invited to dine with an editor and authors that she knew less than nothing about, she had been drafted to introduce the panel at the festival on which they all participated (along with fantasy writer David Coe).

But Kristi had two great things going for her: 1.) she was (and still is) an exemplary student, and 2.) she has a few friends at Bookville who are SF Geeks Extraodinare.

In the following weeks, Kristi became a bit of an SF Geek herself. She read at least one book written by each of the authors she was going to introduce, and she checked up on them online. Her hands only shook a little bit when she got up in front of a room full of misfits to introduce their heroes. The middle-aged women of the Tennessee Humanities watched, agape, at the readings. The teenage boys in the front row grinned like idiots. I'm still proud of Kristi to this day.

That night was the dinner, with each of us Bookville Geeks shuffled in between the Baen Boys and their wrangler/den mother, Toni Weisskopf. It was one for the history books.

I'm not quite sure the patrons of F. Scott's were prepared to be entertained over their filet mignon with snippets of discussions like: "Most Original Demise," "Tracking Mortality Rates on CD-ROM," and "Who in the Publishing Industry is an Idiot." Kristi sat on one end of the table, sharing pumpkin cheesecake with David Weber and discussing the intricacies of Cambodian adoption and Global Thermonuclear War. I sat on the other end, letting David Drake talk me into meeting Andre Norton.

And, to his credit, I think that evening was the most quiet and well-behaved I have ever seen John Ringo. Ever.

The other common topic of conversation was Jim Baen. The boys couldn't say enough good things about him. Jim had his own homegrown way of running the company…commissioning some books on a phone call or a handshake. It was my first glimpse into the real Baen Universe—this publishing company that wasn't broken into authors and editors and executives with anagrams for titles. This was a family, a family so close that I half expected Toni to reach over at any moment and cut up John's steak for him…or at least take away his knife. That Christmas, each of us received a lovely box of Godiva chocolates, courtesy of Toni and the Baen Boys.

Funny how some of the most significant events in my life involve a box of chocolate.

In 2003, Southern Festival came and went, but it wasn't the same. So Kristi and Robin and I talked John and Toni into coming up for dinner anyway. They were on their way to a convention that weekend, so Toni begged off early to tackle the drive ahead. The rest of us closed down the Starbucks before calling it quits…leaving John to go bar-hopping solo.

He showed up at the convention the next morning, wobbly, red-eyed, and smelling like a brewery. It didn't occur to him what impression he was giving until Toni whispered, "Were you out all night?"

"Yeah," he shrugged, forgetting that the boss lady had last seen him in the company of three bodacious buyer babes.

She sighed. "Is there anything we need to apologize to Bookville for?"

I saw John again a year after that; he was on a panel at the 2004 Dragon Con. I sat in the audience, hoping to catch up with him afterward. Honestly, I wasn't too sure if he would remember me. Surely, two dinners in two years does not a best friendship make.

How wrong I was.

John showed up, fashionably late for the panel. I caught his eye as he sat down and waved. His face lit up, and he came running back around the table to sweep me up in his embrace…and then proceeded to tell the entire room that they had to be nice to me.

I wasn't just a friend. I was family.

Later that weekend, the Dragon Con folks had placed John on a panel about writing synopses. After introducing himself, he announced, "Jim doesn't ever make me write synopses. I say, 'Hey Jim, want me to write this book?' and he says, 'Sure.' So I have no idea why I'm on this panel. I'm going to go sit over there." He made his was to the empty chair next to me in the audience, drank all my water, and held court from the corner of the room.

Yup. That's family.

My biological family only sees me at the occasional holiday or reunion, but publishing families…well, there's always a convention somewhere. We're never too far away from one another. We may be lonely, but we're never alone.

When I had a crisis of faith about my writing, Toni was there to tell me that not only did I have potential, I was going to be a great writer. Those of you who read my essay in Apex #4 know the important role the whole Baen gang played after my tumor scare. (Want a girl to forget about her mortality? Put a sharp sword in her hand and cheer her on.)

In the last few years, I've made some amazing friendships that I never would have dreamed I'd have. But they all seem to stem from that first dinner. Crème brûlée and Space Marines. One for the history books.

I regret that despite having gotten to know almost every writer in the Baen stable, I never met their patriarch. But I knew what he meant to them…and in that way, I knew Jim Baen. He was always there, between every word, in every pause. The strength of his presence permeated the air; looking back at them, it's as if he were just outside the frame in every picture. He was the magnet that drew them all in. He defended and protected them. He commanded their army.

He still does.

Somewhere on the internet is an old SFC Bulletin, with a picture in it from the 2002 Southern Festival of Books. (Those of you talented enough will be able to hunt down the PDF on Google.) It's me, Kristi and our friend Leigh, David Coe, David Drake, and John Ringo...all laughing like crazy. I've got it on my wall at home. Kristi only has three pictures up in her office. That's one of them.

Because it's customary to display pictures of your family.

Jim was smiling too, I know it.

Just outside the frame.

He still is.

John Ringo says...

Authors gathered in groups generally talk about money. Which is why you should always leaven any group of authors with normal people.

Alas, once upon a time my publisher decided that it would be a good idea to take three of their authors—David Drake, David Weber and me—to dinner with buyers from Bookville.

(On a side note: I had always imagined buyers to be dull, elderly males, the archetype of the English bookkeeper stuck in the bowels of some firm picking books more or less at random since they didn't read. I was charmed to find that they are generally ladies in their twenties. Not to mention the rather odd contest they have going about personalization of their books.)

This did not fit the definition of 'normal people.'

All three of the authors were conversationalists. Okay, it is generally held that all three hold court and are conversational dominants. But the buyers held their own in the competition. It was an evening of good food, good talk, and good wine, the best of life. We spoke, as Carroll said, of "cabbages and kings."

(Although David Drake's discussion of abyssal nematodes holds place of honor for topics.)

From this less-than-chance meeting I derived not so much "buyers" as friends, people with whom I still enjoy meeting and talking. (And drinking wine.)

Not least among these was Alethea Kontis. Charming, erudite, and fun she and two of the other buyers later accompanied me to Starbucks to continue the conversation. I was to drive down to Huntsville that night but it got so late I ended up, after they left, getting a hotel room and catching a couple of hours sleep.

Which led to the conversation the next day with my publisher.

"So... you didn't get in until this morning."

"Mmmph." (I hadn't even had my first cup of coffee.)

"And you left with three of the buyers. The *female* buyers."

"And?"

"I just want to make sure that nothing happened that will...harm Baen's position with Bookville."

It took me a moment to figure out what she was suggesting.

"Hey, they were fine when they left the Starbucks! Nothing happened! I went my way, they went theirs! Honest! Come on! There were *three* of them!"

Fortunately, I hadn't published *Ghost* at that point or *nobody* would have believed me.

Alethea continues to be a friend and I look forward to every meeting with her. I hope to do so well into the future.

PART FOUR

Points for Bravery

Seventeen and seven numbers
Softly slowly slipping by
A life each day for
An empty soul gone drifting nigh
A reckoning for wrested virtues
Penance paid for wasted wings
The rest will come in time, unbidden
Tried and true and tired things
And what I have here: words unspoken
Paths unwalked and tasks undone
A kiss, a gift, a heart unbroken
A tale yet told, the race yet won.

~ Twenty-four, 2001

The 2006 Southern Festival of Books

(Or: The Search for Robert Olen Butler)

October 16, 2006

One of the first questions a fledgling writer has is about conventions. Which ones do you attend? How do you act? What do you bring? How do you network…or should you?

I have heard lots of advice, and I've given out a good bit myself, but it's always nice to see practical applications of what basics will serve an author well in any situation, at any convention.

Here are six rules I think every new author attending a convention should follow.

There are only six, so they shouldn't be too hard to remember.

I've been going to SF conventions since attending my first Dragon Con as a bookseller in 1996. I've always been a fan, and I love hanging out with other people as geeky as me. I love seeing the lengths to which people will go to show their appreciation—from asking an author to sign every book in their collection to dressing up as their favorite character. SF cons are like family reunions for me—family reunions with lots to look at, more to keep me occupied, and new adventures around every corner.

The Southern Festival of Books is not an SF con. It is hosted by the Tennessee Humanities, who describe it best: "The Southern Festival of Books: A Celebration of the Written Word is a free, three-day literary Festival celebrated each year during the second full weekend of October. The Festival welcomes more than two hundred authors annually for readings, panel discussions, and book signings. Book lovers have the opportunity to hear from and meet some of America's foremost writers in fiction, history, mystery, biography, travel, poetry and children's literature."

Right.

So what the heck was I doing there?

RULE #1: CARRY A COPY OF YOUR BOOK WITH YOU AT ALL TIMES.

I've heard this advice from a lot of people. At an SF convention, you're always walking around with a bag full of *somebody's* books…one of those may as well be yours. At a literary convention, everyone is carrying a book. It's natural. It's a part of you. People are very visual. The next time they see the cover of that book, they will think of you. Just do it.

I carried my book around the Festival all weekend. As you'll see, it served me well.

RULE #2: BRING THE BOOKS OF OTHER AUTHORS AT THE CONVENTION FOR THEM TO SIGN.

It's true, you never know whom you're going to meet at these things...but often times you do. Every Con has a website listing the guests. The best way to break the ice with a fellow guest is to have them sign a book for you.

I learned this lesson after attending a convention full of famous authors that I couldn't find a valid reason to talk to. Trust me: it's worth carrying around all those books. Get a roller suitcase if you have to. They're more common than you think.

I had looked on the Humanities site for Southern Festival a few months ago, and saw that Pulitzer Prize Winning Poet Robert Olen Butler was going to be there. I'm a Genre Chick (and proud of it), so I didn't know Robert Olen Butler from Adam...until a friend handed me a galley of his new book *Severance. Severance* is dark, and brilliant, and I couldn't wait to meet the man who wrote it. I bought two copies—one for me and one for Max—and I carried them around in my bag all weekend, hoping to run into him.

Two things happened because of this:

I never ran into Robert Olen Butler, of course, but I heard he was there...and I forgot to bring any books I had for *all of the other authors* at the convention.

RULE #3: AUTHORS AND ARTISTS ARE PEOPLE TOO.

I completely beat myself up. I sat in the audience of a panel Saturday afternoon for Vivian Vande Velde, T.A. Barron, Barry Yourgrau, and Frank Beddor—all of whose books I had...at home.

Especially Frank Beddor.

I fell in love with *The Looking Glass Wars* and bought a copy when Max and I were in England two years ago. I snagged a galley when it was announced here in the U.S., and then got my hands on a copy of that too when it came out. I was so enamored with the book, I had three copies. At home.

Later, after that panel, my friends (author Jackie Gamber, her husband Dan, and their children Ben and Ellen) and I were walking past a table in the colonnade where Paul Zelinsky was signing books with a line of only one person.

Book or not, I could not pass up the opportunity. Paul O. Zelinsky's Caldecott winning *Rapunzel* is another book on my shelf at home. The man is amazing on many, many levels. And even though I didn't have his book with me, I thought he would appreciate it if I told him so.

I know I would have, had our positions been reversed.

So I stood in line like a moron…and introduced myself…and gushed like a fangirl…and talked about a million miles an hour…and apologized for not having his book with me because I was so caught up in worrying about my own panel on Sunday…and because of RULE #1, I conveniently had a copy of *AlphaOops* right there for him to examine.

He was completely lovely and gracious—said some very nice things about the book, and complimented Bob Kolar's outstanding work. I shook his hand, told him it was an honor, and skipped away, red-faced and happy.

RULE #4: BE BRAVE.

RULE #5: DON'T BE AFRAID TO BE SILLY.

While RULE #4 is perhaps slightly more important than RULE #5, the two go hand in hand. Being brave is scary. It always has been, and it always will be. Being able to laugh at yourself, and putting yourself in situations where people might laugh at you is sometimes even more scary.

But if people are laughing, life can't be too bad.

My ticket for the author banquet Saturday night was for two, so

Jackie and I handed the kids over to Dan, stole his camera, and scooted off to Memphis without them.

I knew at least one person who would be at the banquet: my dear friend, the ever-lovely Pamela King Cable (author of *Southern Fried Women*). So it wouldn't be like we were walking into a party where we knew no one. Much.

Jackie and I decided to use the camera as our ice breaker—and the instrument with which we could make our own fun if this banquet turned into the stuffy AuthorFest we feared it might.

As late as we were, we were still some of the first people there. Thankfully, so were Pam and her husband, Mike. Jackie and I helped ourselves to the buffet and sat down at the huge round table…where I discovered our next obstacle: Not everyone was wearing a name tag. Great.

See, the blessing and the curse about being an author is that you can be ridiculously famous and still shop at Walmart in your sweats. If there *is* a picture on your book jacket, it's probably twenty years old anyway. You change your makeup or your hair color, you put on a few pounds…no one knows who you are. It's the best deal ever. Unless you're trying to meet said authors.

Jackie and I chatted with Mike, while Pam was engrossed in conversation with an older gentleman…if I squinted I could make out the name Jeffry on his name tag (Jeffry John Stein). Next to Jeffry was a young blonde woman, and a soft-spoken older couple. I figured they were all friends of Pam's.

Jackie and I cut up—taking my picture with Curious George and Winnie the Pooh, taking my picture with the centerpiece (a Southern Festival bag with tissue paper and helium balloons, anchored in place with a hidden water balloon and a printed warning not to remove the bag from the table: go buy one yourself).

We all chuckled at the signs and the water balloon, and then Jackie and I did a once around the room. It was then that we discovered our next obstacle: a bunch of introvert writers, when presented with big, round tables, will sit at those tables and talk to only those people *for the entire banquet.*

Well, that wasn't going to do us any good, was it? How was I supposed to find Robert Olen Butler in this mess? (I didn't know at the time that I never would...his talk and signing were at the *exact* same time I was reading *AlphaOops* at the Cordova Branch of the Memphis Public Library.)

Jackie and I took some photos of the buffet...and then decided to just go around taking pictures of the people-filled tables. We figured that later, when we went through the guest list, we would realize whom we had dined with. Jackie turned the camera on the folks at the table where we had sat...and the blonde woman stuck her thumbs on her temples and waggled her fingers at us. It was brilliant.

We laughed and asked everyone at the table to make a face. The older woman made a pug nose. Her husband (I think it was her husband) laughed at us. I snuck in the picture, and Jackie took it. We explained to the blonde woman (she will have to forgive me, or email me, because I completely forgot her name) about our plan to take photos of all the tables.

"No one's mingling," I said. "And hardly anyone has name tags on. How are we supposed to meet anybody?"

The blonde woman pointed at the older woman. "Well, this is Phyllis Reynolds Naylor."

She may as well have said, "Well, this is the Pope," because I instantly blurted, "No, you're not."

And then I remembered where I was. And the blonde woman kept talking about how the *Shiloh* movie was coming out soon...

I went from oblivious to fangirl in under ten seconds. "Oh my *GOD*!"

The banquet just didn't last long enough. Jackie and I descended on five more tables after that, meeting fabulous people and showing off *AlphaOops* to everyone. (You think I forgot RULE #1? *Never*!) We met fabulous folks from the Humanities and Cold Tree Press, and authors and artists galore.

At the second table we went to, I spoke to two women who looked awfully familiar: authors Kathy Rhodes and Susie Dunham. But…how did I know them?

"You know," Susie said at one point, "We were in line at an author signing at Davis Kidd in Nashville a couple of years ago, and there was this girl in front of us who told us all about the alphabet book she was working on."

I can count the authors I'm willing to stand in a line that long for on two fingers, and to the best of my knowledge Anne McCaffrey has never been to Davis Kidd.

"David Sedaris?" I asked.

They nodded.

"Eek! That was *me*!"

We were all so excited.

"We always did wonder what happened with that girl," Kathy smiled.

At the third table, I got to spend some quality time with the very handsome, very talented illustrator Raul Colón and his wife Edie. We took the obligatory picture, and when Jackie and I introduced ourselves and plopped down at the table, Raul waggled his finger at me. "You're the big Paul Zelinsky fan."

I'm sure whatever shade of red I was at the time got one degree darker. Raul and the author Pat Mora (who worked together on the Pura Belpre Award Winning *Dona Flor*) had been sitting right next to Paul that afternoon and had witnessed my gushiness firsthand. At the very least, they had me correctly pegged as a book lover. And who doesn't love a book lover?

Raul and Edie both enjoyed *AlphaOops*. Edie works (she'll have to forgive me if I don't remember this correctly) with a literacy program for English as a second language, and she thought it would be a great teaching tool. They promised to pick up a copy before they flew out in the morning.

Tad Hills (author and illustrator of the hilarious *Duck & Goose*) sought me out and introduced himself…and we freaked each other out over what on earth he and John Segal (*Carrot Soup*) and I were going to discuss the next afternoon on our *two hour* panel.

Jackie and I closed down the party having too much fun with Kimberly Willis Holt, Helen Hemphill, Susan Vaught, Genetta Adair, Patsy Trollinger, Candie Moonshower (yes, that is her real name), and Jamie Adoff.

So where does an author having too much fun go after closing down the Gibson Showcase on a Saturday night in Memphis? Yes indeedy…I took *AlphaOops* to Beale Street and had our picture taken with Elvis.

We all headed to the panel Sunday afternoon straight after church. (Speaking as a girl raised by a Greek Orthodox and a Catholic, I have to say Dan and Jackie really *do* have the coolest church I've ever been to. And no, it's not the one we affectionately refer to as "Six Flags over Jesus." If you've been to Memphis, you know which church I'm talking about: the one that's so huge it has its own exit off the highway.)

It's a good thing I brought my own entourage to the panel, because they made up half the audience. Only two or three random people showed up. Our kind and generous moderator had her daughter Lindsley with her.

Tad brought Paul Zelinsky.

It was a *great* two hours.

RULE #6: BE CLASSY.

Before I get to the end of my adventure, I'm going to back up a bit to that very first panel with Frank Beddor. Being the fangirl that I am, I decided to accost him much as I had Mr. Zelinsky at his signing at the colonnade. In lieu of *The Looking Glass Wars*, I had picked up some postcards and bookmarks that had been set on the table, and I asked him if he minded signing one before his escort scooted him off to the airport. He signed it for me in silver Sharpie, and gave me more tattoos and stickers and fun things to go with the book. I quickly told him the story of the three copies of his book that I had neglected to bring…and the fact that I still hadn't read it but wanted to, now more than ever after his dynamic presentation.

"Why haven't you read it?" he asked, acting put out.

"I've been working on my own book," I said. Thanks to RULE #1, I had it right there in my hands. He was very impressed. And he has an eleven-month old son.

"I'd give you this one," I told him, "but I have to do a reading at the library in about half an hour and it's my only copy."

"Is your book available everywhere?" he asked me. I nodded. "Do they have it here?" They did. He looked to his escort, suitcase in hand. "Do we have time to stop and get one before we leave?"

I was dumbstruck. I snapped out of it long enough to thank him profusely. He and the escort headed back inside the building, and I turned to Dan.

"Frank Beddor's going to buy my book!" I squealed.

Dan gently took the book and bottle of water out of my hands and leveled me with his eyes. "Go. Sign. It. For. Him."

Doh!

This is why I keep Dan around.

I ran after Frank and followed him to the cash register. As he was paying, I quickly signed the book for his son in all the colors and stars and notes I always lovingly decorate my books with. Frank thanked me profusely and gave me a big smiley hug. He breezed off to the airport and I stood in the foyer, letting it all sink in.

That Frank Beddor is one classy guy.

The thought popped in my head before the reason: I had bought his book, multiple times, in multiple countries. It was exceptionally nice of him to have purchased mine in return.

Classy. It was classy.

In that moment, I decided I wanted to be a classy author too.

My signing wasn't much to talk about (except for the fact that Paul Zelinsky kept stopping by and checking in—he was waiting for Tad and John to finish up so they could all ride to the airport together). We signed a few posters and talked about stuff...like the fact that all the people were at the other end of the colonnade, standing in line for Garrison Keillor.

I console myself with the thought that in his line were several fans of *AlphaOops*, distraught over the fact that the Humanities folks had scheduled the signings of their favorite authors simultaneously, and they had been forced to choose.

I don't blame them at all. Hey, if I had had to choose between me and Garrison Keillor, I'd have been standing in that line too.

In my first attempt at being classy, I spent my last forty dollars on books written by my fellow panelists, so that I could have them signed.

The effervescent Candie Moonshower stopped by the table and asked how my panel went.

"Paul Zelinsky was there!" I boasted.

"Kimberly Willis Holt was at mine!" she squealed in return...and we gushed for a little bit. Jackie and I had been waving at and asking after friends we had made at the banquet all afternoon. When Candie left the table, John turned to me and said, "Boy, aren't *you* popular?"

It may not have been entirely true...but it felt good.

I signed one more book and played with my rainbow-colored Sharpies. I calculated whether or not I had enough time to eat before I drove back to Nashville. I stared at the plastic bag Ellen had in her hands—the bag containing my signed copies of *Carrot Soup, Duck & Goose*, and *AlphaOops*.

A wicked thought popped into my head this time. I could be classy…and still be me.

"Ellen, give me that copy of *AlphaOops*." She dutifully handed me the book, and I opened it up to the title page.

"What are you doing?" asked John.

I smiled and picked up the magenta Sharpie. "I am signing a book for Garrison Keillor."

The inscription I composed went something like: "G is for Garrison. Gee, do you know you have a REEEEEEALLY long line? Love, Alethea Kontis: the girl at the other end of the colonnade."

I don't think John ever decided if it was a brilliant move, or a stupid one…but he signed a book for Garrison too.

Dan delivered both books to Garrison's assistant. I heard later that Garrison asked her if there were any more of his books left so that he could sign one for us in return, but they had already sold out. Doesn't matter, though. It's the thought that counts. Know why? Because Garrison Keillor is a classy guy.

When our signing was over, Tad and Paul and John hopped in the minivan like the Illustrator Beatles of the Book World. Garrison Keillor only had three people left in line, so I went and stood in it.

Garrison Keillor is a very tall, very imposing man, with a face that falls naturally into a stern expression. He was wearing a suit…and red sneakers.

I introduced myself as the impertinent author who had signed a book for him, and I pointed to the other end of the colonnade, where we had been sitting. I asked if Dan could take our picture, and he put his arm around me.

"Alethea," Garrison Keillor said slowly, in his Garrison Keillor voice. "Alethea. Is that spelled with an E?" I spelled it for him. "Ah, like Althea, but Alethea. A-lee-thee-a. Alethea." He said it over and over again like a mantra. "Alethea." Like tasting a vintage wine. "Alethea." I just shut up and let him say it. "Alethea." Finally he looked down. "I think I've got it."

It was a long drive home…but it went fairly quickly. I told myself stories, recounting my adventures of the weekend to myself like they had happened to someone else. I thought about what I was going to tell Max when I talk to him on Tuesday. I thought about this essay…and how I was going to write it…and when.

And every so often, even now, Garrison Keillor would pop into my head in that Garrison Keillor voice and say, "Alethea."

I never did manage to find Robert Olen Butler. But I don't mind too much.

Chesya Burke says...

We've all seen that movie, right? *There's Something About Mary.* I've seen it more than a few times, I must admit. But, I gotta tell ya', I never quite understood what the appeal was with Mary. I'm not a huge Cameron Diaz fan; I don't think she's particularly attractive. But, hey, she's hotter than Ben Stiller, right? So, I just went with it. Enjoyed it.

It was several years later that I met Alethea Kontis, and memories of that movie popped into my head. Suddenly, everything just snapped for me. That movie's appeal hadn't been because Mary was so gorgeous or striking that all these men lost their minds over her. No, it was her personality and charm that made her alluring.

This is Alethea Kontis.

There's something about her, something so definitive and beautiful that it's simply captivating.

There's something about Alethea.

It's her smile, I think. The way it never leaves her face. That's the first thing I noticed about her. It's the first thing that everyone notices about her.

There's something about Alethea.

It's hard to remember the first time I met her. It just feels like I've known her for a very long time, at least as long as I've been writing.

I do remember, however, the first time I knew I considered her a good, trusted friend. Alethea was having a writer's retreat at a friend's house in Chattanooga, TN and they invited me up.

It was a beautiful house, the tiles in the bath room were heated to the perfect temperature making me want to sleep right there on the floor. We had a wonderful dinner and great conversation. I had just finished my novel, and gotten a bit of a rise from several agents. That night after all was quiet, our bellies full, I sat down and talked to Alethea about my worries and my options. She told me to take my time and do what was best for me and my book.

Since that time I've had private conversations with her about agents and editors and all things writing related. Each time her advice never fails to keep me going, never letting me give up. Trust me, I've been there more than once. I hope I've helped her a bit along the way as well.

Alethea was always there; just a phone call away. I'm not sure what I would do without her guidance and friendship.

There's something about Alethea. But you probably already knew this. She's one of a kind.

The Princess with Butterfly Wings

for *Orson Scott Card's Intergalactic Medicine Show*
October 19, 2006

Do you ever play Traceback?

You've let your mind wander, and suddenly you're thinking about something totally bizarre and not at all what you were pondering in the first place. Or you're having a conversation that takes an interesting turn…and you wonder just how you came around to that topic. So you stop and try to recall exactly what steps took you from hot air balloons to Kevin Bacon.

I call it Traceback. It's one of those games that people with busy brains play all the time. (And we actually find it entertaining.)

Sometimes I play Traceback with my life, just to be perverse. How exactly did I get to where I am today? If I was making an Academy Award speech, who would I thank? The icing on my Destiny Cake is full of fingerprints: great teachers and horrible bosses, neighbors and enemies, co-workers and ex-boyfriends, distant relatives and friends closer than blood. Like every great production, my life wouldn't be what it is without a countless number of people influencing it just the way they did, exactly when they did it.

The Butterfly Effect. Traceback.

Now I know why many people at the Oscars thank their parents, and God. I suppose if you're going to start, it's wise to start at the beginning.

One of the most popular interview questions asked is "When did you start writing?" I have an answer to that question that reels to the surface a perfect memory of eight-year-old Alethea staring at a poem she had just written and smiling as the world *clicked* around her.

But the stories started with Casey.

My father, fairy tales, and Casey.

In a family steeped in oral tradition, my father is the consummate storyteller. He tells tales of our ancestors, his childhood, his friends, his trips around the world. So inevitably, the first stories I ever wrote in school were essays about my crazy life—or the crazy, magical life of the amazing girl I imagined I could have been—but they were always about me.

Sometime around the age of eleven, I was moping around the house (as eleven-year-olds do). I slumped at my mother's feet and whined, "Tell me what to write."

"Go write me a fairy tale," she said. "A new one."

I suppose if I hadn't been moping quite so loudly, I would have heard the world click again. Like it did later that year, when I met Casey.

She was a bit of a misfit, like me. She had thick glasses, a mouth full of braces, a mop of long, curly champagne blonde hair, and a soul like sunshine. She was affectionately called "Beaker" by the popular kids, but she would just smile at them and retreat back into her own little world…her own little world full of books and princesses and unicorns and notepads and pencils. A little world very much like my own. We didn't pass notes in class—we passed a notebook. Whenever we got bored with one world, we'd just make up a new one.

She was my first heroine.

We started a novel, about the adventures of a silly blonde princess named Casey and a dark-haired Queen of Thieves. We spent days at my house on the dock writing paragraph by paragraph, scene by scene, each page switching between Casey's fat, round scrawl and my neat and tiny letters. We spent nights at her house, playing *Super Mario Brothers* and eating pizza and lying on the trampoline and wishing on stars. I stayed up 'til the wee hours one night teaching her how to count to ten in Greek (which she still doesn't remember). I spent ages one morning painstakingly untangling the rats' nest in the back of her head that had appeared out of nowhere in the middle of the night.

When my first love broke my heart and I cried myself hysterical, she brought me pansies unceremoniously ripped from the bed in her front garden. We got jobs at the same movie theatre and spent the hours between shows behind the concession stand composing ridiculous odes to popcorn. When I was lonely at college in South Carolina, she invited me up to UT Knoxville for the weekend and arranged a gathering with all her friends. When she got married she asked me to be a bridesmaid, and I wrote a rehearsal dinner speech that left the guests in happy tears.

I had a nervous breakdown and moved to Tennessee to work in a library. Casey got her PhD in Victorian Literature and moved to Virginia to be a Professor of Women's Studies at William and Mary.

When I attended Uncle Orson's Literary Boot Camp in the summer of 2003, Casey went with me. Not in the physical sense, of course, but in the age of computers and cell phones anything is possible. Thank goodness, too.

Because I was scared.

I had warned her to be available at all hours of the day or night—especially when we were assigned the inevitable 24-hour story. I had never attempted anything so bold in my entire life. And I knew I would never be able to do it without Casey. I had her on speed dial.

My lifeline was available at the push of a button.

Our 24-hour story had to be based on one of the story notecards we had done for homework the night before. Like a dutiful student, I had completed all seven. I had a young woman who lived in the Black Forest region of Germany in World War Two, a Victorian Royal Society of Lady Etchers and an alchemist, a man with incredibly bad luck who took it out on his wife…right before she found a winning lottery ticket in his pocket while doing the laundry and decided not to share—and four other stories unremarkable enough to be similarly unmemorable.

The World War Two story was by far the best, but despite Mr. Stafford's conscientious tutelage for two years in high school, my knowledge of both the world and that war was sketchy at best. The Bad Luck Man was fun, but cliché. The Lady Etchers was an interesting concept but the story was weak, and once again my disturbing lack of history reared its ugly head.

Which might have been a problem…for someone whose best friend didn't have a PhD in Victorian Literature.

I pushed the button. It was roughly 11pm on Tuesday night. I felt like I was cheating…but I was too scared to care.

Casey and I stayed on the phone for at least three hours, hashing out the details of the story while I frantically scribbled down every bit of Victorian minutiae Casey deemed important.

The words "good-bye" that night were heavy with reluctance, and I forced myself to sleep.

When I got up the next morning, I didn't leave the bed. I crossed my legs, pulled the laptop onto the pillow, and opened up a new document. I had a fascinating idea and a rich world…I just needed the perfect character.

Human instinct is to regress in times of great desperation. Traceback. So I started with my princess. My first heroine. I started with Casey. Only this time, her name was Minna.

Maurice Broaddus says...

I actually made a point to meet Alethea. Whenever I am looking at attending a convention, I make a list of people I want to meet or put a face to. I had long heard about her sweetness and likability and how she was this great person to know and I had to see for myself. So I chose to attend a nearby convention to kill three birds with one stone: Alethea, Max, and Jason Sizemore. I had no idea what to expect from any of them and somehow we all managed to arrange dinner together.

Let me tell you, the evening was a revelation. Alethea was an absolute delight. Don't get me wrong: Max and Jason were okay, too—and sure, we became friends too, however, Alethea stole my heart over a bowl of fried rice. You can't ask for much more than that out of a friendship.

I've said this before and I'll say it again: we're family. In this business, you know that some relationships can be superficial; a sort of "what can this person do for me" dimension to most interactions.

However, there is an utter genuineness to Alethea which takes the fakeness out of things. So we long ago passed the networking phase and are well into that rarified air of relationships that can only be described as family. And anyone lucky enough to be able to call Alethea family is a lucky person indeed. I know that I definitely consider myself blessed.

Much Ado About Driving

Apex Digest
Fall 2006

Fear is different in nightmares. There is no relief that follows the shock, no rational thoughts to council the panicked heart racing, no rhyme or reason. There is only pure, unadulterated fear, the kind that only fades upon waking. Rats. Scorpions. Evacuation. Fire. Tornadoes. Tsunami. Roads like roller coasters and cars I am forced to drive from the passenger's seat. A man who steps into a white room and shoots me in the stomach in a scene that repeats itself over and over again. A burglar trying to break into the house to steal the silverware.

These are my nightmares.

After I met Max, I would periodically have dreams that he was hurt or trapped somewhere in England, and I would be forced to drive somewhere to find him. In England. On the wrong side of the road.

Forget running in dreams…try driving in a backwards world you've never been to and can only imagine with an imagination that has tamed dragons, committed suicide and destroyed worlds.

Imagine, for instance, how freaked out I was after this conversation:

MAX: Babe, we're going to have to rethink the BritRail passes for our London trip. It's going to be something like $900 for the two of us.

LEE: Oh my God. You've got to be kidding!

MAX: Well, I do have another idea…but it would depend on you.

LEE: (comparing her bank account to her sense of adventure) Anything. I'm game for anything. What's the idea?

MAX: We hire a car.

LEE: Okay, anything except that.

My heart went from 0 to 60 faster than Sherrilyn Kenyon's Mustang. He was right, of course—renting a car made the most sense. We would have complete freedom and no time tables for the whole week. We wouldn't have to worry about dragging our suitcases in the rain, or waiting on relatives or taxi drivers.

Only thing is, Max doesn't drive. He doesn't even have a license. He's never needed one, being one of those lucky folks who has always lived in major European cities where public transportation is a way of life and not a premise for urban slasher films.

I was going to have to drive the car. In England. I was going to live the nightmare.

Like any brave idiot, I said yes.

I didn't sleep for three days afterward.

Scared doesn't even begin to describe it. I talked to everyone at work and called everyone I knew on the phone—telling them my worries and making sure they knew I loved them before I went on this crazy joyride. I gathered advice from people who had either lived in

England or traveled there extensively. I read *Rules Brittania: An Insider's Guide to Life in the United Kingdom*, by Toni Summers Hargis (which I can heartily recommend). I spent an entire morning committing to memory the British Highway Code (which can be found online at: www.highwaycode.gov.uk). I printed out the street signs for further study and quick reference. I borrowed an atlas of Great Britain from my friend Susie, who many years ago had traveled to England alone and taught herself to drive. My admiration for Susie knows no bounds. Every piece of advice she gave me I treated like gospel.

Day and night I recited the following mantra under my breath: *Roundabouts go clockwise* and *Max in the woods*. If I could remember those two things, I could stay sane.

At least, that's what I told myself.

Roundabouts go clockwise. Because they do. That part actually made a weird kind of logical sense to me. Driving on the left against oncoming traffic was one thing, but on a roundabout, cars only went one way: clockwise. I could do that.

Max in the woods. This one was more fun to say, but still vitally important. I had faith that on a straight road, I could figure out where to be. But if I had to turn, and if there was no traffic to guide my way, how would I know where to go? Susie had the answer. "Just remember, the passenger is always on the outside. At any moment, you should be able to open the door and kick Max into the woods."

Roundabouts go clockwise. Max in the woods. Got it.

Not that it helped me sleep. I had more nightmares, dreams where we arrived at the rental garage, and there were no automatic cars available (did I mention I can't drive a stick shift?). In one garage, there was a car that folded up into a duffel bag, kind of like that nifty futuristic model George Jetson owned.

Nifty, but not comforting.

I had been so excited about finally having a vacation, about getting away from my work and my house and my life for a while. Only now, every tick of the clock brought me closer to that moment: that moment where I would be sitting in the driver's seat, starting a car, and driving headlong into my own personal hell.

The amusing part was that I knew I was being irrational. I knew full well that my fear of what might happen was far, far worse than reality would be. Susie told me that I was an intelligent woman, and she had complete faith in me. Everybody told me I would be fine. I knew I would be fine.

Roundabouts go clockwise. Max in the woods.

I didn't sleep much on the plane. When I got off and found Max at Gatwick, I made him buy me a Coke and sit for a few minutes. My already trembling body probably didn't need the caffeine, but staving off the inevitable was a knee-jerk reaction. Finally, I bravely downed my soda and followed Max to the rental office.

When we booked the car online, we had specified a small, automatic car. The receipt showed that we would be receiving a compact Ford Focus (Ford, interestingly enough, being one of the only American car brands found on English roads) that got better gas mileage than most hybrid cars in America. So when the girl behind the Hertz counter looked up my account and said, "We have a problem," my imagination ran away with the beast. *They don't have any automatics, and I am going to have to pretend to drive a manual. They don't have any Fords; we'll have to settle for a Peugeot. All the cars had mysteriously folded up into duffel bags overnight, and they were having a hell of a time getting them back in working order.*

Oh, but reality is so much more fun. "We have three automatic Focuses," she said, "but they all came back this morning wrecked."

Hey, God? When a girl doesn't ask for a sign, don't give her one, okay??

She frowned at the computer screen. "Does it have to be an automatic?"

"Yes," Max and I said in stereo.

"Hmm. Let me check something." She went into the back to chat with someone. Those BritRail tickets were looking better and better. A few minutes later, she returned with a smile. "No problem," she said cheerfully. "We'll just upgrade you."

A bigger car. Navigating on narrow roads and worse gas mileage. You know, of all the times a free upgrade would have been nice, this was not one of them. But I smiled and signed the paper graciously, as graciously as everything in England is done.

Tick. Tick. Tick. The footsteps of the inevitable.

The car was lovely, mid-sized and blue. I prayed that I brought it back in one piece. Hell, I prayed I brought *us* back in one piece.

When we got in the car, I took a deep breath. I examined everything on the instrument panel. I flashed the lights. I checked the windshield wipers and the mirrors. I gave Max the rundown on Lee's rules of driving. His role was navigator. I couldn't be concerned with where we were going—I was going to be too busy concentrating on driving. He was to look out for other cars and road signs at all times. He was to keep me up to date on our progress, and tell me well in advance if I was coming up to an exit or a roundabout.

Above all, he was to use the term "correct" when referring to driving. "Right" and "left" were too difficult a concept. If Max told me I was driving on the "right" side of the road, my brain wouldn't know how to process it. It had to be "correct", or nothing. He agreed. I started the car.

We were off.

Susie had also made me promise to think before I pulled out of any parking lot, since that was a time when I wouldn't be following behind anyone, and I would be most likely to fall back on old American habits. I made it out of the parking lot unscathed, headed away from the airport, and almost immediately encountered my first roundabout.

I held my breath the whole time and squeezed through by the skin of my teeth.

According to Susie, I would be able to judge how well I was doing by how often other drivers honked their horns at me. Surprisingly, I only got beeped at once, but it was still pretty easy to track my progress—by how much Max nagged at me.

The most common criticisms from the passenger's seat were "You're too close to this side of the road," and "You know, you don't *have* to drive like an old woman."

The first one is something you just don't think about until you're doing it. When you're sitting on the left side of the car, you're used to seeing the vehicle in front of you from a certain angle. From the right side of the car, the angle is all wonky, and your instinct is to drift to the left. It's a valid comment, because I had no concept of how big the car was on my left side. In fact, for the first part of the journey, I mostly used the windows and my right side mirror for guidance. It took me a while to get used to looking up and to the left for the rear-view mirror.

As to the second comment, my answer was: "I am going to get behind this truck, and I am going to *stay* behind this truck! I don't care if he *is* only going forty miles an hour!"

"Lorry," said Max quietly.

"WHAT?"

"You're in England now. We call them lorries."

It was so ridiculous I burst out laughing—the first time I had laughed in four days.

To be fair, the people in England *actually know how to drive*. It isn't some anarchistic free-for-all video game like it is here in the states. In England, you can tell what kind of road you're on by how many lanes it has. Most motorways only have three lanes. The outside lane is for slow cars, caravans, and lorries. The middle lane is for people who drive at a decent speed. The inside lane is for passing only. And the amazing part is, *that's actually how they do it.* All of them.

It was a while before I was comfortable enough on the motorway to get out from behind a lorry and pass another car. But it happened eventually.

Another big help is that almost every road is marked on the pavement, cluing you in to what lane you need to in be based on your destination. What a concept! None of this squinting at signs and realizing at the last minute that you're in the right lane when you need to be turning left. Kudos also goes to the AA Route Planner—Great Britain's version of Mapquest. It details every distance and direction and roundabout, even sometimes going so far as to mention which lane you should be in to get to a certain place.

The only thing it didn't tell you was where the parking lots—excuse me, car parks—were.

Our destination that first day was Nottingham. We had made plans to have dinner with Lindsey and Rik Priestley from Games Workshop. The AA Route Planner reckoned it would take us two hours to get to our hotel from the airport. We had told Lindsey that if we made it into town early, we would stop by the offices and have a tour. We got into town right about 4:30pm. We drove straight to the hotel…

…and we drove straight past it because we couldn't find a place to park.

No problem, said Max, we'll just drive on to Games Workshop. Only…our AA Route Planner didn't give us directions to Games Workshop. I was relying on the sketchy memory of the last time Max had been in Nottingham and walked there from his hotel.

Right.

Two hours of driving around Nottingham later ("Look, Lee, there's the famous Robin Hood castle." "I *can't* look, honey, I'm trying to *drive*."), one accidental turn down a pedestrian-only street and two stops to a.) get directions to the hotel and/or the public car park and b.) discover that the security guard at the new Boots factory had no idea where Games Workshop was (never mind that the GW offices are in the *old* Boots factory building), we made it back around to a car park two blocks from the hotel. I jumped out of the car like it was on fire, my legs wobbling more than they did after my first ride on the Mind Bender at Six Flags Atlanta.

We had made it.

I wasn't getting into that car again if they paid me.

Lindsey and Rik graciously met us at the hotel and we walked to the restaurant, which thank *God* was right beside where we were staying. I didn't want to touch that car again with the proverbial thirty-nine-and-a-half-foot pole. We had a lovely Indian meal and a lovely conversation, and when we got back to the hotel I fell into my lovely bed and slept for the first time in 36 hours.

The next morning, the idea was to visit Games Workshop and walk around the town a little bit. According to Max, the GW offices were five minutes' drive down the road…or an hour's walk. I begged and pleaded not to have to get back in that car. Max tried to smooth my ruffled self-confidence, tried to remind me that I had done just fine the day before, tried to reason with my penny-pinching by saying that not using the car for a whole day would be a waste of money. I would not yield. Finally he relented. We arrived at GW a bit unkempt due to the unseasonably warm weather, but I had one whole relaxing day without having to worry about that damn car. To me, it was worth it.

From Nottingham we drove to Newcastle, and then stopped over in Birmingham on our way down to Bath. I never became entirely comfortable with driving…but I didn't necessarily want to be. Comfortable meant letting your guard down. Instead, I just let my brain make a mirror of everything. If I forgot all I knew, threw "right" and "left" out the window and just *drove*, I was fine. I realized that roundabouts weren't as difficult as I thought—I wasn't just getting lucky every time, there actually is a natural progression to them that makes sense. If you get in the *correct* lane when you approach, you get off at the correct exit. As long as you know where you're going, you won't have a problem.

And we did know where we were going, thanks to the AA Route Planner…and Max. I have to give him all the credit he deserves: he was an invaluable co-pilot. The nagging eventually turned into reassuring comments that we were going the *correct* way, and that I was doing well. When I was thirsty or hungry, there was always a drink or snack at hand. He handed me my sunglasses when it got bright. He read the manual to figure out exactly how the lights worked. Whenever we approached a roundabout, he would tell me exactly which exit we would be getting off onto. When we drove over the scariest bridge in Newcastle, he murmured encouraging comments all the way that would have soothed a woman in her twenty-fourth hour of labor. When the access road was blocked on the way to Bath, Max pulled out Susie's trusty atlas and figured out a route around the city that would access it from another direction.

I was proud of him. He was proud of me. We were proud of us.

That pride gave me the boost of confidence I needed to agree to a side-trip to Stratford, the birthplace of Shakespeare.

We were in Birmingham at the time, a city with lots of shops but not much else that appeals to a girl with little spending money, no head for fashion, and a disturbing uneasiness when surrounded by large crowds of people. Max suggested the Stratford trip, and I had to make a choice. I could repeat the Nottingham Wimp-Out Day of Walking, or I could bite the bullet and drive.

I've said it before and I'll say it again: being brave is scary. But once again, I said yes.

We arrived in Stratford a little after 5:30 and found a car park immediately. Since most of the shops closed at 6:00, the nice old gentleman at the car park didn't charge me a brass farthing, and informed me politely that I could leave anytime. We walked down the street and followed the signs to various and sundry places of interest.

At which point I discovered something: a semi-deserted tourist town after the shops are closed is just about the most *perfect* place in the world.

We strolled along the uncrowded cobblestone streets and peeked in closed shop windows. We passed by the birthplace of Shakespeare, but we didn't need to go in to feel the history that permeated the place. We admired statues and gardens and buildings with stunning architecture. We passed by a small tea shop that was still open, the only populated place on the street.

"Have you ever had cream tea?" Max asked me. When I shook my head, he pulled me inside. Cream tea is simply tea served with scones and jam and clotted cream. Easy peasy.

When my sister and I were very young, my Greek Anglophile Grandmother (aka Nana) taught us how to take our tea and eat eggs with the Queen. We also sang constantly, asking not only after the price of the doggie in the window, but who would eat the fishy on the little dishy and when the Bells of Old Bailey might expect their payment.

I was teased in high school because I didn't know proper American children's rhymes…but having sung about a knacker coming to chop off your head before you went to sleep never did lose its coolness factor.

Her Majesty didn't happen to be in Stratford at the time, and despite the fact that cream tea involved dishys sans fishys, I poured my tea and took a lump of sugar and a splash of cream like I had been doing it forever. The scone was scrumptious and the tea…well, the tea tasted just like Nana used to make. Happy memories swirled inside my cup. It was perfect. Wonderful, amazing and perfect. I had been brave, and this was my reward. I will always remember that little tea shop as being one of the best parts of the whole vacation.

I do wonder what wonderful thing I missed in Nottingham by chickening out that first day, but what's done is done. No sense worrying over it. But I'll definitely think twice about being a coward the next time I have to make a tough decision.

The other reward was the hotel we stayed in the last night of our road trip. By a grand stroke of luck, England's version of Hotwire had picked the most elegant hotel room I had ever been in. In the morning, when we packed up to return the car, I almost wished we were still driving.

Almost.

I left the car in the lot and signed the receipt—we had gone over a thousand miles in that week. We had done the whole of England pretty much from top to bottom…but there were a few places we missed. Brighton. Stonehenge. Lime Regis. Hay-on-Wye, the world famous Book Haven. You can only get to Hay-on-Wye by car. It will definitely be on the agenda next trip.

Back in America, I made a couple of realizations. The first is that Americans really have absolutely no idea how to drive. None at all. And not only do they not have any clue what they're doing, but you cannot drive safely unless you adopt the same degree of insanity. I've finally stopped jumping when I get cut off from both the right *and* the left, but I now flash the offenders an irate two-fingered British gesture. They probably think I'm saying "peace."

They can keep thinking that.

The other realization was that despite my affinity for Starbucks' frappuccinos, I am—and always have been—a big, fat tea drinker. I haven't yet been able to replicate that wonderful cup of tea I had in Stratford, or even the tea Nana used to make, but I went to four different grocery stores hunting down the Red Rose Tea she always swore by.

Red Rose Tea. It was blast from the past to open up the box and find a tiny porcelain figurine in the corner…just like they've always had. My sister and I used to have huge collections of these animals, our menageries long since donated to some charitable organization along with the rest of our childhood play toys.

Best of all, the nightmares have stopped—at least, the ones involving cars and foreign countries. In the mornings I awake to a hot cup of tea and a tiny, brown porcelain spaniel on my sill. It reminds me of England and Stratford and bravery, my Nana, my childhood, and songs of similar doggies in similar windows.

Helen Kontis says...

August 28, 2007

I am Alethea's Nana (that is *Nah Nah*, not *Na Na* to rhyme with banana).

The two sisters Alethea and Sami grew up in Vermont, so my interaction with them during their developing years was limited.

However, from time to time they would visit me here in Florida where I worked in the fashionable department store, Jordan Marsh. I always bragged to my co-workers about my beautiful family and my adorable grandchildren. I am sure the response to that was, "Uh-huh, oh sure, Grandma!"

But one day they came to the store. Two smiling dimpled little girls—one four, one six—dressed like models came bouncing down the aisle into my open arms. My co-workers stared in disbelief at one child with shining dark brown hair around her shoulders and the other with flowing golden curls. The comments from my friends did not surprise me when almost in unison they said, "You really do have a beautiful family!"

Looking back at those two beauties I wish I could have at that very moment stopped the Earth's rotation just long enough to cut out that picture and freeze frame it for all time. In an art gallery it would have rivaled any Renoir.

But the cute little girls grew up and blossomed into lovely talented young ladies.

Alethea is a published author and Sam, an accomplished artist.

How lucky can one Nana be?

Recently I visited Alethea in Murfreesboro, Tennessee where she lives and works and I learned that her second book is about to be released and Sami's wedding date is set in October.

I have kept that freeze-framed picture in my memory for a long time and I recall it nostalgically from time to time. But the pull of gravity has come into play and now it has migrated down around my heart. That is where it is now and where it will stay forever.

Blood Oath, Take One

Apex Digest
Winter 2007

Some of you may know this, and some of you might not remember. But before there was an all-star SF anthology, before the picture book, even before Apex…there was a little horror movie called *Blood Oath*. It was local and low budget. It was a bunch of us running around the woods of Tennessee with digital video cameras. It was four years' worth of mistakes in the making, and valuable lessons learned.

On Monday, October 23rd 2006, *Blood Oath* premiered at 7:00pm at the historic Belcourt Theatre in Nashville.

Finally.

THE EX FACTOR

4:30pm CST

Lee: Hey, busy man, what's up?

David: Hey, Miss Associate Producer. Bob and I are picking up a new projector. Belcourt neglected to mention theirs was broken. I swear…this damn movie is cursed.

Lee: No such monster. So what time should I be there?

David: We probably won't start it until 7:30 or so. Get there a little bit before 7:00 and you should be fine.

Lee: Will do, boss.

David. Um…you do know that your Ex is going to be there, right?

Four years ago, three guys were sitting around my dining room table discussing horror movies: David Buchert, Robert (Bob) Ziegler, and my ex-boyfriend. I don't remember where I was at the time—it was four years ago after all—but this wasn't a rare occurrence. I don't want to think about how many shot-on-video/direct-to-DVD movies I had seen as a result of this triumvirate's passion. (Of course, if I ever want a refresher, all I have to do is go visit David's home video library. Sheesh.)

Most of the time the boys club was in session I was in another room reading, or editing, or watching cheesy romance movies out of spite. But I might have been at that table and probably was, since Bob's quiet, zenlike presence was a rare occurrence that I always enjoyed.

I'm not sure any one of us remembers exactly. It was four years ago, after all.

So it was a day just like any other day…right up until the Ex said something about a "woman in the woods," and we all heard the bolt slam home on our cell door in Fate.

I figured the Ex would be at the premiere of the movie. He had every right to be there. It made sense for him to be there. It wouldn't be a surprise for either one of us.

A lot had happened—at least, to me—in the three years that I hadn't laid eyes on him. I was the better person (and the helluva lot famouser one too, thankyouverymuch), so I knew I could handle it.

But that didn't mean I wasn't going to look awesome.

It occurred to me, after curling my hair and trying on the third outfit, that these sorts of insane reunions must happen in Hollywood all the time. Virtual lifetimes pass between the conception, production, and release of a major feature film. Who knows how many people, behind the scenes and in them, have gone from adoration to apathy…and vice versa? Who knew how many Exes would be seen tonight for the first time in happy forevers?

As I carefully applied my make-up I wondered if directors planned it this way, or if they just laid back and reaped the benefits.

Think about it: if you want to have a movie premiere where everyone looks *fabulous*, invite all the Exes. The girls will be dressed to the nines. The guys will have taken showers. Everyone will be at their most glamorous, on their best behavior, and smiling for the cameras.

Flash. Vogue.

It was brilliant, really.

On the way out the door, I threw my camera in my bag.

FAMILY REUNION

The theatre lobby was packed.

I didn't recognize a soul.

Deftly I skirted around an older couple pondering the showtimes and a younger couple signing up for the Belcourt e-mail list. I navigated through the velvet-wrapped poles and past the concessions bar advertising a Campfire Drink special (that consisted of a lot of vodka and a little bit of something blood-red). At the back of the room I spotted a table with a huge TV on it playing a trailer for *Blood Oath*, so I headed that way.

Behind the table was an exceptionally cute girl selling t-shirts, soundtracks, and mini-posters for the movie. On either side of the table were frames with the full-size *Blood Oath* poster, and various promotional pictures from the film. Like a real movie.

My god, it was a real movie.

I was incredibly impressed.

I was also comforted by the fact that behind the table were a couple of familiar faces: David and Bob. David was busy signing a poster so I caught Bob's eyes first, and he signaled me over. We hugged and I asked after the projector (which they had miraculously procured) and his birthday (which was the very next day). In kind, Bob asked after *AlphaOops* (which I had brought with me of course—yes, I am the sort of woman who brings a picture book to a horror movie), and he pointed out David's parents in the crowd.

David's parents were there. For the opening night of his horror movie. How awesome was that?

Our reunion was all too brief, but I expected as much. David and Bob were the Men of the Hour. It was a bit like going to a wedding when you only know the bride. You see her for five lovely minutes, and then spend the rest of the reception milling around the outskirts holding up walls and trying not to scan the enormous and boisterous crowd for your Ex. I picked a nice spot on the sidelines behind the table next to a tall, slender man with dark hair and a skullcap.

"Hi," he held out his hand. "I'm Enrique."

"Alethea," I said. "Nice to meet you."

"So what did you do on this thing?"

Oh, why stand on ceremony. "I was the money. Not all of it, of course, just some of it. You?"

"I was in it."

I squinted at him. Now, granted, I had not seen every single minute of the film—there's been a rough cut sitting on my coffee table at home for months, but I decided to wait until the premiere to watch *Blood Oath* in its chronological entirety. However, I knew I had seen just about every scene at some point, in some way shape or form, and I totally did not remember this guy.

He sensed my skepticism. "I got to make out with Tiffany Shepis."

"Oh my god, *RIQ*!" I lit up immediately. The scene where he and Tiffany make out in the car (before being brutally murdered of course) was the first scene that was ever shot. I wasn't on the set those two days, since they filmed it at night and I was working two or three jobs at the time, but I had seen hours and hours of footage. "Sorry, David never calls you Enrique. I didn't make the connection. And I completely didn't recognize you."

"Yeah," he said, "my hair got long again, and then I cut it, and then it got long again. A lot happens in four years."

"Tell me about it," I said. "I got married and had three kids."

His eyes were like saucers. "Did you really?"

"No. But I could have."

I had a great time with Riq. It's so much fun, when you barely know one another, and you have so much to catch up on. He told me all about Tiffany Shepis and his days on the set; I told him stories of Tina Krause and my scattered few days on location here or there. We reminisced over the neverending horror that was his beheading and the scene that literally wouldn't die. Neither one of us had seen the whole movie from beginning to end, and we were really looking forward to it. We were also thrilled by the enormous crowd that still filtered into the almost-packed theatre.

We humored Matt Dyer as he circled the room with his camera in hand (once a DP, always a DP). We reintroduced ourselves to quasi-familiar passersby as the river of people continued to flow into the theatre, and decided that name tags would have been a handy thing to have around.

Not that the labels of "Lady Money" and "Shepis Boy Toy" would have identified us in any helpful way, but they would have been fun.

Another tall guy walked past us, and then backed up. "Patrick," he said to me, and this time I did remember the handsome face beneath the disfigured monster. "Where do I know you from?"

"*Blood Oath*," I said glibly. And then in response to the slant-eyed stare, "I was at the farmhouse one day." The infamous farmhouse, a few months before it was completely destroyed right along with all the props inside it. The day Adrian took the famous picture of Natalie tied to the chair that became the first signature poster for the movie. Was that right before or after James asked Adrian to marry him? They've been married for three years now. The day Natalie hacked Patrick's body to pieces and got covered in blood. She was such a trooper with that sickle. God, Natalie was barely old enough to vote back then. Now she's a Coyote Ugly girl and a spokesmodel for Red Bull.

"Right," Patrick nodded.

I imagine his thoughts were running along much the same lines.

MEMORY LANE

It was showtime.

I parked myself in the back row. After a short introduction met with wild screams and thunderous applause, David, Bob, Riq and Matt stood along the wall by the door—either because they forgot to reserve seats together, or because they wanted to masochistically get a record (on video, even, since Matt still had that camera) of who left the theatre, and when, and why.

Suddenly, the screen was full of Tiffany and Riq—or, rather, Janet and Marc. There was a plethora of cheesy dialogue, scads of sexual innuendo, a healthy amount of foul language, plenty of screaming, and lots and lots and lots of blood. All before the opening credits.

Excellent.

It's a great audience that cheers for every name in the credits...even mine. I raised my arms in a V to the chorus of deep hoorahs that came from the gang by the back wall, which is all that mattered.

Then came the campfire scene, with Natalie, Jamie, Roger and Katie. I hear Katie's in New York dabbling in both acting and real estate and that Roger's somewhere in—Africa, was it?—though I'm not sure if that comment was said in seriousness or jest. I remember campfire day on the set too, one of the first ones when everyone was still excited about the project and enamored with each other. The car-cam, the bags of Doritos, the McDonald's hamburgers, and Roger and Katie's kissing scene.

The four young characters on the screen may have been starting off down the scary, dark road to the Krupps' house, but for me they were walking down memory lane. To others, this was just a low-budget, B-rate slasher flick. To us, it was scrapbook bits of our lives that we hadn't thought about in ages upon ages.

There was Tina and her Polaroid camera and the bit about the squirrels...there for a few minutes and then gone in an instant. I remember how concerned David was over Patrick's rough handling of our guest as he sliced through her guts and ripped her clothes off. I remember the pictures floating down the red-tainted stream and the water gun filled with blood, how annoyingly bright the sun was that day and how much we laughed. I remembered the night before the shoot, full of black-light bowling at Gillian's and appletinis. I still have my cool martini glass with the wavy stem.

The restaurant is still there, but it's called something different now.

Half of me flipped through the mental photo album, and half of me just enjoyed watching the film. It was very much a first-time effort—there was an odd sound mix here or there, and that beheading of Riq's never was going to be perfect—but it had energy and sarcasm and all the essential elements. It was *fun*. It actually struck me how much laughter constantly circulated throughout the theatre.

It was our *Evil Dead.*

And yet, even through the ennui there were some diamonds. There were heart-pounding moments of shock and eww. There were times when the dialogue between the actors was so natural it was flawless. Katie freaked out, and you freaked out too. Natalie went back for the lamp, no matter what you yelled at the screen to try and stop her. Roger's running through the woods and the delivery of that one word, "Beverly," as he stops was met with as much applause as if it had been Bruce Campbell uttering "Woodshed."

How many takes of that shot had there been? Roger must have run ten miles that day. It was worth it.

And then…it was over. The credits rolled, the theme song echoed over the clapping, and nobody threw tomatoes. Four years in the making, and it was over in eighty minutes.

Like the longest Thanksgiving ever.

A IS FOR ALBATROSS

That day at the farmhouse was also the day I asked David why he named his company Albatross Films.

"It's for this albatross on my back," he answered.

I forget how many months into shooting that was at the time, but there had already been an avalanche of problems, mishaps, and complications—not the least of which was actually *finding* the farmhouse where we finally did the shooting. They were having difficulties with day-for-night scenes. A chunk of the script was going to have to be scrapped because they couldn't find the girls to be in it. Some of the actors weren't getting along. Money was tight, but it had to be spent. The scheduling was insane. David had broken up with his girlfriend and moved out, and my soon-to-be Ex was fast on his way to becoming so himself.

"Isn't the albatross supposed to be around your neck?" asked my smartypants literary self.

David didn't miss a beat. "It's for the one on my back *and* the one around my neck."

We all learn from our mistakes, and four years gave us all plenty of time in which to make them. Everyone had their own thoughts about what they would do next time.

We're going to have a budget, and we're going to stick to it. There's going to be a definite shooting schedule, and we're going to stick to that too. And then came all the minutiae about the shots and the cameras and the sound equipment and every little other thing we could think of. The theme of the evening seemed to be: *Now that we've done it once, we're going to do it better next time.*

Next time.

I did see the Ex, in passing, as I lingered by the table with Riq and he flowed by in the stream of people heading to the theatre. "Congratulations on the book," he said. I saw him again, in much the same fashion on his way out. "Good to see you." And that was it. Yet another mistake over and done with.

After the show, David visibly relaxed. There was more excited meeting and greeting, and posters and Sharpies were passed around. The ever polite and appropriate Bob took the time to write me out his thanks and "this couldn't have happened without you." David cursed him for always saying the perfect thing as he snatched the poster out of my hand to scribble on it himself. I didn't have a chance to see what he wrote because I was whisked away by Jennifer, who demanded that I sign her poster with something clever that somehow involved *AlphaOops*.

Right. Clever. Picture book. Horror movie. Right. The Sharpie hovered above the poster, and I worried about it drying out.

It doesn't really take as long as it feels like it does for inspiration to strike. With a twinkle in my eye I wrote, "B is for Beverly!" and signed my name. I signed a few more after that, and then we cleaned up and went off to the after party. Bob had a customized birthday cake with the famous Natalie picture printed on it. We all sang, more than once. There were pictures taken for "next time."

Oh yes, there will be a next time. According to the Albatross film site, *Blood Oath* made more at the box office in its one-night showing at the Belcourt than the fifteen million dollar-budgeted 20th Century Fox film *The Marine* did in its two week run at the multiplex downtown. I wonder how many Exes were involved in that one.

I have no doubts that our little slasher film will be sold to a respectable company very soon and will eventually be available on DVD in several countries. Bob and David will make their money back. Maybe not in spades, but it will come. I've told them both—and I'll say it again here—I don't ever want to see any money from *Blood Oath*. Whatever share of whatever profits is deemed as mine, I want them to use on the next movie. Next time.

See, I wasn't just investing in a movie; I was investing in people.

Some people dream things, and some people do them. It's those people in the second group that are the real heroes—the people who fall down and stand back up again over and over despite all obstacles, emotional or physical. They dance with the muse, they let her use them and toss them away like so much tissue. They throw themselves on that bed of nails again and again until it's done. They brush the dust off their knees and straighten their ties. And then they do it all over again.

We need more people like that in the world, people that will take the harder path and the road less traveled. People who will accomplish things. I will give those people whatever support I can, every single time.

Bob might have been right that it couldn't have happened without me, but it couldn't have happened without any one of us making *Blood*

Oath what it was. All the ups and downs, the great ideas and the mistakes, we needed all of those. Kind of like life, really.

I promised I would stay at the party for one drink. I ended up saying goodbye sometime before one in the morning.

I hugged Bob and wished him a happy birthday again. I hugged Natalie and told her she was beautiful. I hugged Matt and we spoke of next times. I had already hugged David so many times that night I lost count, but I did it once again for good measure.

"I can't thank you enough," he said solemnly for the umpteenth time.

I smiled and gave him a squeeze. "Just make another one."

There were a million things going through my head on the drive home, my own list of next times. Next time, I'm going to spend more time on the set. Next time, I'm going to know the crew a lot better. Next time, I'm going to get my hands on that script. Next time, I'm going to be more involved. I'm going to call David more than four times a year. I'm going to buy a *Blood Oath* t-shirt and tell everyone I know about the movie and frame my poster with names scribbled all over it.

My poster.

I pulled into the driveway and turned on the dome light to see what David had written. Underneath Bob's thoughtful inscription were the words: *You helped my dream come true.*

Well, what do you know.

Some things you *can* do right the first time.

Earth Angels

November 7, 2006

Some of you might remember my mother's hard and fast theories about guardian angels—most importantly, that they exist. They are all around us, just waiting for us to ask them something. And I don't just mean wishing your heart's desire on stars, though I'm certainly an expert in that department after so many years of experience.

You have to ask your guardian angels everything, my mother says, the big stuff and the little stuff. Especially the little stuff. Parking spaces, lost keys, free car washes, and specials on laundry detergent. They're best at those.

I don't ever wish any of these things out loud of course (normally if you see me talking to myself it concerns something far less vital), but I always ask. Angels or not, my belief is that it never hurts to throw helpful suggestions out into the ether. You never know who might be listening. And you probably never will.

But—like my father taught me—the worst thing they can say is "No."

Over a year ago, I started wishing like hell that I could go to World Fantasy Con. Thanks to *Elemental*, Sharon Shinn and I had been exchanging emails even before the 2005 event in Wisconsin. I knew I didn't have the resources available to go then, so I started looking ahead to next year. I went to Google and typed in "World Fantasy Con 2006, Austin TX." When the site popped up, I squealed.

I immediately emailed Sharon back with a link. The lovely background artwork was from one of her books—my personal favorite—*Jovah's Angel.* The illustration was also done by my favorite cover artist in the whole wide world: John Jude Palencar.

It was fate. It was the internet telling me my trip to World Fantasy was meant to be. I would be in Austin in 2006, by god, and the machines of the universe were going to make that happen. I was going to see my friends, the *Elemental* authors, and John Jude Friggin' Palencar. I didn't even bother to hope. I just took it as a given.

I clung to that dream until about a month ago, when I pried my sad, desperate fingers from around the edges and set it free. My anorexic piggy bank had checked itself into rehab. I couldn't do it. It wasn't going to work. I needed to accept that. I would just have to save up for next time. Next year. It was okay.

Didn't mean I had to be happy about it.

I moped around the Codex board, and sent pouty emails to Sharon and Lynn Flewelling steeped in self-pity. I asked them to please tell JJP that his biggest fan in the world wanted to come and hated to miss him, but not to worry too much, because she still planned on having him on the cover of one of *her* books someday.

The last week of October, I got an email from Southwest Airlines. They were having an internet special to Texas, but the "featured destination" was Dallas, not Austin. Out of curiosity (and sheer masochism), I pretended to book a flight to World Fantasy. Just to see.

Round trip from Nashville to Austin was $230. A ticket to the Con was $150. Mary Robinette Kowal had said that if I managed to find a way to get there, she would be more than happy to let me room with her. And if I brought a bunch of Power bars and skipped a few meals… My hand hovered over the phone. I had promised myself I wasn't going to do this. But it was Sharon and Mary and Lynn…it was John Jude Palencar. It meant that much to me.

I dialed the number.

"Hey, Mom? Remember when you said you'd lend me some money if I was desperate?"

Two hours later, I had a ticket to Austin, a convention membership, and a new lease on life. If mom can have her tenets about angels, I can have my own personal riders to the Chaos Theory.

On my first ALERT field trip in elementary school, one of the instructions in our study packet insisted that we "be flexible." Flexible? When I was in gymnastics, I got a blue ribbon for being able to do all three splits, but I knew my friends had no such pretzel-like tendencies. How could the instructors have suggested something so impossible? I learned soon after that "flexible" meant being open to change. Being poised for spontaneity. Being able to go with the flow.

Sure. I could be that kind of flexible too.

Not only is it surprising how many people do not possess the ability to be that kind of flexible, but also how much better your life is when you are. You accept that things will happen that you have no control over, that you cannot change, and it's far easier to go where the wind takes you.

From experience, I must say the wind is a fabulous tour guide.

The wind brought me two fantastic hours sitting with Sharon Shinn in the corner catching up on life. Bonding with Nina Kiriki

Hoffman over rainbow-colored pens and a forged Charles DeLint signature. David Drake scaring the hell out of Steven Erikson by way of introduction. Chatting and laughing for not-long-enough with F. Paul Wilson and Tom Monteleone. Mary Robinette Kowal being asked to tell the marionette story again…and again…and again until Jay Lake almost swallowed his tongue. A very important hug from Tim Waggoner. A party of thirteen at T.G.I. Fridays, Ken Scholes signing his thirteenth book to me, and a Pirate Party in 413. Arrrrgh! Pirates, Black Death, and bloody tattoos courtesy of *Shimmer*. My new best friends: Julie Wright and C.E. "Catie" Murphy. Making plans for next summer with Tim and Serena Powers. Sandra Bullock ahead of me in line for ice cream at the Austin airport. Kicking the back of David Coe's seat on the airplane all the way home.

And John Jude Palencar, of course. I'm still swooning. He signed my gorgeous 2007 JJP calendar (a Barnes & Noble exclusive), and I told him he was going to do the cover of one of my books one day. Edmund says he probably hears that all the time. Just maybe never with so much conviction.

Above all of that, though, were my real life guardian angels.

Eric James Stone was the wheel man, and let me check my email on his magical internet connection. Rick Fischer was in charge of looking after my jacket and making me laugh so hard my stomach hurt for three days after the convention. (Beth Wodzinski brought down my jacket once and asked if that officially made her part of my staff.) Julie, who took care of my bag when I left it behind in the mass autograph session. The lovely hostess at the pizza place who chased after me with the water bottle Michael/Onyx gave me the first day that saved my life the whole weekend. Theresa at the Austin Lost & Found, who tracked down my John Jude Palencar calendar where I left it at the Southwest check-in and FedExed it to me the very next day. And Edmund Schubert—dear Edmund—my hero from the first minute he talked to the cab driver, who took care of everything else, and kept me in line.

I suppose I should worry that I need so much looking after, but I'm not.

A person could certainly have more to complain about than an abundance of angels.

TOP TEN QUOTES FROM WFC 2006

10. "American cheese is the muzak of cheeses." *—Rick Fischer*

9. "I'm not going to submit to you anymore." *—Alethea Kontis (to Edmund Schubert)*

8. "A cliché is a trope done badly." *—Eric Flint*

7. "Excuse me, mister?" *—Alethea Kontis*

6. "Let me shoooooooow you how to hoooooold it." *—Mary Robinette Kowal*

5. "It's *only* this big." *—Edmund Schubert*

4. "...because the rest of us aren't as perverse as you. Why are you beating your banana?" *C.E. "Catie" Murphy (also to Edmund)*

3. "I'm not as old as I used to be. Wait..." *—Alethea Kontis*

2. "When people quote me, that's a 'smart quote'." *—Rick Fischer*

1. "Losing my virginity is *nothing* compared to not getting a donut." *—Julie Wright*

Edmund R. Schubert says...

It was November of 2006, and I was hanging with Alethea at a party at World Fantasy Con in Austin TX. At this party, in an overstuffed arm chair pushed almost all the way into one corner of the room, sat an assistant editor who shall remain nameless because a) I'm sure he's a wonderful person, b) you'd know who he is and I'm not here to embarrass him, and c) this story really isn't about him; he's only here for contrast.

So why I do I bring him up? Two reasons.

First, he was sitting in a particular, specific chair (I'll get back to that in a minute), and second, because he was indisputably one of the 'cool' kids at this party. You know the type, everybody wants to be around them, near them; doing what they're doing.

And you could tell that's what he was, too—one of the truly cool kids—because as our aforementioned assistant editor sat on his overstuffed throne...excuse me...arm chair, drink in hand, he also had a troop of groupies clustered around him, hanging on his every word.

In case you hadn't noticed, assistant editors don't usually have groupies. 'Cool' kids do. Cool trumps all titles.

Of course, groupies don't call themselves groupies. If you have any familiarity with the concept of 'cool,' you know that it rubs off. It's contagious. Everyone 'in' the group gets cool by association. Then these people go out, disciples of cool, and spread their gospel. Well, it's not actually gospel, but they're out there spreading *something.*

Spreading it pretty thick, in most cases…

It's enough to make regular folks sick.

That's why Alethea and I get along so well. Very shortly after we met, we both realized we were 'not cool' kids. Always had been, always would be. And the stink of 'not cool' had been on us for a long time. For most folks, that label goes back to high school if not earlier. So it was for the two of us, and it drew us together into one of the best friendships I've ever had.

Here's the thing, though: more important than which side of the 'cool' equation Alethea fell on is the fact that she embraced her status with such vigor that she transcended it. She relishes—even wallows in—her '*not* cool' role. And when you embrace who you are the way Alethea has, you become a better, stronger person. You end up being 'super cool.'

Now, I know that 'super cool' might be considered a radical concept by some, akin to cold fusion, too good to be true. And (to go on a slight tangent), I've been married for many years to a woman with a scientific background. So if there's one thing I know, it's that if someone is going to make these kinds of outrageous assertions, they have to have evidence to back them up. I also know that for any scientific theory to be considered valid is has to be tested, and the success of the test must be repeatable. These scientific tenets have been thoroughly drummed into me.

So what's my evidence for Alethea being 'so-*not*-cool-she's super-cool'?

Remember that overstuffed armchair I mentioned before, the one doubling as a throne for our 'cool' kids? Well this is where it comes back into the story. You see, on the opposite side of that chair (both literally and metaphorically), sitting on the floor in a little cave formed by the chair's arching back and two intersecting walls, Alethea and I sat with another friend, Julie. We sat back there for what seemed like hours, drinking juice and soda (cool kids do not drink juice!). In fact, we hung out all weekend and told each other stories that ended with phrases like, "And losing my virginity was nothing compared to not getting a donut!" and "I know I'm not supposed to, but I grabbed Gordon Van Gelder in the men's room…" (yeah, that one was mine—I don't want you thinking any of the ladies were in the men's room). Sitting in our little cave, we were so *not* cool it hurt. There aren't words for our uncoolness.

So the not cool part is easy. Nobody claims to be not cool unless they really are; it's one of the defining traits of the condition.

Yet over that same weekend I saw award-winning author Tim Powers seek her out for a hug and hello and conversation. At a previous con that year, (Dragon Con—Alethea and I hang out at a lot of cons), I saw *New-York-Times*-Best-Selling-I-Write-Five-Novels-Every-Year author Kevin Anderson and his wife Rebecca Moesta seek Alethea out to give her tickets to the big celebrity banquet. Also at Dragon Con that year we had lunch with Sherrilyn Kenyon—who's so big she has her own convention—talking about Sherri's kids (right before she hand-picked Alethea to co-author the *Dark-Hunter Companion*). At Chattacon in Tennessee the next year, over the course of the weekend we had late night pizza, and then lunch, and then dinner, and then lunch, dinner, and lunch again with Rob Sawyer and Kevin Anderson, talking about B-movies and comic books and all the things cool kids eschew.

I could go on and on, and that's kind of the point. To go back to my science-minded wife, this has been the ultimate in repeatable experiments. Alethea doesn't have any groupies. Nobody sits at her feet while she pontificates (there's no room to do so behind pieces of hotel furniture). If you'll notice, there's nothing 'cool' about any of it. Come on, kids and comic books? No, there's nothing cool about any of it—nothing but everything. Every time I see Alethea out and about, the most successful people in the SF and Fantasy world all shine on her. When you've transcended cool far enough to talk with these kinds of people about these kinds of things, you are, without question, super cool.

In a nutshell, that's Alethea. She's *not* cool. But she's embraced her not-coolness with more enthusiasm than can be contained by man, beast, or machine. Heck, she's embraced it with more enthusiasm than can be contained by man, beast, and machine furniture caves (though apparently it can be contained by furniture caves).

And you want to know a secret? That's the real reason why she's super cool. She makes fun wherever she goes.

She's open to anyone who wants to have fun with her.

She makes me proud to be one of the *not* cool kids.

Tradition

December 17, 2006

Among the many sayings in my family new and old, there's one I can take credit for having made up myself. It's about tradition: Once is an event, twice is a coincidence, three times is tradition.

It fits, really—three is a powerful number to the Greeks. If you do something three times, it's a given that you're pretty serious about it. You may as well go on and call it a tradition.

I've been doing a lot of thinking this month—kind of a surprise, since my plate's been so full I've barely had enough time to breathe. The great thing about thinking is that you can fit it in all those tiny in-between times: in the bathroom, in the middle of the road while a cop kicks at your flat tire, at your desk when the program you're using freezes up and you're forced to reboot your whole system if you have any interest in ever again connecting to the internet.

Of course, that's the awful thing about thinking, too. You do it in those times whether you intend to or not. All of those things you try to avoid and shove in the back of your mind come creeping around the corners and sinking their claws into the shadows so that each time it's harder to make them go away again.

There seems to have been more than a few of those inescapable moments lately (Sharon Shinn said only I could turn a flat tire into a bonding experience with the local police department), so a great deal of quality thinking has gone on in my busy little head. In fact, I've thought myself straight into a nice, healthy holiday depression.

What's up with *that*? The self-proclaimed Cheerleader of Life should never have to worry about being depressed for heaven's sake. It's all about point of view, so I should be able to shake this with minimal effort, shouldn't I? Some peppy music, a couple of projects completed, an evening out with friends, a partridge in a pear tree and Bob's your true love, right?

Right?

Right.

So.

STEP ONE: PEPPY MUSIC

I've compiled a Christmas CD for every year I've been at Bookville. In 2001, it was eleven songs on a plain, text-only, two-color label given to maybe twenty people tops. In 2002 I found a great pic of a Vargas girl in a Santa hat, and a few friends brought CDs by to broaden my musical horizons.

These last few years the CDs have been jam-packed with songs from near and far, old and new, traditional and not-so-much, well-known and obscure. The labels have sported art by professional artists who are personal friends of mine. (This year's featured Janet Lee's Aviator Girl—the original piece she did for the Biography page on my website.)

And I'm not sure how many I made this year. I stopped counting after the first hundred and twenty or so. I put all the Technicolor envelopes in a basket and made my rounds to each department, doling out my peppy, bright blue discs full of holiday cheer to the masses.

It's a little something that makes everyone happy, and in turn, that makes me happy. So many people stop by to tell me how they leave my CDs in their players every December—for the whole month and sometimes beyond. Everyone has a different favorite song, but they always look forward to the next year's surprise installment.

I always see the smiles and hear the kind words of gratitude, but it didn't hit me how great an impact it had until I handed a bright green CD envelope to Diana. "Hooray!" she said with a smile. "You know, this is the only tradition we have left around here anymore."

The company's Christmas parties stopped happening at Bookville the year after I got there, and with them went the annual Christmas turkeys. The Product Group stopped having their White Elephant lunch after the first director left. The holiday gathering has evolved from a scary off-site dry karaoke party to a couple of gratis boxed lunches. In a world where no one likes change, each year has been less certain than the day before it. No one could count on anything…except me.

How right she was: I am a tradition.

The weight of the responsibility of those words scared me to death, and at the same time made me immensely happy. I could be a tradition—this one, at least. I don't mind being the Christmas Fairy once a year. I think I can handle that.

I walked away from Diana's office, swinging my basket and whistling that song from *Fiddler on the Roof*.

STEP TWO: PROJECTS

Last year at work, someone thought it would be a great morale booster if people decorated their cubicle walls and office doors for the holidays. As an added motivator, they turned it into a contest with prizes and stuff.

Yeah.

Everybody immediately assumed I'd do something. At the time, I was in the middle of my first novel and copyediting the manuscript for *Elemental*—like I had the time for such corporate nonsense. So I decided to surprise everyone and not do anything.

See, I've gone this route before, every year of grade school. I was the Teacher's Pet, the curve-buster, the effortless overachiever. My Spanish teacher begged me not to switch to French, because she enjoyed the stories I told in my test essays so much. For a homework assignment in U.S. History, Mr. Stafford had us shade the thirteen colonies in on a worksheet. I shaded them in with the flags of the states those colonies now represent. The class voted to give me extra credit.

From my point of view, if anyone else wanted a chance at winning whatever prizes there were, I really shouldn't be entering this contest. The part I didn't realize is how much it was *expected* of me to stun people with some fabulous show of creative genius.

As the deadline grew closer, people started to notice that I wasn't doing anything. Worse, they started giving me "helpful" ideas to jumpstart my imagination. For a week or two, I graciously stomached suggestion after suggestion. I considered putting out a box with forms for them. And then I started getting insulted.

Do you want to know why Van Gogh really cut his ear off? Because he got sick of hearing people say, "Dude! Know what you *should* paint?"

Yes, yes, I understand everyone meant well. And they were just trying to be helpful. But the camel's back finally broke upon the proposal of this brilliant straw: "How about I come up with the idea, you do all the work, and we split the prizes?"

I wish I was making that up.

That was actually said to me, word for precious word.

After I stopped flipping between baffled and furious, I took it as a challenge.

You want a display? Fine. *You'll get one.*

The next day, on the wall outside my office was the outline of a Christmas tree in green crepe paper (you can do amazing things on cubicle walls with crepe paper and straight pins—I made the Eiffel Tower outside Nicole's office with crepe paper once…but I digress). The tree was decorated with actual garland and ornaments. Underneath the tree were a few construction paper presents with real bows. Beside the tree, going up the pole to the ceiling, was a huge gray chimney made out of cardboard and butcher paper. On the chimney hung two real socks, one magenta and one purple. Opposite the chimney was a dark alcove with the silhouette of a sleeping child covered in blankets. It was all a very simple and pretty and traditional Christmas. People commented about how artistic it was, and how much they liked it. And I chuckled to myself every time they did.

Because I had plans for that weekend.

When everyone came in to work on Monday, the day of the contest judging, they passed my office to find that Cindy Lou Who had gotten out of bed and caught the Grinch shoving the Christmas tree up the stocking-stripped chimney.

It had taken me forever to draw and color those characters, and that chimney, and back them all on cardboard, but it was worth it. It was BRILLIANT.

And it took second place.

The woman who won was the woman who organized the contest.

Yeah, I was a little bitter. [*Edited to add: It's 2018. I am still bitter.*]

Enter 2006, and a resurgence of the hugely successful Decorating Contest. When the committee put out feelers for category ideas and generic suggestions, I offered up that the committee members be exempt from the judging. Not that I cared, of course, because I had no intention of participating.

Nope.

Nada.

Zip.

None whatsoever.

Enter Janet.

Janet Lee sat down in my office with her coffee one morning and asked me if I was participating in the contest. I told her no. I had too much on my plate, and so did she. Janet is one of the only women I know who can out-Wonder Woman the Whirlwind. I'm a writer; she's an artist. On top of our day job, she does just as much as I do—possibly more—*and* she has children to boot. I bow to her supreme task-performing skills.

She also has really great ideas.

Damnit, Janet.

She thought a few of us should work together to have interconnected displays throughout the department. It was a cool idea, if enough people would participate. Too bad I wasn't participating. Until she told me the theme: *Frankenstein Wraps a Present.*

Our favorite children's book this year by a landslide was Adam Rex's *Frankenstein Makes a Sandwich*—a selection of hilarious illustrated poems that were plays on all the classic monsters. Among them are gems like: "Frankenstein Makes a Sandwich," "Zombie Zombie," and "The Phantom of the Opera Can't Get 'It's a Small World' Out of His Head."

In that same vein, our display theme would be a play on Adam's book. Kitti was all lined up to decorate "Frankenstein Wraps a Present." Janet had dibs on a Christmas version of "Zombie Zombie." And if Alethea would only do…

"The Phantom of the Opera Can't Get 'The Twelve Days of

Christmas' Out of His Head," I blurted. The words fell out of my mouth before I could stop them.

On the twelfth day of Christmas
The Phantom heard a song...
For eleven days now
Thoughts kept the cadence
Darn greedy true love
Did his best to fight it
Sung a bit of Opera
Hummed "It's a Small World"
Ignoring as his phone rang
FIVE GOLDEN RINGS
The more that he heard
The more lines kept
Counting in his head
...and he kept singing all night long!

Suddenly, I wanted to do this display more than anything in the whole world.

It was going to take forever. I had a week.

It was going to be *awesome.*

On Monday morning, I came up with the poem. (How sad was it that I had to work out the last verse of "The Twelve Days of Christmas" first? I can't ever remember if it's six geese, or six swans, and who's leaping, who's piping, and when.) That afternoon I went to the Teacher Supply store for poster board and butcher paper. That night and the next, I burned through five black markers working on the title board. Wednesday, I drew the Phantom (one more black Sharpie and an entire black Crayola pencil) fleeing down the stairs. Thursday, I got the poem down on the third poster board. Saturday morning, I stretched out on the floor with a pencil and a yardstick and wrote out all the lines of "The Twelve Days of Christmas" on the four-foot-by-six-foot butcher-paper background (two more red Sharpies, one green one, and half a big eraser).

I met Janet and Ethan on Sunday to assemble everything. I stared at it for a while. After all that work, I expected it to explode into lights, or stream confetti and balloons from the ceiling, or launch a parade or something. But it was still very cool. I still have the poem stuck in my head.

It placed in "Best Musical Entry."

"Best in Show" (as well as "Most Colorful") went to Jeannie S. and her awesome cubicle, tastefully wallpapered entirely in bold, stripy wrapping paper.

I'm not bitter this year—Jeannie's office was gorgeous, and could have starred in a Target ad. (Besides, she deserved it simply based on the fact that on Dessert Extravaganza Day our little diabetic wore a shirt that said "Got Insulin?" Jeannie rocks.)

I'm not bitter, but I have no intention of participating in the contest next year. It takes way too much time that I don't have—way too much time to bother once again not winning first place.

No intention. None. Nada. Zip.

Again.

That's three times, right?

Voila. Tradition.

It will be interesting to see which Muse bites me in the butt next year.

STEP THREE: FRIENDS

Once upon a time, Lee had a very depressing Christmas.

I suppose I should preface this whole thing by saying that according to my mother, I've always been depressed about Christmas.

As a child not depressed in the clinical sense of the word…but sad. Everything at Christmas hinged upon magic and wonder and that miraculous unnamed present I was always hoping would be under the tree the next morning that would transform my life into the most fantastic life ever lived. I was so adamant that Christmas *mean* something, and it always ended up being relatively mundane and over far too soon.

Of course, I've been looking for magic for most of my life, so I'm not quite sure what exactly made Christmas different from any other day.

But, once upon a time, not so very long ago, Lee had the most depressing Christmas ever. This time, it was depressed in the clinical sense of the word. I cried so hard I couldn't get out of bed. It was my first Christmas in Tennessee. I was in my parents' house at the time, and Memere (my maternal grandmother) was with us…but I just couldn't make myself get up. Mom came in and gave me a hug and tried to convince me of all the wonderful things I had waiting for me out in the living room. Presents had a habit of cheering people up.

Only, I didn't really want to be cheered up.

I told her I would come out soon, but I really didn't see how. I just missed everyone *so* much. I missed all the friends I had left behind in South Carolina, and some friends who weren't even in South Carolina anymore. I missed my little sister. I missed people I hadn't met yet. I missed everybody in the whole world, life was wretched, and I just couldn't do it.

But I had to. I had promised my mother. So I made a decision: if I was going to go out there, my friends were coming with me.

I put on the ring I have that matches Casey's, and a necklace my sister had made. I donned my college boyfriend's Nine Inch Nails t-shirt, and some warm, fuzzy socks Fontaine had given me. There may have been more things, but essentially everything besides my sweatpants and my underwear had at some point in time been in someone else's possession, someone else I cared about a great deal and who cared about me in return. I wore their love over my troubles and prayed it would protect me from that horrible world.

Thusly armored, I made my way into the living room. I only cried through the first couple of presents, and things got better. Presents do have a habit of cheering people up…eventually.

But it's a Christmas I really don't want to repeat.

This year, I had fair warning that I was going to be alone for Christmas. I had been alone before and weathered it just fine…well, okay, maybe I wasn't fine. But memory always has the benefit of being sugar-coated and double-dipped in 100% all-natural hindsight and that amazing ability the human body has for forgetting pain.

I survived them all, which means they were good.

Halcyon yesteryears or not, December 2006 was barreling headlong toward its end with a boatload of unresolved issues and that ever-so-wonderful holiday funk I was already wading in. I'll admit it. I was worried.

I forced myself to put up the tree—Eddie helped me lug containers out of the attic one weekend, and then after he left I trimmed the tree…and cried. I stopped putting ornaments on when I figured there were enough, and I couldn't see anymore anyway from the tears.

It got to the point where I was sick of myself. I had to be around this weepy, simpering brat 24/7, and boy, I was seriously getting tired of putting up with her. Couldn't she just snap out of it?

I turned on the Christmas lights every day when I got home. I worked on my project. And I planned for Christmas morning.

I made a lovely dinner on Christmas Eve, and went to bed at a decent hour. When I got up in the morning I turned on the tree lights, pressed play on the CD player, and went to make breakfast. Mom always made us pigs-in-blankets and other things to munch on while we opened our gifts, but I decided to go a step further.

I was going to bring my friends to breakfast.

First, I made tea in my "Eric Screams" mug—the Best Christmas Present Ever that I received from Eric James Stone. The mug sports a picture of Eric's tortured face over Edvard Munch's "Scream." He'd posted that picture on the Codex Writer's board when I had my tumor scare. The tumor—and the scare—were both over, but the mug was a perfect reminder of how our little writing family had conquered that particular adventure.

I made my tea the way Jackie Gamber taught me, with a little bit of cinnamon. Then I baked some brie (wrapped in phyllo dough I had leftover from making baklava the day before) and an apple cranberry scone that Patty (my former boss and now Harlequin rep) had given me along with a ton of other little goodies to remind me of England and my sweetheart. I made some toast for the brie and opened up Kristi's pot of homemade ginger pear preserves to have on top of that…wow. It was awesome. I'm craving it again just thinking about it. Tummy happily sated, I started opening the few gifts I had under my sparkly, tear-stained little tree.

My big sister Cherie gave me a beautiful fairy ornament and a tin filled with her scrumptious traditional homemade flesh-eating turtles (the first time she made them there was a caramel accident, and she had to go to the hospital with third degree burns). My mother gave me—well, in my house you have to understand that "Mom and Dad" didn't give a lot of gifts. The names on the from-tos were more often things like "Mrs. Claus" (who always gave us underwear and girly things) or "Rudolph" or "Elf Number Four." So I wasn't surprised to find gifts from both Santa and Cinderella in the box from my mother.

From Santa I got a fantastic Frog Prince ornament. From Cinderella I got a little pearlescent picture frame in the shape of Cinderella's pumpkin carriage…and inside the pumpkin was a picture of my sweetheart. I set it up beside the ginger pear preserves so he could share my lovely breakfast with me. From Mom I got a bag full of her traditional homemade Chex mix.

Food and family, food and friends, food and love. To Greeks, they're all one and the same.

The other wrapped gift inside my parents' box was from my Nana, but written in my mother's handwriting. I figured it was another piece of jewelry from her stash—it's common knowledge at this point that Sami gets all the pretty stuff, and I get all the stuff with stories behind it. Last year it was an inexpensive but pretty metal flower bracelet that was the first gift my grandfather gave my grandmother. It's one of my most treasured possessions. I never knew my grandfather—he died before I was born.

Out of the box I pulled a very old, very thin locket on a long piece of black leather cord (the default necklace in our family; it's usually more helpful when Sami's around to put a clasp on it). I carefully popped the catch with my fingernail. Inside were tiny, black-and-white pictures of my grandfather, and my father as a baby.

The tears shed in the weeks up until that moment had been nothing—I sobbed over that locket, those big, gasping sobs that shake your whole body and require so much oxygen they make you dizzy.

I could invite imaginary friends to breakfast; I could build my House of Cards—or in this case, Great Wall of Food—all around me. My friends and family could send me their love…but my grandmother had given me her heart. There is no magic in this world more powerful than that.

Thankfully I had saved Sami's pile of little gifts for last—Sami, who is always so good at pulling me out of a funk and making me laugh at the insanity of the world. With tears still fresh on my cheeks I laughed hysterically as I opened up a bottle of Tylenol PM… a box of Pepto Bismol chewables… Benadryl… Bonine… Airborne… cough drops…

Superman band-aids…

It's no secret that I get ill so rarely that I never have unexpired medicine in my cabinet. This last flu that knocked me for a loop over Thanksgiving sent me running to the pharmacy in search of Robitussin, throat spray…and I still forgot the Tylenol. Sami was sick at the same time—we commiserated over the phone a lot that week. Of course, her shelves are always fully stocked with the latest and greatest; she's who I'd pick to room with if there was ever a national emergency.

I guess she got sick of my complaining. God, I love my little sister. I miss her.

But I guess that's tradition.

A little magic…and a little misery.

Happy New Year, everybody.

Kill Me Then

Apex Digest
Spring 2007

2007 has been a long time coming.

I've dubbed 2006 "The Year of the Dark-Hunter" for all the work I did on *The Dark-Hunter Companion* (look for it in stores this October!). But after swimming in Sherri's brain for an entire year, living with, dreaming of, and cataloguing vampires, I was more than ready to jump back into the deep end of my own twisted psyche. I started off the year with a list of projects, a burning desire, and a blank Word document.

It was like trying to remember how to walk.

I stared at the big white nothing on the screen for a very long time, and then I walked away from the computer. I threw myself into my day job so hard I came home every night exhausted. I initiated a complete purge and reorganization of my entire house. I caught up on my emails. I surfed message boards. I even started working out again.

You know it's bad when *going to the gym* is the lesser of evils.

About a week or two (and 2000 paltry words) into 2007, someone in the Codex Writers Group started a thread with a story about how she had accidentally been a bit too creative on one of her medical school writing assignments. It had almost gotten her in serious trouble with the department. She asked if anyone else had had similar experiences—if their love for the written word had ever caused problems for them. What followed was a spectacular slew of crazy stories.

Mine among them.

NINTH GRADE

After years of writing stories, notes and travelogues that friends loved and teachers didn't quite get, I was really looking forward to high school. Higher Education. English Honors. A place where intelligence is praised and creativity is encouraged. A place where I would finally be understood.

Oh, how wrong I was.

Ninth grade brought the indomitable Mr. Hendrick. Just to give you an idea—the quote I remember most from Mr. Hendrick was, "Thoreau is right, and you are wrong." His favorite editorial comment was the unadorned question mark, and I was the one student upon which he most often bestowed this beloved symbol. I probably should have contacted Guinness after receiving one red-ink-stained paper boasting thirty-three question marks—over six marks per page.

What do you do with that, I ask you?

We had to rewrite our *Member of the Wedding* paper three times, our *Raisin in the Sun* papers "had coffee spilled on them" and were never seen again, and we were forced to read *Sister Carrie*. I hated *The Sea Wolf*; it was where I learned to despise anything having to do with yeast, and the term "universal truth." We even read some Dickens that year. Which is a shame—I might have actually enjoyed *Great Expectations* otherwise.

The only bright spots were the 5+ on my poetry portfolio (five-plusses were about as widespread as whooping cranes, but I had at the last minute added a four-page unassigned narrative poem), and the time we were given extra credit for memorizing the *Romeo and Juliet* balcony exchange.

I memorized the whole scene. It was about three pages of our Literature textbook.

[...would through the airy regions stream so bright, the birds would sing and think it was not night...]

At the end of that year Mr. Hendrick and I parted quietly and civilly. I was not sorry to see him go.

TENTH GRADE

Tenth Grade brought Mrs. Watkins—a soft, charming older woman who never understood me no matter how much I loved her. She couldn't comprehend why passages from *A Separate Peace* sparked all these abstract thoughts in my brain. If you didn't get out of the book what you were supposed to get out of the book, you weren't doing the assignment.

Cliff's Notes were a godsend. It wasn't cheating; those little yellow booklets taught me how and what the rest of the world expected me to think.

The most revealing unit was the peer editing. Historically the most evil, thankless experiment, the class broke into groups of three and anonymously co-edited three similarly anonymous papers. Let me tell you: fifteen-year-olds pull no punches. (Had we known that one of the papers we hacked to pieces was written by our Vietnamese friend for whom English was a second language, we *certainly* would have acted differently…talk about embarrassing.) As a saving grace, Mrs. Watkins went over the papers and put her own, compassionate, *real* grade on top of the peer grade. No pressure, right?

This assignment would have made Hitler sweat.

Ever the overachiever, the paper I turned in was a thirty-five page handwritten fairy tale edited down to four typed pages with non-existent margins. My biggest fear was that I had abridged so much that the readers wouldn't be able to follow the plot. But I shouldn't have worried—my ruthless peers gave me an A.

Mrs. Watkins gave me a B-.

I was as surprised as you. And more than a little confused—if the purpose of peer editing was to successfully please my readers, then what was the problem? I knew from our experience with Trien's paper that had the grammar been an issue there would have been machete evidence right there in red and white. I was never popular enough—even among the Nerd Clique—for the A grade to have been a gift, that was certain.

Baffled, I whispered an inquiry after class about the lowered grade.

"I gathered it was supposed to be a fairy tale," she said casually. "But it wasn't appropriate for children."

I may not take any of that nonsense now, but I was not one of those teens who walked around with a "Question Authority" T-shirt. Hell, at the time I was still too shy to ask for extra ketchup at the McDonald's counter (a fact about which Tom Piccirilli takes great pleasure in torturing me). There was no way I was going to put up a fight.

But my brain was screaming.

Had she never actually read the original Grimm's "Cinderella"…the one where the evil stepsisters *cut off parts of their feet* to squeeze into the slipper? Or "The Goose Girl," where the disloyal maid unknowingly suggests her own punishment in the form of being placed naked into a barrel full of nails and dragged down the street by two white horses?

Apparently not.

Mr. Hendrick may have been a jerk, but at least he was well read.

Not knowing what else to do, I silently took the grade and waited for my life to get better.

ELEVENTH GRADE

Thanks to the luck of the draw, Mr. Hendrick decided to teach eleventh grade English Honors that year. I wept when I received my class assignment. I dreaded every moment…and blocked out most of them.

I do remember that I read William Goldman's *The Princess Bride* that year as an independent movie tie-in project. I was amused to report that Goldman's universal truth was ironically: Life Is Not Fair.

Mr. Hendrick and I fought over whether the book was written before or after the movie. He finally ended up taking points off, probably because he thought I should have hunted down the original S. Morgenstern version instead of Goldman's "abridgment."

Our very last assignment was a poetry analysis. It wasn't even really for a grade—we either got a check or a check plus. The purpose was to test our skills to see if we were ready for AP English the next year.

Because of the Advanced Placement program, there was no English Honors offered in our school in the twelfth grade. If you didn't go into AP, you had to settle for College Prep English with all the "normals."

Of course, I had already made up my mind—I had no intention of wasting my senior year stressed and overworked while reading books I didn't like and writing papers teachers hated all to exempt the easiest 4.0s in college to procure. I may have been reticent, but I wasn't stupid.

Only four people in the class received one of Mr. Hendrick's parsimonious check-plusses.

I was one of them.

Oh yes, shy girls can still be smug.

TWELFTH GRADE

Mrs. Smith's College Prep English Class of 1992-3 was like one of those TV sitcoms where the nerdy chubby girl is surrounded by jocks and pretty girls who can't read. The first day, someone asked Mrs. Smith what we needed to do to exempt the exam. Her answer: "Don't piss me off."

Yes, ma'am. Piece of cake.

I didn't have it so easy in my other classes—my schedule was crammed full with AP Chemistry, AP European History, AP Government and Economics, and AP Calculus. (On top of my dramatic duties as a lettered Thespian.) I figured I'd just sit in the back and do my Calculus homework and cruise through this class without a care in the world.

Mrs. Smith sat me in the front row, right beside her desk.

I rebelled by turning in four-page papers when the minimum requirement was one, and yelling out the answers to the classroom every time she gave us a pop quiz and then left the cubicle to go smoke a cigarette or flirt with her favorite administrator.

We read *A Tale of Two Cities*, *Tess of the D'Urbervilles*, and *Canterbury Tales*. I loved them all. When I was bored in class I simply flipped around in the Literature book, enraptured with T.S. Eliot, e e cummings, and the short stories of Ray Bradbury and Roald Dahl. Sure the class was crap, but I actually had *fun*.

All the "normals" thought I was crazy…and I let them. (I still do.)

The only real snarl Mrs. Smith and I had was during the Chaucer unit. I got back my paper to find the word "microcosm" circled, with "plagiarized?" written above it in red pen.

"Plagiarism" is a word that makes every honors student's heart stop.

"Microcosm" was a word we had learned in our ninth grade spelling book. At least, it was a word the English Honors kids had learned. When I asked Mrs. Smith about it, she told me that there was no way I could have come up with that word all by myself; I must have seen it in the Literature book and subconsciously memorized it and stolen it for my own.

Riiiiiiight.

It's not like she was ever going to expend the energy to get me in trouble, so it was never a big deal. But I have to admit, I'm still wondering how one plagiarizes a *word.*

Reading a word, comprehending it, and using it again properly...isn't that how one learns vocabulary in the first place?

GRADUATION

I ran into Mr. Hendrick again in the bowels of the USC Coliseum when everyone was lining up before graduation. Having acquired a teeny bit more gumption, I walked right up to him and said, "You know, you made me hate English."

In retrospect, that was a horrible thing to say. Just because it was true didn't make it okay.

He came up to me later after the ceremony and apologized, but I shrugged him off. I didn't have to like English—I may have been writing since I was eight, but my parents had told me in no uncertain terms that English was not an acceptable college major. We had toured colleges up and down the eastern seaboard the summer before and I had tried to make it work, looking at journalism and mass communications and any other career path that might have had to do with the written word.

Ultimately, parental pressures and budgets decided for me. I stayed at home, worked like a madwoman, and went to the local University. I ended up majoring in chemistry, but only because I was good at it. I dropped out of college after three years—ironically, after all those AP classes I had enough credits to get a degree. Technically, they call that "graduating."

Funny how life works out.

I never had a proper writing class until 2003—ten years after high school—when I was accepted into Orson Scott Card's Boot Camp. Not much slimmer but oceans braver, it was all I could do not to burst out laughing when Scott instructed us all to *never* pursue an academic English career. He maintained that kowtowing to professors and "learning" how to write was the worst thing a writer could ever do.

Mom always said that everything happens for a reason.

A universal truth if ever there was one.

So here I am—a girl who mixed up the alphabet, who brought together an international SF Legion of Superheroes to benefit victims of the worst natural disaster in history, who had the privilege of assembling a book of facts on one of the most popular paranormal romance series of all time, and who publishes silly stories about herself in a horror magazine for the Best Boss Ever.

I've taken up permanent residence outside the box, and I spray paint rainbow graffiti on it in my spare time. My family is belowstairs in the genre ghetto; my misfit siblings post on a board called Shocklines, my honorary Uncle is Orson Scott Card, and my guardian angel is Andre Norton.

Even the shyness has come a long way—I now have a life goal of acquiring as many friends as humanly possible. I'm not as brave as I still could be; there I'm still a work in progress. But I *have* actually walked into a room and said, "The party can start now."

I have had to fight upstream in order to do what I'm doing right now. But I think because of that, I appreciate every aspect of my very long list of jobs. I carpe diem, noctem, and every hour in between. Every opportunity is a miracle. Every publication is a gift like no other.

Beauty and Dynamite.

It's a pretty amazing life.

I wouldn't have it any other way.

OH, BUGGER.

That's the end of the essay.

I guess that means I have to go finish that short story now…

**When this essay was published in Apex, I signed a copy and sent it to Mr. Hendrick, who was still employed by Richland District 2 at the time. I don't know why I did it—spite?—after being so horrible to him that day of graduation. I can't remember if I sent a note along with it, but I must have included my card or something, because he sent me an email in return. He told me that the magazine had arrived on one of the worst days of his life. All he wanted to do was quit teaching…and then he got this. Instead of depressing him further (amazingly), it reminded him why he loved being a teacher so much, and he was writing to thank me for that.*

Never in a million years would I have ever believed that Mr. Hendrick and I would become friends. But time is an amazing healer of both wounds and perspective. When I stopped in South Carolina on the Enchanted *book tour, he showed up early (and excited!) to see me…and I finally had the chance to apologize for all of what you just read, in person.*

Route 666: Road Trip to World Horror 2007

Apex Digest
Summer 2007

The Free Online Dictionary defines "adventure" as *an undertaking of a hazardous or questionable nature*. Think about that the next time you wish someone else an adventure...or wish one on yourself.

You may as well live in interesting times.

If an "adventure" is the best thing someone can say, be prepared for the worst. But the rest of the Rules of Life still apply: Keep an Open Mind, Be Flexible, and—above all—Be Brave. At the very least, you'll have one hell of a story to tell when it's over.

When Jason Sizemore, esteemed founder and publisher of this very Apex Digest, asked me to accompany him to the Stokers in support of *Aegri Somnia*'s nomination, I thought it over. When he told me we'd be driving to Toronto, I immediately said yes.

It would be an adventure.

A writer is always up for an adventure (and if you're not, shame on you! What kind of writer are you? Not a very good one, I'll warrant), and she will certainly summon up the energy for an adventure with the greatest potential to go spectacularly wrong.

Otherwise, what stories are there to tell?

I've got to hand it to Jason—our trip to Toronto was not the makings of an 80's movie starring Tom Hanks, Richard Pryor, or Chevy Chase. (Thank the gods.) But it did have its moments.

THERE

I was already running on fumes by the time we got to Kentucky; the aftermath of MidSouth Con the weekend before. Do yourself a favor and try not to schedule two conventions two weekends in a row.

But The Best Boss in the World had asked me, and since I love Jason dearly, I figured out a way to go. I worked out how to get the days off of work. I got my ticket to World Horror ($$$!). I set aside some moolah for the hotel and gas. I even got the Boss a bonus *Aegri Somnia* author! By way of timing, Max was along for the ride.

Being at the Stokers was important to Jason, so it was important to me. Everything else was secondary.

At a convention, sleep is kind of secondary anyway.

You just don't usually start out that way.

We left for Kentucky on Wednesday night. Things were being thrown into the car right up to the moment we pulled out of the driveway: suitcase, CDs, iPod, laptop, fancy dress, fancy shoes, curlers, case of water, suitcase, power bars, books…including my limited hardcover *Aegri Somnia,* the mass signature sheet of which our Stoker-nominated editor Jason had somehow neglected to sign.

I always like a trip better once I'm on the road, because at that point there's no sense worrying about what you've forgotten. You really do—and should—leave all your cares behind. And if you happen to leave your razor with them, they do have drugstores in Toronto (hallelujah).

We made it to Jason's house that night in time to settle in, make up the pullout couch bed, have dinner, and crash. In that order. The next morning, we tried to hit the road early. We unloaded the contents of the Volvo into Jason's SUV (we left the baby car seat in place, since we had more than enough room and Jason swore it would be a bear to take it out and put it back in again). Jason crammed in the rest of his maps and gear, while I entertained myself with getting the owner of the car seat, Jason's two-year-old daughter Lindsey, all riled up.

First, let me say that Lindsey is *reeeeeeally* not a morning person. I used to think my mother was the worst specimen to come across at daybreak, but Lindsey takes the cake. She was sitting in the living room when I came upon her, her high chair parked in front of Dora the Explorer. Her hair was half plastered to her face, and half straight up a foot in the air. She stared at the television like a zombie, unresponsive to either the calling of her name or the presence of food put before her. I half expected Jason to walk up with a sippy cup full of Bloody Mary and say, "Here, sweetie. Hair of the dog."

Of course, no child—morning person or not—can withstand the awesome power of Fairy Godmother Lee. Lindsey was no exception. Within half an hour, we were chasing each other around the kitchen and giggling like maniacs. All in all, it was a lovely way to start the day. Mad game of tag, followed by Starbucks. I really must do that more often.

Here comes the uneventful bit, so I'll William Goldman it for you: What with one thing or another, nine hours passed.

Jason and I took turns driving in stints (Max can't, you'll remember). And kudos to Jason, who introduced me to one of the best gadgets I've ever owned: the Belkin TuneBase FM transmitter for iPod. Oh, yes…download a ton of songs onto your iPod and listen to them for uninterrupted hours on your car's stereo system. It's the best thing invented for interstate road trips. And since it comes with a handy-dandy cigarette lighter/holder, your iPod stays charged. Jason even had great taste in songs.

What the Big Kahuna didn't have, however, was a proper judge of time and distance. We were at the border well before expected…and I was at the wheel.

Which meant everything was going to go wrong.

The first thing that went wrong was that I was muscled into the Humongous Trucks Only lane. Luckily, they don't hold that against you, and they'll begrudgingly take your toll money anyway. (In that SUV, they probably just thought I was trying to compensate for something.) Next came the bridge—the bridge with *very* narrow lanes. Not that I was concerned about falling off the bridge at all, since I was surrounded on all sides by Very Fast-Moving Humongous Trucks. Hoorah.

And then we were at the border. I pulled right up to the window with no waiting, and handed the grim young man our passports.

GRIM YOUNG MAN: Where are you from?

LEE: Murfreesboro, Tennessee. (Why can't I say that without a southern accent?)

GYM: What are you bringing?

LEE: Clothes…and books.

GYM: Where are you going?

LEE: World Horror Convention in Toronto.

GYM: What kind of convention is it?

LEE: It's a literary convention.

GYM: Who are you bringing?

Who am I bringing? Really? Wasn't he holding their credentials? I looked at Max and Jason, then looked back at the Grim Young Man skeptically. The first answer that sprang to mind was "My pimp and my John." Fortunately for us all, I have learned the ability to think before I speak. Sometimes.

LEE: Um...my two friends.

GYM: Then what's all that stuff in the back?

LEE: Clothes and books. (Was he nuts?) We're going to be there for a few days.

GYM: Then why didn't you say that when I asked you what you were bringing?

LEE: I thought you asked me *who* I was bringing.

And he had, too. I know, because the editor in me wanted to correct him and say "whom" the first time he asked the question. But I thought before that outburst too (clever me). Honestly, he could think I was as stupid as he wanted as long as he let us pass.

Finally, he reluctantly handed me back the passports and waved me on. And I drove ahead...kind of.

What is it with Canada? Do they think we know instinctively where to go? Like geese or something? There were *no* markings on the road. Most of the cars seemed to be going in a left-erly direction, so I steered that way. I gently approached the exit, hoping that at some point there would be official designated markings that prevented cars from just bashing into each other willy-nilly. Happily, there were. But I didn't have to deal with them for long.

I pulled into the nearest fast-food parking lot, nerves still jangling, and handed Jason the keys.

A few things to note about Canada: paying with American cash gets you a horrible exchange rate, your cell phone will work but it will be bloody expensive, and Europeans have a hell of a time getting cash out of the ATMs.

Jason got us to the Official World Horror Con Overflow Hotel, and checked in. We unloaded the car in bits and pieces, went up the elevator, and opened the door to our rat cage.

Oh, the hotel was fine enough. The room was just the *size* of a rat cage. Inside the room were two twin beds. I looked at Max and Jason in turn, and did the calculations. I mentally cursed myself for yet again having gone against instinct and not grabbed my Aero Bed on the way out the door. I kept cursing myself, loudly enough to drown out most of Max's fascinating lecture on the definition of a standard European "double" room. I stopped just in time to hear his suggestion that we just tough it out and "get romantic." I could not, however, stop myself from laughing at the idea.

I do love Max, and I will vote Romantic any day of the week. But the practical side of my Mini Wheat did not want to hate him bitterly in four days' time, and the two of us trying to share a twin bed was the surest way to do that. Jason asked after another room—which of course there were none—and as a last-ditch effort the hotel staff offered us a rollaway bed. For a small (*ie*: exorbitant) fee, of course.

I sighed, and offered to pay for the bed. Max may have been a little dismayed and not a little surprised at my final judgment under pressure, but I've been to enough conventions. I've learned my lessons, and your lessons, and then some. Sleep may indeed be secondary, but it's still *second.*

The rollaway bed wasn't so bad. I had brought my own pillow along for the car ride, so that was a bonus. The mattress on the rollaway was much softer than the beds in the room, and perhaps even a tiny bit bigger. In fact, it was just a tiny bit bigger than there was space in the room. We shoved one twin bed up against the wall and the other up against the air conditioning unit, and all three of us still had to lift and shove and squeeze to get the whole rollaway in enough to lay flat. But we finally did it. We stood back and admired our handiwork…and realized that our room now consisted of a small entranceway, a bathroom, and one slightly wonky Great Big Huge Bed.

It was every twelve-year-old's dream. Had I been an hour more overtired or an hour less hungry, I probably would have gone whole hog and built a fort with blankets. But the men needed their food, so they dragged me out of dreamland and down two blocks to the main hotel. On the way, they wondered casually which friends they might run into first.

We made it three feet—and I'm not kidding when I say *three feet*, count 'em, thirty-six inches—when we were embraced by the very vivacious Robert J. Sawyer and whisked off to the bar. Our very own personal Multi-Award-Winning Canadian Representative of 2007 World Horror Welcoming Committee, and a round of drinks.

The convention had officially begun.

AND BACK AGAIN

What with one thing or another, three days passed.

By now you've read the World Horror 2007 Con reports and seen the pictures in *Locus* (Michael Laimo still owes me five bucks), so I won't bore you with more details. Suffice it to say that many friends were met—new and old—many books were enthusiastically defaced, many deals were witnessed, and many *many* alcoholic beverages were consumed. I didn't get any rest…and Jason got food poisoning.

But like a certain chart-topping Torontonian rock band reminds us, the point of the journey is not to arrive.

Max was a champion. On Sunday he marched Post-Banquet-Food-Poisoning and Far-Beyond-Overtired past the angry bus driver and poured us into the car. I curled up into a ball on the backseat, and Jason drove around the same block three times before finally finding his way out of the city. Max turned the music up, played DJ, and chattered constantly to keep whoever was at the wheel alert and awake. Jason looked progressively worse and worse; Max took the keys from him as soon as we stopped for lunch and handed them to me. No one argued.

No one bothered to check the gas gauge either.

The "almost empty" warning light never worked in the first Saturn I owned, but it was never an issue. I drove to school and drove to work and filled up like clockwork every week (back when ten dollars got me change back from a full tank). Happily, the little orange icon in my Volvo is in proper working order. It's saved my carcass more than a few times on the way to and from work.

But the way to and from work in Murfreesboro, Tennessee is fifteen miles long, with three exits between origin and destination. Conversely, the way to the U.S. from Toronto is a wasteland.

When I noticed the warning light in the SUV, I started praying.

It's pretty bad when I resort to praying, and I am not selective in my deity. I go through God, Buddha, Allah, Kali, Ganesha (and any other Hindu god I can remember), Mother Mary, Mother Earth, The Unnamed Ones, The Machines of the Universe, and my own personal guardian angel, Murphy. Not that praying to Murphy ever gets me anywhere—he's usually the one laughing his ass off at whatever predicament I've gotten myself into this time. But I digress.

Prayers led me to Exit 17. I followed the tiny blue sign with the tinier white arrow to the left and drove. And drove. And drove. We finally found ourselves at a four-way stop, at the center of a conglomeration that had given up on the wish to be a town when it grew up. Staring back at us was a dusty one-pump service station with a giant LEASE sign in the window.

Of course I'm not kidding. This is all part of the adventure, you see. The heart pounding, the gut-wrenching fear…this is all part of the adventure.

Since the female was driving, I sidled up to the first pedestrian I spotted and rolled down the window. When I asked after a gas station,

I was informed there was none. When I conveyed my sheer desperation, he asked where we were headed.

"Home," said Max.

"Kentucky," I said at the same time.

"The States," our Samaritan translated sagely. He gave us directions that led us far down one road, turning right, and going farther down another. Farther into the wasteland. My gut clenched.

Jason tried to be sympathetic and hopeful all at the same time. "What's the worst that could happen?" he asked. "If we run out of gas, we walk to the gas station and get some more. Don't worry. It's okay."

On one level, I knew what he said made perfect rational sense. But had he just been to the same convention I had? Every horror fan on the planet recognizes those famous last words.

How long had that gas station been closed? Did the Department of Canadian Wasteland Transportation know about this…or care? What if that little blue sign was just a lure for desperate travelers, the locals of the "town" forced by some ancient demonic geas to direct said travelers into the depths of said wasteland from whence they never returned…

…and there it was.

I was so elated that I filled the car up while the men relieved themselves, and I sprang for the full tank. That dingy little gas station had rescued me from my terrible imagination. That dingy little gas station was my salvation, my oasis in the desert. That dingy little gas station…was the same dingy little gas station we had stopped at on the way up.

You have to appreciate the irony.

According to Max, there was graffiti in one stall proclaiming that "This Place Sucks." Considering ourselves recent experts on the area, we had to agree.

Our last hurdle was the U.S. border. Here was where we would find out if they would let Jason back into the country, and if they would scold Max for having left it in the first place. We were given plenty of time to contemplate this and countless other scenarios because, unlike Canada, the wait in line for the U.S. border was over an hour.

We watched as car after car was searched. We watched as a woman in line who got out of her car was yelled at and approached by tetchy armed officials as if she might explode at any moment. We made up stories about how the furriners in the sedan ahead of us were the refugees responsible for defacing our dingy gas station. We postulated a slew of questions the border patrol could possibly ask us, and what our serious—and not-so-serious—answers would be. Offhand, I added, "What if they ask us about the empty baby seat?"

There was a pause; it was obviously something the men hadn't considered.

I put my hands on my cheeks and, suppressing a wave of giggles, screamed: "Oh my *gawd*, WE FORGOT THE BABY!!!"

Our proud author was the talkative one at the border; I think our publisher was doing his best not to throw up. For some reason the guard's interest was in neither of them, but in *me*. (I was as surprised as you.) Author and publisher he got; he wanted to know how I fit into the equation. That quip from before rose up in my throat and I swallowed it down, mechanically spouting a succinct description of my job at Bookville that apparently sufficed. He waved us through.

And that was it.

Well, that was it apart from the rest of the grueling hours home. I don't remember a whole lot more than the road, the thunderstorms, and black raspberry ice cream in the Ohio town I will forever remember as "Wikipedia."

Okay, I do remember more than that, but I won't bore you with the details. After all, if what happens at the convention stays at the convention, it follows that whatever happens in the car…well, you get the point.

The things some people will do to get home and sleep in their own bed...and I did that night (technically, the next morning), and it was wonderful. It wasn't a decadent foreign city surrounded by three hundred of my closest friends, but it was home and it was sleep and it was wonderful.

It was a week later, when we were finally unpacking the last World Horror box, that I realized I had traveled across North America—to Kentucky and Canada and back—and never gotten my *Aegri Somnia* signed.

Jaaaaaaaaaaaaaasoooooooooooooooooon!!!!!!!!!!!!!

Five Things Few People Know About Me

March-May 2007

About a millennium ago, my dear friend Eric James Stone tagged me on his blog. The challenge: to write five things about myself that few people know about me. From me, the girl with the big mouth who doesn't keep secrets. I knew it would have to be more than just a list…and I was immediately outdone by James Maxey's Five Things. If you haven't read them, I encourage you to do so. Especially if you like really spicy chili.

So, without further ado, I will now endeavor to meet the challenge. As a twist, I won't be choosing five more people to tag with this task—number one because I don't propagate such things as a rule, and two because everyone else I would have had on my kickball team has undoubtedly been chosen already. It is a fun exercise, though…I do encourage you to think about and post it on your own blog at some point. No pressure.

#1: I DREAM OF BIG HOUSES

Some songs just hit you in the right place, at the right time. Bowling For Soup's "Belgium" was one of these.

The lyrics, in their entirety, center around the emotional turmoil of a lover left behind. I'm sure Bowling for Soup had no intention of bringing to tears a lonely woman who was missing the world at the time. But when I heard the chorus it dredged memories up to the surface…for very different reasons. Not the least of which was the song's title.

Dad worked for a European-owned company and traveled for most of my grade school years. All over the country, all over the world. Sometimes he would find a way to bring Mom along with him. A workaholic like his daughter, he was often forced to use his previous year's vacation days in January, under threat of losing them.

Practical Capricorn that I am, my parents were in Belgium for many of my adolescent birthdays.

When my little sister was too young for me to handle in their absence, we spent the week with Memere, or at our neighbor's house. This neighbor made me chocolate cake (I prefer brownies, but Dorie's chocolate cake was possibly the best I've ever had), gave me presents, and did her best to cheer up a melancholy little introvert who only spoke to people when the spirit moved her. (And when it did, hoo-baby, try to shut her up.) All the years after that, Sami and I were old enough to stay home alone.

Our two-story Charleston-style house on the lake was massive enough in its emptiness as it was; with only half the family in residence, it was palatial.

I often turned up the stereo in the spacious ballroom (there was a formal sitting area by the fireplace, Mom's computer desk at the far end, and the front windows where our Christmas tree went every year—the acoustics were fabulous) and danced in my stocking feet across the gleaming hardwood floors. Sami and I would rearrange the furniture willy-nilly, and clean our dishes as we used them so that they never piled up. We littered the banister and steps with our coats, schoolbooks, and shoes. We stayed on the phone as long as we wanted, and we never had bedtimes.

Once, we even had a ska band [Less Than Jake] spend the night.

But the lake was always scary when the fog rolled in. We never went up to the third-floor attic at night, if it could be helped. I watched *The Shining* once by myself in the empty ballroom…and was brave until the shadows chased me up the stairs. Sami did not stand for shadows. Whenever I worked late at the movie theater, I often came home to a light on in every room and a sister asleep like the dead.

When we lived in Vermont, with my older sister and brother, I admit we were cramped. (Though we did well with six people in a one-bathroom house.) When four of us moved to South Carolina, the split-level with the tiny yard was plenty. Granted it was ugly as sin, but Sami and I had our own rooms. Life was good. And yes, the neighborhood with the big house was this side of perfect—the near-acre of land on the lake, the great schools, the tons of friends, the active community…I get it.

But I still don't understand why anyone would want a house that large.

I can't tell you if the houses in my dreams were substantial before or after that house in South Carolina, but I'm sure the brick behemoth only reinforced the images. Every time my dreams take place in a house, hotel, or hospital, there are endless stairs and elevators that climb to infinite floors. There are planters as large as houses, filled with trees. There are hidden rooms and multi-story attics—some that I know about, some that I discover, and some that I get lost in. There are bathrooms that put professional locker rooms to shame. There are magnificent entryways with wrought-iron banisters and extensive grounds that often lead to the ocean.

Freud might have something to say about them…I prefer to think I was a duchess in a former life. A duchess who gave lots of parties, just as Mr. Stafford predicted.

I've only had two birthday parties in all of my double-digit years (the Apex readers know which ones). The first was when I was twelve—a Rip-Roaring Slumber Party filled with lip-sync contests and movie marathons and caramel brownies. The second was for my thirtieth birthday—a Writers' Slumber Party disguised as a three-day weekend mini convention, filled with slush readings and knife-fight instructing…and caramel brownies. Both were events so successful, the attendees reminisce about them to this very day.

I didn't get to have LeeCon this year—I had to use up some of my held-over vacation days (like father like daughter), so I went to Florida to visit my parents.

I'm thinking next year—the 20th anniversary of that first fabulous party—I should host LeeCon again. I'll announce it way ahead of time so everyone can make arrangements to come, and this time I'll invite my parents. They definitely shouldn't miss out.

Good lord.

I'm gonna need a bigger house.

#2: WISTERIA IS THE COLOR OF BLACK RASPBERRY ICE CREAM

You guys know Murphy, my ersatz Guardian Angel. He makes my life hell because he thinks it's funny. He loves nothing more than to see me bruised and embarrassed and downright annoyed. He's the pestering little brother I never had, and the big brother that didn't miss the bullying age.

But he has his moments.

When life gets me down—way down—he's still around. Maybe he even feels a little guilty for doing all he does on the days when I'm not so blue. Murphy puts little surprises in the cracks of life for me to find. A song on the radio. A free candy bar with a fill up at the gas station. A message on a license plate. An email from an old friend. A fan letter. Sunshine caught in the palm of my hand on a cloudy day.

I've learned to look for them now. It's a game we play.

The love of my life thinks I'm nuts. (Okay, so maybe it's a little past thinking at this point.) He laughs and sighs: "Only you would have a Guardian Angel with his own law." He knows me so well.

They both do.

I'm still worn out from World Horror Convention. Fifteen hours driving each way and 72 hours in Toronto in between is enough to tucker anyone out. Of course, this came right on the heels of MidSouth Con.

You know, I accidentally wrote "hells" just now. It's pretty appropriate. I'm just not myself when I'm that exhausted. I have so much fun at the convention—I love meeting all the friends I've known for so long and never seen, and getting to know better the ones I still keep in touch with. I love the stories and the gossip and the pranks, the jokes and the laughter and the commiseration. I love that we're a family, no matter what country you find us in.

But bad things happen as well as good. Life throws curveballs, and sleep becomes elusive. And as everyone knows, sleep at a con is a precious commodity.

Somewhere around 7pm on Sunday I was curled up on the backseat of Jason's car, staring out the window with my allergy-puffed eyes (I'm betting the rollaway bed I slept on hadn't been pulled out of storage in a few years anyway) and contemplating the misery of the world. Max gave me one of his antihistamines, and I took some

Excedrin for good measure, braving the caffeine despite desperately wanting sleep. I knew there was still eight hours of the journey to go yet, and I wanted to be at home in my bed at the end of it.

Heck, I wanted to be in my bed right then. But if wishes were airplanes…

We pulled off in Wikipedia (okay, that wasn't the name of the town, but Max called it Wikipedia and now I can't remember the real name. Wapakoneta or something) for a pit stop, and decided to get dinner out of the way. I vetoed the Taco Bell and the Arby's, and Jason (post-food poisoning), thought maybe he could handle fries from Wendy's.

There was a diner called the "Comfort Zone" right next to the Wendy's. Something fun. Different. Adventurous.

I caught the last of the waning sun with my fingers and let the wind take me.

The diner was nice and clean. The menu was plentiful. We ordered, and I stared alternately out the window and at the dessert menu beside the salt and pepper shakers at the end of the table. Ice cream did sound good. My comfort foods are ice cream, Chinese food, and six hours of *Pride & Prejudice*. I don't get much of any of those anymore.

The Comfort Zone had its own specialty brand of ice cream. And on the list was black raspberry.

Black raspberry ice cream was my favorite ice cream when I was a kid in Vermont. Then I moved to South Carolina. Either it was something that only existed north of the Mason-Dixon line, or it just went out of style. I guessed the latter when Ben & Jerry's retired the flavor. It wasn't something I even looked for anymore, and it never would have occurred to me to ask for it.

But there, in the hollow of my Pit of Despair, my Guardian Angel resurrected an ice cream flavor that had been extinct for me for 20 years. It's nice to know that Murphy's still there for me when the world goes to hell.

We made it back to Nashville in the wee hours of the morning and fell into bed. I took yesterday off work sick, mustering up enough energy after six hours of napping to drag myself and a book out onto the back porch.

I didn't read a lick.

It was amazing how much had changed in the few days we'd been gone. The trees had started filling out with their new green leaves. The forsythia had shed its gold and gone green. The violets stuck their tongues out at the lawn-mowed grass. The bulbs I replanted in the fall exploded to the edges of their beds. And the wisteria...the bee-laden wisteria wept off the vine in a quiet purple snow. A snow that will no doubt be gone after tonight's storm.

A snow the color of black raspberry ice cream.

Thanks, Murphy.

#3: DANNY WAS MY FIRST LOVE

My favorite moment at the Stoker awards was when Stephen King's *Lisey's Story* won the award for best novel. Michael Marshall Smith's announcement was met with polite applause, but no one came forward to receive the statue. Our lovely M.C., Sephera Giron, didn't have anything in her notes as to who might accept on Mr. King's behalf.

There was a moment of awkward silence.

Michael Marshall Smith looked around, and then leaned in to the microphone. "This is like that nightmare you have," he said, "when you're standing in front of a roomful of people staring at you...and you're not Stephen King."

Stephen King was Danny's favorite author.

I think I was born in love with Danny. His much older brother and my much older sister were high school sweethearts, so we were thrown together a lot. We would play Star Wars with his toys; I was always Princess Leia. When Cherie and Billy got married, I was six.

Danny was nine. We danced at their wedding. I kissed him on the cheek.

It was the bravest thing I had ever done.

Our family moved away not long after that, but we went back to Vermont almost every summer. The adults would talk or go shopping—the kids would go down to the camp on Lake Champlain and go swimming. My favorite visit was the year I was eleven and Danny was fourteen, chubby and pimply and awkward. We played video games all day long. I commented on his homemade bookshelves full of Stephen King titles, and he told me how he had written a few novels himself already.

I was in so much awe of him. By eleven I had decided that writing was what I wanted to do with my life, but I knew I wasn't old enough to complete a decent novel. I also knew that my imagination was one that wouldn't let me read things like Stephen King without scarring me for life. It made me sad, because that was a part of him I couldn't share.

A few years later, our ramshackle camp was torn down and his family built a mansion on the property. The built-in bookshelves still framed the collected works of Stephen King, but the world around them had changed too much. Including us. He took me to see *Total Recall*—not a date at all; his family owned the movie theatre—but it wasn't what I wanted it to be. We weren't the dream of what I thought we might have been, and we never would be.

And that was that.

I have a theory about boyfriends. As a serial monogamist, I've had quite a vested interest in the few boys I've loved. At the end of each one I realized that there were things in them that called to me...but none of those things by themselves had been enough to sustain us. Deep down, though, I was cataloguing all of the facets that magnetized me: the overly-sensitive artist with the comic book and video game collections; the movie-obsessed misfit film director; the passionately creative dreamer with a head full of ideas. I thought that if I paid very close attention, maybe I would recognize the person who had all of these qualities. It was true enough; each one of these boys had certain elements of the other.

But none of them had elements of Danny.

I thought about that, in that awkward silence after Stephen King's name was announced. There I was, at the Bram Stoker Awards, the shy girl now a slasher film producer and dark fantasy publisher and author and Bookville Buyer. I sat at the fancy table dolled up in my pretty dress, between Brian Keene and Michael Laimo, and thought about the man I'm going to marry.

Meeting him was the bravest thing I've ever done.

He is all of the best of those boys—every single one—right down to the bookshelves full of Stephen King. Of course he's not perfect; I wouldn't adore him half as much if he were. But there's something he's given me that none of the others did: the dream of what we could be…and the promise that we will.

Perhaps it wasn't Danny I was born in love with after all.

#4: I HAVE NEVER BETRAYED A LION'S OATH

We were all a bunch of stinkin' liars.

I'm sure I've told you before: I grew up in a TV sitcom. We lived in the perfect brick two-story house on a lake in the perfect neighborhood. My high school had about 2500 students in it, over 600 per class, and we were broken up into all the stereotypical cliques. There was the Popular crowd who reigned over the cafeteria (called "The Commons"), the trenchcoat-wearing, cigarette-smoking Back Porchers, the Nerds (who pretty much ran the school), the Band Geeks, and the Drama Freaks.

We had it all.

All of these groups were mutually exclusive save one—the Nerds.

Thankfully there was a hoard of us large enough to warrant our own department, and the T&G (talented & gifted) Room to escape to when the rest of the world went to hell. The problems in that room were always bigger, real life concerns—test scores and parental pressures and future college plans—concerns that did not discriminate from teenager to teenager. So neither did we. We each belonged to all of those other groups, but inside that room existed no boundaries. We kept quiet in the hallways, but behind the T&G Room's closed doors we were confidants.

A bit like science fiction conventions today, really. Only now we wear it as a badge of honor.

In addition to the T&G crowd, I was a Drama Freak.

The Drama Freaks spent before school, lunchtime, and after school in the Drama room or the auditorium. When we got kicked out of those places during the reign of the new teacher, we camped out in front of the Drama Room door or, on sunny days, we picnicked outside.

It might have been difficult to pick us chameleons out of a crowd, but it was never hard to track us down. We were as close knit a group as any family—and closer than most. We were places to escape to, ears to hear secrets, and shoulders to cry on. Most importantly, of course, we were a reliably attentive audience. We told jokes, told stories, told blatant outright lies in the name of entertainment. We created a world around us where the line between reality and fantasy constantly blurred.

The trouble with chameleons is that sometimes they change colors so much, you forget what shade they were to begin with.

I think it was James who originally came up with the concept of the Lion's Oath. To swear a Lion's Oath was to vouch for the fact that what you had just said was the absolute, unquestionable truth. It was an amazingly handy thing to have around.

How many times have you told someone something you knew they wouldn't believe? Or something they should believe, but don't? Imagine having a way to ensure perfect trust, an instant path to belief in another person, no matter how strange his circumstances.

It was one of the most brilliant ideas ever set forth in this age or any other. Imagine a world where a suspect could get on the stand and swear a Lion's Oath and walk free because we all knew, without a doubt, that his testimony was the truth. I would like to live in a world like that. But the only way it would work is if we all vowed to never betray a Lion's Oath. Ever.

So we did.

We've all grown up now and moved away from each other. We each have our own lives and families. We have our own places to escape to. We have different ears to hear our secrets, and different shoulders to shed our tears on, and different audiences to hear our stories.

Oh, we're all still a bunch of stinkin' liars—heck, some of us even get paid for it.

But I know that if Casey or Margo or James or Patrick ever called me out of the blue and told me to head underground because—Lion's Oath—the sky was falling, I'd grab my laptop and spelunking gear as soon as I put the phone down.

We might not be fifteen anymore, but forever is still forever.

#5: I LOVE LINES

It's taken so long to make this post because I made Max a promise that I wouldn't blog until I finished another chapter of *Sunday*. Technically, I finished two, so I should be good to go.

Without further ado, I bring you the fifth and final thing that few people know about me: I love lines.

Now don't get me wrong—I'm about as impatient as the next person. And, just like Inigo Montoya, I hate waiting. But standing in line is a different thing entirely.

Most people hate standing in line. Lines at the DMV, the theme park, the airport, the mall at Christmas. It's an obsession, and something people are very passionate about. When people are in a line, it's all they talk about; have you noticed?

It's so incredibly difficult to get most people to do anything, but once they're in a line they are suddenly in a very great hurry to get on with their lives. The whole logic behind that confuses me.

Whenever folks ask me how I am, my standard answer is, "busy," because it's the truth. At any given time I have a list of things I'm currently doing, a list of things I should be doing, and a list of things I have yet to do. I believe in living my life to the fullest. (It's exhausting, but it's fun.) An idle minute is a minute wasted.

Unless you're in line.

Standing in line is just part of life. It's something everybody has to do. It's inevitable and unavoidable. The world comes to a halt and you are forced to linger wherever you are—sitting or standing or behind the wheel. That's the best part.

None of those places is at a desk staring at a computer.

There are so many things you *can't* be doing while you're waiting to buy your groceries, milling about the doctor's office, or stuck in traffic. You are completely off the hook where life is concerned; the responsibility is removed from your shoulders. Look around. Smell the proverbial roses. Take a deep breath and relax. Indulge in a daydream. Tell yourself a joke. Listen to the music.

Lines are the world telling me to relax and take it easy. So I do.

I once stood in line at the LaVergne post office (a line of maybe four people tops), when a woman decided to vocally berate the postal staff about how another location had no lines and no waiting, this was ridiculous, didn't they know how important her life was, and couldn't they open more registers? The staff became *gushingly* (and slightly facetiously) courteous, which only infuriated the woman more (to the amusement of the rest of the line). She yelled at the top of her lungs that she would never be back, and slammed the door on her way out.

"I suddenly feel much better about my life," I said in the stunned silent wake of her dramatic exit, and everyone laughed. But it was true! If waiting in line at the post office is something you categorize as a personal tragedy in your life, I envy you.

A toast to you all: May waiting in line be the worst thing that ever happens to you.

Gray Rinehart says…

Alethea peered over the edge of the long-forgotten tomb into the darkness below. She dropped a flaming torch into the chamber; it fell until it was barely a pinprick of light on the stone floor below. The brightly clad creatures below scampered back from the torch's unfamiliar heat. A few lost their tall caps.

"Gnomes," she said. "Why did it have to be gnomes?"

After the ordeal at the tomb, Alethea eventually overcame her aversion to gnomes enough to adopt Seamus…though some have said that Seamus actually adopted her. It's hard to tell with gnomes.

—from "*Indiana" Kontis and the Lost Fairie Temple*

Alethea and I attended Orson Scott Card's two-day Writing Workshop in Greensboro, N.C., in the summer of 2003. She, of course, was one of the chosen few who would stay for the week-long Literary Boot Camp, and I—a mere workshop mortal—did not dare approach her greatness at that time. I relinquished my chosen seat in the front row to one of her Boot Camp peers, and joined the rest of the unwashed in the back of the class.

However, Lady Alethea, ever full of charm, wit, and grace, eventually deigned to accept my humble offering of friendship, and even my hospitality. But she had to bring that blessed gnome Seamus along with her, and he is nothing but trouble. He got all the gnomes in the neighborhood riled up, and now it's always, "Can Seamus come out to play?" and "When is Seamus coming back?"

Gnomes. Why did it have to be gnomes, Lee?

Soulmates and Lost Faith

June 7, 2007

If you can force your heart and nerve and sinew
To serve your turn long after they are gone,
And so hold on when there is nothing in you
Except the Will which says to them: "Hold on!"
—Rudyard Kipling, *If*

I am smack dab in the middle of a month of madness—four states in four weekends: South Carolina, North Carolina, Florida, and Tennessee (the last one I get to count for Hypericon in Nashville). I've seen family, made new friends, and connected with old.

Technically Casey's not the oldest, but she is the most important.

You might remember my best friend from her influence on the short story "Small Magics." Well, her birthday was Sunday, June 3rd (happy birthday, Casey!) so I plotted with her husband to surprise her.

And it was a surprise too—the last time I saw Casey was at her baby shower. Thea's two now. (I am such a crappy friend.)

It was just like old times...you know, except for the kid and the big house in the suburbs. We had fancy brunch with Mom, we talked until we were hoarse, we watched movies (*The Prestige* is a fabulous flick), we even made Lee's Caramel Brownies—the staple of every fantastic birthday. It was the most delicious batch we ever made. Probably because we didn't eat all the batter.

We finally put ourselves to bed on Sunday night, but before passing out I signed on to the internet to check on my absent sweetie.

I started crying before I finished reading his email.

Goodbyes have never been easy for me—curse of being born a child with an overwhelming sense of mortality. You never know what's going to happen: something that can be both good and bad. So we make the most of our lives, find out what it is that makes us happy, and strive for that thing with all our heart and nerve and sinew.

And once we have those things, it tears us up to have to leave them again and again. I had one soulmate seven hours away, another seven timezones, and I missed them both that night with all my heart.

I delayed as long as I could Monday afternoon, leaving after a very long lunch with enough time for me to make it home and relax before bed. I made fabulous time through the mountains; I couldn't wait to get home and call my sweetie and tell him all my great stories...and then the truck in front of me kicked this three-foot, solid metal bar into my path. There was no swerving—by the time I saw it I had already run over it.

I should be happy it didn't smash up my car, or crash into my windshield. I should be glad it only punctured the back tire, and not both on that side. I should have been glad the air leaked out slowly, and didn't completely blow. I should have been counting a thousand blessings instead of shaking and screaming a very nasty word on the side of the highway outside Johnson City as Humongous Trucks whizzed past just shy of the sound barrier.

It was 6:15 pm. If I hurried, maybe I could find a tire before everything closed.

A guy stopped to help me. He seemed slightly annoyed that I had already almost finished changing the tire by myself. I refrained from being uberrude and asking him to speed up the process. He suggested I try the next exit and go into Johnson City to find a service station, as opposed to driving the extra forty miles and trying my luck in Knoxville.

Two gas stations, a Napa Auto Parts store, a Walgreens, and 4 sets of dodgy instructions later, I found the Super Walmart. Their service area closed at 8:00. It was just after 7:00. I was so happy, I didn't care what the stupid tire cost.

And I was proud of myself—not once did I ever cry or lose my cool (apart from that vehement, and well-deserved, nasty word). I had a problem; I was going to find a solution. And I had. Easy peasy. I walked around the parking lot under the ominous sky, making copious phone calls to assure everyone that I was all right.

At the very least, the adrenaline had masked the depression.

Gassed up, re-tired, and on the way back to the interstate, I set my camera on the passenger's seat. There had been a Miller's restaurant with a great mural on the side of it, and I thought it might be fun to stop and take a photo as a memento of my adventures in Johnson City. Once again, I got more than I bargained for.

Some of you might remember an essay I wrote called "Faith." It was the morning after the Winter Solstice of 2004, the Longest Night, four days before the Tsunami, eight days before I met the love of my life in the middle of London. I was a mess, as usual. My life had been turned upside-down so much by a succession of amazing things, I started daydreaming about being normal. I was incredibly torn up inside, wondering if the insane and surreal path that I found myself walking was the right one. I had slept past my alarm, taken my time that morning and was late to work. And on the way, the Machines of the Universe (as Quinn calls them) gave me a sign. A double rainbow, perfect in the sky.

On the way back from Johnson City, they gave it to me again. Only this time I had my camera.

Whatever path I'm on, for better or worse, I'm going to keep walking it.

Ken Scholes says...

She did not always have the magic hat. She did not always have the struck pose or the graceful sway. And the tattoo on the upper swell of her breast, she said, was utterly and completely removable, fake, untrue. But the jazz hands were real. As was the rest of her.

What is truth? I wondered.

She was not always a goddess. Or if she was, it was unknown to her. My favorite brand of deity—one promoted up through the ranks of mortality. One that grasped our precarious and uninvited position in the Cosmos.

When I saw her eyes there was an inner earthquake. Equilibrium gone amok. They were large and round, twin holes in the space time fabric that drew unsuspecting rabbit-chasers into Wonder. And there was sadness there with truth and hope. But when I looked to her smile, wide and white, it was something I could cling to until the world stopped shaking.

"What should I do," she didn't ask.

"Save the world," I cried, "by simply being yourself."

Her smile became more secretive. "I can do that if I ever find out how."

She found the magic hat in a store in Saratoga Springs. It was of the sort that made snowmen become real, begin to dance, attempt to sing. I knew this because just like she once had been mortal, I'd once been a snowman. It wasn't straw, that hat. It was black as starless night with her hair waterfalling down beneath it, long and silky. A redemptive bowler.

I did not see her save the world though I would've liked to. She surged into the lobby and struck the pose, I'm told. The universe looked on with shackled breath. Feet shuffled, shifted as the head cocked and the hands came up. Jazz hands, bright and shimmering like moonlight over water. The eyes went wider if wider was truly possible and the smile poured out from her. It was a defining truth and then she shifted into the sway.

Somewhere, somehow a stranger was healed of their infirmity. Somewhere, somehow a child laughed in delight at the alphabet they learned. Somewhere, somehow an untrue and unkind deed was redeemed.

"What is your name," a curious world asked.

"Verity," she said as she danced from side to side.

"What is your quest," it asked her again.

"Verity," she said as the jazz hands wove hope into the despairing.

"What is your favorite color," it asked in finality.

"Again," she said, "Verity."

And as always, Alethea was true.

Unwarranted Serendipity

By Jason Sizemore

So I'm at a rest area off the Bluegrass Parkway doing my business when I started to smell cigarette smoke floating over from the stall next to mine. Smoking in the boy's room in public areas wasn't something uncommon in these parts, so I paid it no mind. But when the smoker took things to that next level he caught my attention.

"Going to Hypericon," he said more as a statement, less as a question. The voice sounded familiar but, without the face, I knew I'd never place him.

Even so, I hated to be rude and not say anything. And I figured trying to ignore the man would only encourage my new stalker. I grunted out a non-committal "I guess."

Smoke rose above the wall separating our stalls. I willed my body to hurry and finish its business. It was like trying to urinate while standing up to the high school bully. It just wasn't going to happen.

He spoke up again.

"Keep your eyes open, Kid."

"Who the hell are you?" I asked. "What do you mean 'Keep my eyes open'?"

But whoever he was, he had nothing more to say. His stall-door opened and I heard him walk out, his boots making clacking noises against the filthy concrete bathroom floor in his wake.

Hypericon 2005 was to be the "coming out" party for a little publication of mine, *Apex Science Fiction and Horror Digest.* I'd just received issue two from the printer and was heading south to Nashville to thrust it upon the unsuspecting horror-fans in attendance. The first issue had been a modest success, both financially and critically, so I fully expected to sell several hundred copies over the weekend to throngs of adoring fans.

This would also be my initiation into the world of fan conventions. I'd heard of such strange things before, where the freaks (like me) could get their freak on. I knew better than to expect the madness as described by the news networks: furry parties, orgies, yiffing, BDSM, creepy roleplay. I figured the convention would be a small gathering of like-minded fans of the genre.

But the real question as to "why" did I choose Hypericon 2005 as the jumping point for *Apex Digest* when there were so many larger, more popular fan conventions held in the region? I don't know. Truth be told, you could hold a loaded gun to my head and I'd still draw a blank. Maybe it was luck? Pure genius? Thinking back, I liken it to something I call "unwarranted serendipity."

Arriving in Nashville, it didn't take me long to find the hotel and to get myself registered. I found my hotel room and unloaded my luggage.

It wasn't until I went back downstairs and walked around the dealers' room that I realized something: I didn't know a single person there. Images flashed through my mind. There was me, without friends, watching lame porn all weekend in my hotel room. There was me playing Marco-Polo by myself in the empty hotel pool. There was me watching from a distance as other convention members had fun, sharing experiences over a beer. Hell, this was going to be high school and college all over again! I was trapped. My little dark secret of being a closet introvert was going to make this the worst weekend of my life. It just wasn't in my wiring to enable me to randomly speak to strangers.

"Don't mess this up, kiddo."

I jumped, startled. It was that voice again. And that damn cigarette. I spotted him, standing in the shadows of a large ficus in a far corner of the hotel lobby. I couldn't make out any features, but I got a distinct Rod Sterling vibe from the man. But hell, for all I knew, it could have been Harlan Ellison standing over there giving me the finger.

The stranger nodded and I followed it to the lobby elevators. Okay, I thought, I'll play this out. After all, I had no better plan.

I sauntered over and pressed the 'Up' button. I was checking my watch when I heard an Enchantress speak: "Redheads are the scourge of the earth. When I'm in charge, they will be the first up against the wall!"

I'm a redhead, therefore I found this particular declaration to be quite disturbing.

"Excuse me," I said. I was probably blushing.

"Not you, those other redheaded assholes."

The Enchantress spoke with a sexy, educated accent—my favorite. My gaze fell to her face. It could have been Greek…certainly Mediterranean in design. She had long, shimmering curly brown hair, and she wore a radiant smile punctuated by dark red lipstick.

Accompanying her was an attractive lady adorned in full Goth regalia. Both made quite striking impressions.

My hand shot out in greeting. "I'm Jason Sizemore." My hand was probably sweaty.

She smiled and I thought I would crumple to the floor in a heap of helpless boy hormones. "That accent, how cute!"

She was talking about my thick hillbilly drawl. It was certainly much worse than usual. I was nervous.

"I publish *Apex Science Fiction and Horror Digest*," I said, finally managing to string together a full sentence.

"Whores?" She sort of backed away, glanced nervously at her Goth friend. "You do what with whores?"

"No, no! Not whores, hor-ror."

"Oh, I see."

We shared a laugh. I glanced over to the man in shadows. His shadowed face nodded and I knew he was pleased.

Ding.

The door opened, vomiting a load of angry-looking horror fans (turns out most horror fans are angry looking), and admitted me and the two ladies. I pressed the button for the sixth floor where, according to the registration desk, all the action was supposed to be happening.

"Let me give you a copy of my magazine." I dug through my backpack like a crazed rabbit rooting through an abandoned warren. The two ladies looked at each other and giggled.

I found it. "See, *Apex Digest.* That's me." I proudly shoved the first issue, with its aliens and stark landscape, at them.

"Oh, nice magazine," the Enchantress cooed. She took it from my outstretched hand and proceeded to show it off to her friend (who, as it turns out, was Sherrilyn Kenyon!).

Ding.

The elevator doors opened and the two women turned to depart.

"Wait," I blurted out.

They paused and stared at me.

"Will I see you again?"

The Enchantress smiled, and again I was overwhelmed.

A wink. "Keep your eyes open, and you just might."

The elevator doors closed on me, and I took an unplanned ride back to the lobby.

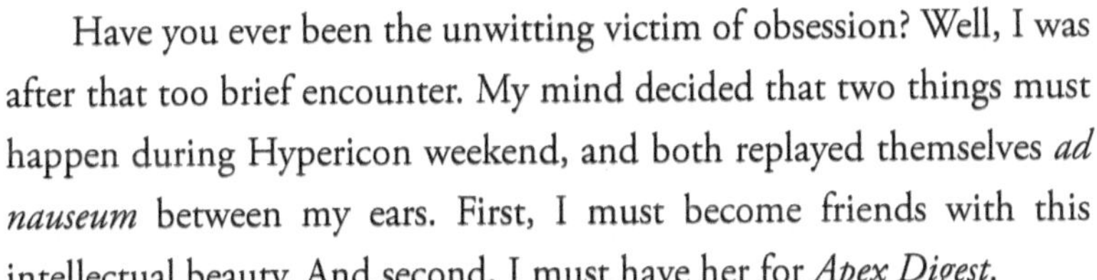

Have you ever been the unwitting victim of obsession? Well, I was after that too brief encounter. My mind decided that two things must happen during Hypericon weekend, and both replayed themselves *ad nauseum* between my ears. First, I must become friends with this intellectual beauty. And second, I must have her for *Apex Digest*.

In retrospect, I can readily admit that the "friends" part was nothing more than that base need shared by all chest-beating males since the beginning of time: the urge to get close to the pretty girl. But the second part was more practical. One thing I had gleaned from the business of publishing a genre magazine was that you needed something to set it apart from the rest. Although I couldn't tell you what this mystery woman could bring to the publication, I only knew that Apex needed it.

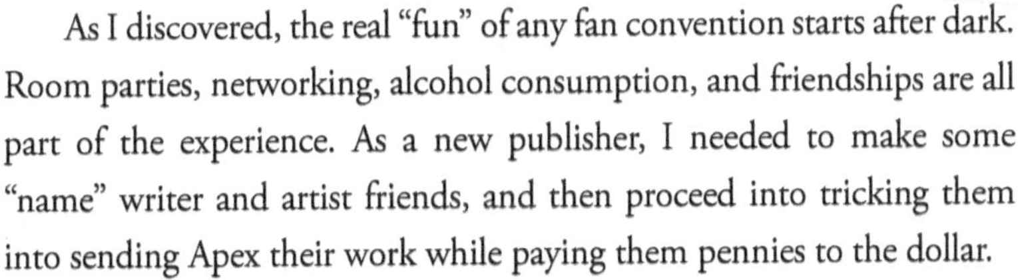

As I discovered, the real "fun" of any fan convention starts after dark. Room parties, networking, alcohol consumption, and friendships are all part of the experience. As a new publisher, I needed to make some "name" writer and artist friends, and then proceed into tricking them into sending Apex their work while paying them pennies to the dollar.

Having no friends, I went alone to the designated party floor. An elderly man in chaps being led around with a leash and collar by a younger lady cornered me as soon as I got off the elevator. They sported sexy BDSM gear.

"You're *Apex Digest*, aren't you?" he asked.

I gulped. Although having attended a liberal arts college (Transylvania University) and being a rather open-minded person (or so I thought), I'd never encountered such a thing before. An elderly man on a leash just wasn't my "thing." I fought to keep eye contact with him, refused to allow myself to look at the pair of studded leather briefs he was wearing.

"Yes, in a sense," I answered.

"Brian Keene was looking for you."

My heart lurched. Brian Keene was looking for *me*. Landing a Brian Keene story would be big business for an upstart like Apex. Back then, Keene was (and still is) the King of Our World. And for good reason…he's one of the best writers in the business—a man among boys.

"You mean like, Brian Keene?" I asked, dumbly.

"Yes, room 508. He's having a private room party."

My excitement waned. If it was a private party, I couldn't just waltz on in. Keene and his entourage would kick my ass and send me whimpering back to the private confines of my hotel room. Lonely hotel porn became a real possibility once again.

"Here, I'll take you there," the collared man offered. His young mistress had not spoken a word, or even bothered to acknowledge my existence. "I'll introduce you, tell him you're a friend of mine. They'll let you in."

"Do I have to wear a collar?" I asked.

The elderly man's bushy left eyebrow arched and he looked at his keeper. She shot her nose up into the air and said in a disgusted manner, "No."

Quietly, the pair walked me down the hallway, snaking through the crowds hanging outside the hotel rooms. We stepped through a crowd of people in large animal costumes. The most disturbing of these was a squirrel marked with large band-aids and blood. The furries were mostly interested in a room that emitted a light blue glow. Inside, groups of…animals were frolicking on the floor.

I looked up to the elderly man for an explanation. His eyes told me to not ask.

We pushed forward.

We encountered another large crowd. They stood outside a room blasting techno-music. An angry looking man stood around holding a meatloaf. I took a quick peek inside and saw a full-fledged orgy that would make Bob Guccione a proud man.

Finally, we reached room 508. Somebody knocked on the door. It cracked open and we were admitted inside.

The room was veiled under a fog of cigarette smoke. I heard lots of swearing. My survival senses told me that at any moment, a blade could be pulled and somebody would lose a finger, a toe, or even an ear.

A large man blocked my way further into the room.

"Mr. Keene is not signing at this time," the big guy said. "Please leave."

"It's okay, Big Joe, let he who steps into my room face the master of the guard."

Big Joe. I recognized the name. He was the famous bodyguard of Brian Keene.

Through the clearing haze, I see Brian Keene. He's holding a tumbler full of Knob Creek in one hand, a cigarette in the other. He squinted at me.

"Who the fuck are you?" he finally asked.

The elderly man with the collar spoke up. "This is Jaso…"

"Frank, I don't remember asking you a goddamn thing!" The murmur of the crowd died. Everybody turned to look at me.

I couldn't help but notice that room 508 was a Mecca of famous writers. I saw Tom Piccirilli leaning back in an uncomfortable hotel chair in the back of the room. He was watching the proceedings much like a bemused crime boss. Bryan Smith relaxed on an ottoman, nursing a beer and a cigarette. His face was a mask of indifference. I could be gutted and tossed out the window and he'd not give a shit. James Newman was sitting on the floor, hard to read behind his dark glasses. Deborah LeBlanc popped her knuckles, her expression grim. Other famous horror writers sat around the room, each looking equally annoyed.

"I asked you, who the *fuck* are you?" Keene demanded again.

I closed my eyes, summoning courage. When I opened them again, I saw the stranger. He was standing in the darkened far corner of the room. A plume of blue cigarette smoke drifted to the ceiling from his mouth. He, too, was awaiting my answer.

"I'm Jason Sizemore."

"So?" Keene said.

My heart palpitated. Sweat formed on my brow. At that moment, I realized I'd made the biggest mistake of my life. I should never have gotten into the publishing industry. I don't have cojones. All the naysayers were right, you can't produce a profitable magazine. I should just go home, tail between legs, and forget this all ever happened.

"I'm sorry, I'll go," I said.

I turn. But in mid-stride, I heard that voice of beauty and dynamite.

"He's cool, Brian. That's *Apex Digest*."

"Wait a minute," Keene said.

I stopped, frozen. When Keene bellows out an order, everybody, including God and Satan, stops to obey. He's got that kind of voice.

Keene held up the copy of *Apex Digest* issue one I'd given to the Enchantress. "You mean he's this."

Then she stepped magically out of the crowd. "Yes, he publishes Apex."

"Goddamn. Then come inside, buddy! Have some Knob Creek. Big Joe, take care of the man."

In record time, I found myself holding some bourbon. I looked over to my angelic benefactor. She smiled and my heart melted.

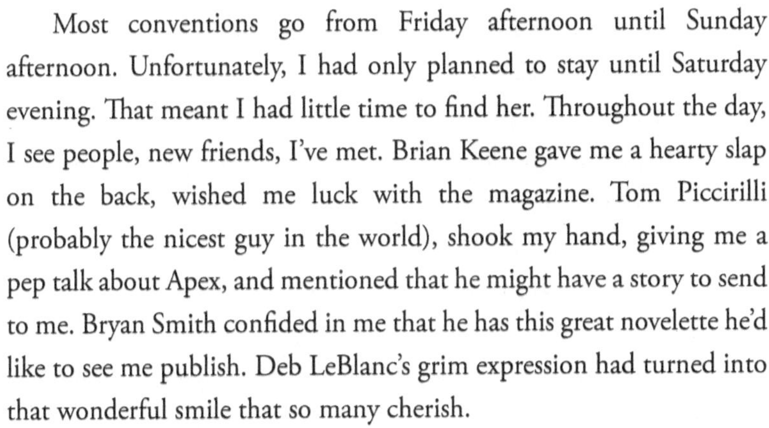

Most conventions go from Friday afternoon until Sunday afternoon. Unfortunately, I had only planned to stay until Saturday evening. That meant I had little time to find her. Throughout the day, I see people, new friends, I've met. Brian Keene gave me a hearty slap on the back, wished me luck with the magazine. Tom Piccirilli (probably the nicest guy in the world), shook my hand, giving me a pep talk about Apex, and mentioned that he might have a story to send to me. Bryan Smith confided in me that he has this great novelette he'd like to see me publish. Deb LeBlanc's grim expression had turned into that wonderful smile that so many cherish.

Life was grand.

But I couldn't find her. I made my final trek through the hotel, worked my way back around to the lobby.

Was I never going to see her again?

Ding.

The elevator opened and out she came. I hopped up, full of courage and initiative. From of the corner of my eye, I saw the smoking man smiling at me.

"Hey!" I called out, perhaps a bit too enthusiastically.

"*Apex Digest*!"

She gave me a light embrace. I have somehow befriended this beautiful person.

She crinkled her nose. "Do you smoke? You always stink like cigarettes."

I smiled. "Well, not technically, no, I don't smoke."

"Have a good time last night?" she asked.

"Absolutely." I paused. "I need to ask you something."

"Yes?" The apprehension in her voice made me wince.

"Do you write?"

She shook her head. "Not much. I write movie reviews. I blog sometimes. Nothing impressive."

"Would you work for me?"

"What do you mean 'work for me?'"

I explained to her my plans for global domination. I told her that we already printed stuff like reviews and standard non-fiction fare in Apex. I described to her that I need content that would help make Apex different from the rest of the crowd.

"I can't pay much," I warned her. Unfortunately, writers are use to hearing this.

"I'll do it," she said. We giggled and embraced, spinning around in each other's arms.

"Not bad, Sizemore," the now familiar Rod Sterling voice said from across the lobby. "Not bad at all." From over her shoulder, I watched as he faded away like a dying television image. After a couple of seconds, only a spent cigarette remained in his spot.

As I was about to leave, I realized that I had yet to ask the Enchantress her name. This drew embarrassed chuckles from us both.

Again, there was that smile. "Alethea," she said. "Alethea Kontis."

—Jason Sizemore

2007

Don't miss *Enchanted,* Book 1 of the Woodcutter Sisters series!

Gelett Burgess Award Winner
Garden State Teen Book Award
Kirkus Best Teen Books
Andre Norton Nebula Award Nominee
Audie Award Nominee, Best Teens Category

It isn't easy being Sunday's child, not when you're the rather overlooked and unhappy youngest sibling to sisters named for the other six days of the week. Sunday's only comfort is writing stories, although what she writes has a terrible tendency to come true. When Sunday meets an enchanted frog who asks about her stories, the two become friends. Soon that friendship deepens into something magical.

One night, Sunday kisses her frog goodbye and leaves, not realizing that her love has transformed him back into Rumbold, the crown prince of Arilland—and a man Sunday's family despises. The prince returns to his castle, intent on making Sunday fall in love with him as the man he is, not the frog he was. But Sunday is not so easy to woo. How can she feel such a strange, strong attraction to this prince she barely knows? And what twisted secrets lie hidden in his past—and hers?

Want to be notified when the next book comes out?
Subscribe to my monthly newsletter (princessalethea.substack.com) or follow me @ Amazon or BookBub!

If your life could use more smiles, join Princess Alethea's Brute Squad on Facebook! (facebook.com/groups/aletheasbrutesquad)

You can always find me @ AletheaKontis.com

THE RYOGAN CHRONICLES
by ERICA CAMERON
ISLAND OF EXILES
ERICA CAMERON
SEA OF STRANGERS
ERICA CAMERON
WAR OF STORMS
ERICA CAMERON
IN KHYA'S WORLD, EVERY BREATH IS A BATTLE.
"Cameron expertly blends worldbuilding and intriguing characters with page-turning action scenes and a story that builds in tension and complexity... This is rare gem of a book that has a lot to offer readers, including magic, action, and intrigue on the edge of a knife."
—Kirkus, Starred Review
★ ★ ★ ★ ★
"*Island of Exiles* is imaginative, bold, and as electrifying as a Shiara storm."
—Lori M. Lee, author of *Gates of Thread and Stone* and *The Infinite*
Available now!

BOOKS OF ARILLAND

~The Woodcutter Sisters Series~

Enchanted

Hero

Dearest / *Messenger*

Thieftess (Coming Aug 2024)

~The Trix Adventures~

Trixter

Trix and the Faerie Queen

Trix & The Fire Witch (Coming 2025)

~Other Tales of Arilland~

Tales of Arilland

The Glass Mountain

The Unicorn Hunter

For Angels to Fly

ALSO BY ALETHEA KONTIS

~The Harmswood Academy Trilogy~

(Nocturne Falls Universe)

The Truth About Cats and Wolves

When Tinker Met Bell

"The Meddlesome Misadventures of Merri and Bright"

(novella in the Merry & Bright anthology)

Besphinxed

~Short Story Collections and Essays~

Wild & Wishful, Dark & Dreaming

Starfish and Coffee (Coming 2025)

Beauty & Dynamite

~The Dark Hunter Universe~

(w/Sherrilyn Kenyon)

The Dark-Hunter Companion

The Simi's ABCs

~Children's Books~

AlphaOops: The Day Z Went First

AlphaOops: H is for Halloween

Diary of a Mad Scientist Garden Gnome

The Little Witch & Wizard

Oodles of Doodles

The Wonderland Alphabet: Alice's Adventures Through the ABCs and What She Found There

~Poetry~

Patchwork Poetry (and Other Gibberish by the Saturday Songwriters)

ABOUT THE AUTHOR

New York Times bestselling author and stormchasing princess Alethea Kontis has written over 20 books and 50 short stories. She has received the Scribe Award, the Garden State Teen Book Award, and is a two-time winner of the Gelett Burgess Children's Book Award. She has been twice nominated for both the Andre Norton Nebula and the Dragon Award. Alethea also narrates stories for multiple award-winning online magazines, contributes book reviews to NPR, and does freelance work for Writing the Other. Born in Vermont, she currently resides on the Space Coast of Florida where she watches K-dramas with her teddy bear, Charlie. Together they are ARMY, VVS, and Black Roses.

Follow all my adventures!

aletheakontis.com
FB: facebook.com/AletheaKontis
IG: instagram.com/aletheakontis
TikTok: TikTok.com/aletheakontis
YouTube: youtube.com/user/Thieftess
Patreon: patreon.com/princessalethea
Amazon: amazon.com/author/aletheakontis
BookBub: bookbub.com/authors/alethea-kontis

www.ingramcontent.com/pod-product-compliance
Lightning Source LLC
Chambersburg PA
CBHW031307210726
48287CB00005B/1448

* 9 7 8 1 9 4 2 5 4 1 3 2 5 *